ON RACE AND RELIGION

MY JOURNEY FROM JIM CROW TO MYSTICISM

LAUREN JOICHIN NILE

Rainmaker Publishing

First published by Rainmaker Publishing 2023

First edition

Paperback ISBN: 978-1-961351-90-5

Cover Design by Lauria

ON RACE AND RELIGION

MY JOURNEY FROM JIM CROW TO MYSTICISM

LAUREN JOICHIN NILE

FOREWORD

This is my story. It is the story of my experience of race and racism in the United States, and it is the story of my spiritual journey.

My racial memoir is the story of me as a child who grew up seeing both the best and the worst of her country, the United States. On the one hand, it is the story of my seeing, very early in life, a deep desire and attempt on the part of some people to maintain a societal system of birth-based privilege for some and birth-based oppression for others. On the other hand, it is the story of my seeing, at that time, a deep desire and attempt on the part of other people to transform the country into one that lives up to the vision declared in its founding documents, a nation in which all people are treated equally and with compassion.

My racial memoir is also the story of my mother, a woman of principle, strength, warmth and deep compassion, and of a community of adults who were inspiring examples for the children they raised. Finally, my racial memoir is the story of me as a woman who devoted her life to opening minds and softening hearts - to helping people see all human beings as equally deserving of dignity, as members of one human family with many more commonalities than differences, and as deserving love.

My spiritual memoir is my other story, the one that most deeply defines my life. It is the story of my childhood curiosity about some of the deepest mysteries of reality, and the deepest theological questions. It is also the story of my adult quest for the source of my life-long, deep, intuitive feeling that there is something more to the universe than we experience through our senses, and specifically, that that "something" is a loving Divine Creator. It is the story of how very early in life, I not only felt the existence, but also a genuine love for The Creator, and grew up to embark upon a life-long journey to find The Creator. My spiritual memoir is the story of a journey that took me from science to philosophy, and from philosophy, ultimately, to mysticism.

I invite you, dear reader, to embark with me upon an adventure. On that adventure, you will witness first-hand the two themes of my life. The first theme is social justice—my desire for all human beings to be both seen and treated as equally human, worthy of equal respect and love. It is my desire for people to both **want** to do good toward their fellow human beings, and to **do** so. It is, in essence, my desire for humanity to mature. The second theme is my desire for wisdom, Ultimate Truth, and Divine Knowledge—the overriding hallmark of my life. Let us now hoist our sails and commence our adventure!

CONTENTS

PART ONE

MY RACIAL MEMOIR

THE MAKING OF A COMPASSIONATE ACTIVIST

I dedicate my racial memoir to my mother, Mrs. Selina Gray Joichin, whose indescribable love and powerful life lessons of compassion, poise, maturity, dignity, citizenship, deep concern for the less fortunate and hope for a just and compassionate world, have been my foundation throughout my life. My mother's example continues to inspire me to this day.

ACKNOWLEDGMENTS

I thank my loving wife, Barbara, for her extraordinary patience throughout my writing process. For your understanding on all of the evenings and weekends during which I did nothing but work on this project, and for your faith both in me and in this work, I am exceptionally grateful. I love you, honey.

My sincere gratitude goes to my brother, Lambert, who helped me to fact check my memories of people, places and things from my childhood. You were a tremendous help during all of those long phone calls. Thanks, Lambert.

A genuine thank you to my Aunt Johnnie for keeping and sending me the only picture of Grandpa Jim that survived Hurricane Katrina. For all of our long, delightful conversations about our family history, thank you as well, Johnnie. They mean a lot to me.

My heartfelt appreciation goes to my dear friends, Theresa Sayles and Jack Straton, for agreeing to be my readers on this project. Theresa and Jack's editorial suggestions have been utterly invaluable. Theresa and Jack, sincere thanks. Special thanks to you, Theresa, for the time you spent working with me on all of the edits, and for encouraging me to write this, the story of my racial journey.

I would also like to acknowledge Dean, the staff member of the library of California State University, Northridge, for researching and finding all of the photos from the archives of the New Orleans Public Library that I have included in this memoir.

INTRODUCTION

I was born black and to non-college educated parents in the Deep South, New Orleans, specifically, at a time during which the southern states were still enforcing the last legally sanctioned vestige of slavery—segregation. The year was 1953.

I **loved** my childhood!

I was enormously blessed that four extremely fortunate circumstances severely limited the potentially devastating negative impact that the larger society into which I was born could have had on my development as a healthy human being. They were, indeed, my emotional sanctuaries.

First, I was born to a mother and grandmother who showered pure, total and complete love upon me from the moment I was born. Second, in addition to her deep love, my mother also provided me with a powerful example of how to live a conscious life of integrity, poise, dignity, compassion, generosity of spirit and civic engagement. Third, I grew up in a beautiful, middle class African-American community in which I had many role models of adults who, even while living with the daily indignities of segregation, led lives in which they modeled self-respect, maturity and community involvement. Fourth, I was born with a fierce intellectual curiosity, the result of which was a childhood love of science, and an incredible inner life of fantasy, imagination and wonder. I was, indeed, a little science geek.

Gramzie, my grandmother, my mother's mother (**Miss** Gramzie to all the kids in her neighborhood), told me that beginning as an adolescent, my mother "always" wanted a daughter. My mother, an avid reader, wanted a daughter so badly, in fact, that in high school, she began saving her favorite books for the daughter she dreamt of having some day. After having two sons, my brothers Lemar Jr. and Lambert, born respectively nearly ten and six years before me, and then losing a baby girl at birth, my mother **really** wanted me. She wanted me so desperately, that even though she was a practicing Methodist (and Methodists decidedly do not pray to statues), she made a novena, a special prayer, for a little girl, to a statute of the Virgin Mary every day after discovering that she was expecting me. The story, as Gramzie told me, was that my parents' Catholic neighbor told my mother that if an expectant mother wanted to have a little girl, upon learning of her future bundle, she had to make a novena to the Blessed Virgin every single day without fail until the baby's birth, asking the Virgin to bless her with a baby daughter. My mother wanted a little girl so badly that this, Gramzie said, is exactly what she faithfully did to a little statuette of the Virgin Mary every single day for eight months prior to my birth. Then, two weeks premature, I was born on August 15th, the Feast Day of the Blessed Virgin![1] It was a sure sign, as my mother saw it, that I was indeed the literal answer to all of her many prayers. And oh my goodness—how my mother loved me.

1 Within Roman Catholicism, the Feast Day of the Blessed Virgin is celebrated as the day on which The Virgin Mary's physical ascension into heaven is believed to have taken place.

And I loved her too, more than life. She faithfully recorded all of my infant milestones in my baby book.

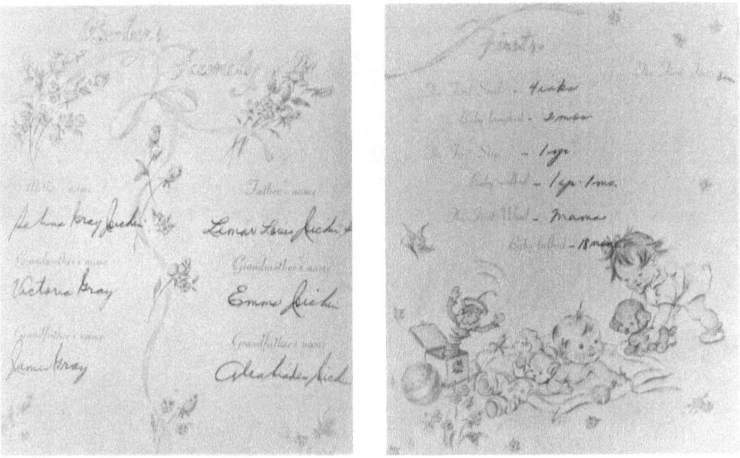

My Baby Book

Gramzie, for her part, had five grandsons before me, Lemar Jr. and Lambert, and my cousins Joseph, Gerard and Drexel, the stepson and two younger boys of Mama's older brother, my Uncle Isaac. Need I say it? Right. From Gramzie, I had a second dose of extreme love, extreme in the sense that extreme sports are extreme—intense, powerful and concentrated. I know, though, that Gramzie didn't love me any more than she loved my brothers and cousins. In watching her with the boys, it was absolutely clear to me how very much she also loved them.

My being her first granddaughter, Gramzie's deep love for me was as much the result of the happiness that my long-awaited birth brought to her Selina, the eldest of her three girls, whom, like her two younger daughters, my aunts Verlie and Johnnie, she adored beyond description. Because my birth so delighted and thrilled my mother, I was also to Gramzie, a blessing from heaven.

So, late on the Saturday afternoon of August 15, 1953 at precisely 4:58 P.M., I entered the world with my very own little personal double halo.

Me at Three Months and Nine Months Old

Despite the fact that I was the little girl my mother wanted so desperately, it was completely clear to me that, like Gramzie, who loved all of her grandchildren the same, Mama loved Lemar Jr. and Lambert every single bit as much as she loved me. I heard her say more than once, "I don't believe in making a difference between children. I love all my children the same." I knew that that was categorically true.

My mother and I were **always** together. While Lemar Jr. and Lambert were either at home or with their friends, Mama and I would be together, running her many errands—grocery shopping, buying our school clothes and supplies, getting something for the house, doing Gramzie's food shopping and picking up her medications, or buying some item for the church, among numerous other tasks that always seemed to need doing. Mama and I were together so much, in fact, that she told me numerous times, "Laurie, you're my little shadow."

My mother took surprising pride in my smallest accomplishments. The first time I combed my hair without her help when I was about nine, she called Gramzie and said with such love and happiness in her voice, "Mother, my little girl just combed her hair and put it in the cutest little pony tail, all by herself!" Overhearing that conversation from my bedroom, I smiled from ear to ear, happy that I had made Mama proud.

On the morning of my seventh birthday, my mother woke me, said that she wanted to show me something, took me by the hand to my brothers' room (the window of which faced the backyard) and opened the curtain to show me, to my utter surprise, the swing/sliding board gym set that I wanted so badly. On the morning of my fifteenth birthday, my mother was already at work, but I woke up to see on my desk, a wonderful surprise that I hadn't even asked for—a portable, electric, Smith Corona typewriter wrapped in a bright red ribbon with a big red bow on top. Next to it was a beautiful card on which my mother had, as always, written a very touching inscription. My swing set, typewriter, telescope, microscope, piano and bicycle are the surprises that I remember. The many little surprises that my mother often had for me upon returning home from shopping are just too numerous for me to remember.

Shortly after my fifteenth birthday, my mother began having "the talks" with me. At one point during one of those conversations, she asked me what I would do if I liked a boy, was alone with him and he asked me to become intimate with him. I told her that I wouldn't do it. "Even if no one would know?", she asked. "**I'd** know Mama", I responded. "I have a conscience." Within a minute, I overheard yet another conversation in which Mama had called Gramzie, and with her voice trembling from the emotion she was obviously feeling, said, "Mother, I was having another talk with Laurie today and I asked her what she would do if a boy wanted to be intimate with her and no one would know, and you know what that child said to me? She said, 'Well **I'd** know, Mama. I have a conscience.' I was **so** proud of her, Mother". I'm sure Mama didn't know that I had overheard that conversation as well, but as I did, hearing how deeply she had been touched, I also became full, my eyes welling up with tears.

During my high school years, after school, I'd sometimes take the bus uptown to my mother's office at the New Orleans Urban League and then ride home in the car with her. On one such afternoon, I walked into her office when Gloria Bartley, her much younger colleague and friend happened to be sitting in Mama's office when I arrived. Gloria looked at me, and with a big warm smile, said, "Oh, there she is—Laurie Joichin.[2] That's all we hear about—Laurie, Laurie, Laurie. Laurie did this. Laurie did that. Young lady, you're all your mother talks about!" Whether it was the progress I was making in my piano lessons, my ninth-grade science project having been chosen for a regional science competition, getting my driver's license, or any of my other quite ordinary adolescent landmarks, my mother's pride in me was endless.[3]

The love I felt so intensely from both my mother and my grandmother when I was a child was powerful. It was tender. It was adoring. That double dose of indescribable love from the two women who directly preceded me in my birth line was unquestionably the source of both the happiness which was ninety percent of the emotional template of my childhood and the strength, dignity and compassion with which I have tried to live my adult life.

My mother's example, the second thing that helped emotionally shelter me from the effects of the segregated New Orleans of the 1950's and '60's, came in the form of a two-tiered lesson. On one level was her message, very lovingly taught, that it is important

2 I changed my last name to "Nile" when I was in my late 30's. Even though I hadn't actually done the research to unequivocally establish it, I assumed, quite safely I believe, that "Joichin" (pronounced "Joysin" – the "h" is silent) was the name of one of my father's ancestors' French enslavers. I decided at that point, that while I could do nothing to change that tragic history, I did not have to carry its vestige in my very identity. I chose "Nile" as a name that connects me with both the African continent and with the great Nile Valley Civilization.

3 Lemar Jr. and Lambert were out of the house by then so it wasn't that my mother wasn't also proud of them. They were just no longer in our everyday family life at that point.

to have poise, charm, a beautiful smile, and a genuinely warm personality. There were lessons in good good grammar, good posture, and good manners - how to hold a fork (that I received when I was so young that I don't remember ever holding my fork any other way but in the manner she taught me), covering my mouth before yawning, answering questions in complete sentences, and saying, "Yes please", "No thank you" and "You're welcome" among many others. On a far deeper and more important level, however, were Mama's lessons of character. She taught me that no matter how attractive a person may be on the outside, if they have "ugly ways", i.e., if they're ugly on the inside, their looks do not matter one bit. Mama taught me how to be compassionate and empathetic to others—all others, especially those less fortunate. They were powerful lessons—lessons of true character. All of my mother's lessons were powerful for me because she exemplified them so exquisitely herself. Her sincere concern for and kindness to others and her social activism were also profound influences in my life.

My third childhood sanctuary was my neighborhood, Pontchartrain Park, a wonderful African American community named for Lake Pontchartrain which was walking distance away. "The Park", as it was widely known throughout the city's African American community, is recognized as one of the first (if not the first) middle class African American sub-divisions in the country and is a National Register Historic District. The Park was a brand new, beautiful, middle and upper middle class African American community of single family homes with meticulously manicured lawns. African American couples began touring the subdivision's model homes (which were very nice in the 1950's but quite modest by today's standards) immediately upon their availability. Pontchartrain Park was officially dedicated in January of 1955 and was truly one of the most beautiful neighborhoods in the city, black or white.[4]

4 As an interesting historical note, despite how amazing a place Pontchartrain Park was in which to grow up, it was built for a disturbing, nefarious reason - to keep the city's new and growing Post World War II middle and upper middle class African American population from moving into white subdivisions during the Jim Crow era. Fortunately, as children, we were

Now as for my fourth emotional shelter, that imagination of mine. Consider: On a hot summer day when I was about nine, while waiting my turn at bat during a day camp softball game, I picked a blade of grass from the ground, looked at it for several seconds, and then asked Mrs. Green, the camp director sitting nearby, "Hey Mrs. Green, you think maybe there's a whole nother universe on this blade of grass, or maybe a whole lot of universes on it? And you think maybe our universe might be on a blade of grass in some other, really big universe?" Mrs. Green turned, and as she looked at me in utter astonishment, responded, "Little girl, there's that imagination of yours again! I've never **seen** a child with such an imagination!" I was a genuine little science geek. Curiosity and imagination truly were my two best childhood friends.

Because of the love that Mama and Gramzie showered on me, Mama's example, my childhood neighborhood and my rich inner life of curiosity, fantasy and wonderment, I was for the most part, amazingly happy as a kid. The small part of me that wasn't happy, was the result of my father's behavior and parenting style. Four things about Daddy made me uncomfortable when I was young and caused me, during my childhood, to never really emotionally bond with or even get in touch with any feelings of love toward him.

First, and characteristic of many men of his era, my father, Lemar Louis Joichin, Sr., was somewhat emotionally detached and unavailable. Shortly after my eighteenth birthday, after several years of wanting to but never having the nerve, I finally asked him, "Daddy, can't you show any emotion?" "No. My daddy didn't do it and I'm not going to do it. Men don't do that." His response deeply hurt. After that conversation, I lowered my expectations of

---

totally unaware of the community's perverse raison d'etre. It was also built just behind the all-white Gentilly Woods subdivision. The two communities were by either accident or design, separated by a trench. It was a very clean trench, with thick, neatly cut grass that grew on both sides and the bottom, but it was a trench, a divider, nonetheless. Ironically, in its location, Pontchartrain Park was closer to Lake Pontchartrain than was Gentilly Woods, which I believe made its location more desirable.

my father and never again expected him to be emotionally available. I was very sad, but it also felt tremendously liberating.

Second, despite the fact that he was a quiet, reserved man, my father expressed his anger in bouts of yelling. When something upset him, as when one of my brothers or I had the volume on the stereo too high, he'd stew in bed quietly for as long as he could take it, then suddenly storm into the living room and yell, "Turn that G_____D_____music down!" We would, then he'd go right back to the bedroom. The whole thing lasted about five seconds. It didn't happen often, thankfully, but I didn't like it when it did, and it frightened me.[5]

Third, Daddy drank excessively on weekends. He was as straight as an arrow during the week, and went to work every day during the week. (In fact, in all of the years during which he worked as I was growing up, while I'm sure he must have, I don't remember my father ever missing a single day of work from his job as a U.S. Postman.) Then, every Friday and Saturday night, he'd gorge on beer at the neighborhood clubhouse, the Golfers' Clubhouse, qualifying him, perhaps, for the term, "weekend alcoholic". Fortunately though, Daddy wasn't abusive toward my brothers and me when he drank. Indeed, it was after he'd been drinking that he became much more animated in a somewhat pleasant way toward us. He'd sometimes come home and actually talk quite pleasantly with me in a way that he otherwise never did. The end of those conversations was always the same, "Li'l girl, you know your Daddy loves you." Then pointing to his right cheek, "C'mon, give your Daddy a kiss." I would, then he'd smile and give me a five-dollar bill. Those conversations happened perhaps every tenth time he'd come home sloshed. Usually though, he'd just go straight to the refrigerator, and after staring into it for a good five

5 I'm painfully aware that there is a bit of that temperament in me. While I'm not a yeller, I can be exasperated by a situation. I feel exasperation almost exclusively when behavior that I consider to be absent of concern, understanding and compassion is directed toward either myself or another. When that does happen, I try my absolute best to handle the challenge with my mother's poise. I am not always successful, but fortunately, it is seldom that I'm in that position.

minutes, grab a left-over pork chop or piece of hot sausage, make and eat a sandwich, then go to bed.

I am thankful both that my father drank only on the weekend, and that he was not abusive when he drank, but his drinking nevertheless hurt me deeply when I was a child because I witnessed how much pain it caused my mother, whom I **dearly** loved. I am infinitely thankful that my mother and grandmother's love was for me, an extraordinarily strong emotional counterbalance to my father's weekend drinking.

Fourth and finally, and more than his emotional unavailability, his stints of expressed anger **or** his weekend beer binges, the thing that saddened me most during my childhood was my father's emotional distance toward my mother. She bought him Christmas presents every Christmas, made him a big Easter basket with his favorite candy every Easter, reminded him of their anniversary every July and gave him a birthday card and present every September. I saw my mother trying so hard to make her marriage what she wanted it to be, but never saw my father respond to her in kind. I wanted him to be as loving and as kind toward her as she was toward him. Tragically, he was utterly incapable. His lack of emotional warmth, his temper (expressed toward her in arguments, usually about the fact that he thought she spent too much money on either us or on the house), and his weekend drinking, hurt my mother deeply. It was a very difficult marriage for my mother. I knew that, and because I loved her so deeply, it also hurt me tremendously.

Many years later, sometime in my mid-thirties, in thinking about my father in comparison to the very loving, nurturing fathers of many of my childhood friends, both in my neighborhood and at school, I realized that my father had himself been raised by an emotionally unavailable father. I realized that he was an absolute product of his time, one during which being raised to be a nurturing father, although fortunately not for all, was for many men, not a part of their socialization. I also realized that he was a very responsible man who provided well for us, and that after I left home, during my young adulthood, he showed, in a number of ways, that he loved me. I realized then that he had always loved my mother, my siblings and me. I also realized—that I loved him.[6]

My father was indeed a very responsible man. The January 18, 1949 official transcript of his World War II military record reads as follows:

- **Civilian Occupation and Number**: Student X-02
- **Summary of Military Occupations**: Cargo Checker—Checked cargo from ship to shore. Kept records and tally sheets of all materials. Turned records in to be filed. Supervised four men working as checkers. Checked all records and tally sheets of men under him to check correctness.
- **Battles & Campaigns**: Normandy, Northern France
- **Decoration & Citations**: EAME Campaign Medal, 2 Bronze Service Stars, Good Conduct Medal and Victory Medal WWII

My father was a young man of 21-24 years old during the years of his military service. He was there, on D-Day, not fighting, but supporting those who did, at the Battle of Normandy.

I am fortunate that even though I didn't have a very close emotional bond with my father during my childhood, because of Mama and Gramzie's powerful love, I nonetheless grew up feeling cherished and adored. It was that tremendous love that I received so early in my life that has in large measure inspired me to write this book, for I have written it out of my great love for humanity, a

6 One of the most loving things that my father did for me occurred so early in my life that I do not remember it. My mother told me that I was quite small when I was born, weighing in at a mere 5 pounds, 4 ounces, and that after giving birth to my brothers who were much larger than me, she was actually afraid to hold me, for fear of hurting me! She and Gramzie both told me that it was my father who when I was two weeks old, "handled" me in order to take the measurements for my christening outfit. My father, who sewed quite well on our old foot-pedal singer sewing machine, then made the outfit for my christening the following week.

love which I am able to deeply feel only because of the great love that I experienced upon entering this world and throughout my formative years.

The seeds of My Racial Memoir: The Making of a Compassionate Activist originated very early in my childhood, about which you now know a little. I cannot, however, represent that I am its source. It feels far more honest to say that I was merely its recipient, and that its source is far greater than I. My fervent hope is that this work will help to heal our species and to guide us into a future in which racism, all other "isms", and all other prejudices are relegated to the ashbin of history, where they belong. My fervent wish is to be of service in guiding humanity to a future of wisdom, of compassion and of maturity.

What follows is the story of how the passion to do so was cultivated in me.

CHAPTER ONE

MY CHILDHOOD

SEGREGATION WAS EVERYWHERE

I received this card from my dear friend Tom Finn thirty years ago:

Picture: A little girl about ten, sitting on Santa's lap wearing Harry Potter glasses, a pencil behind her right ear, reading quite deliberately from a spiral notepad.

The words on the pad: "Let's see now, did I mention world peace? And of course, cures for all the horrible diseases in the world, places for everyone to live, an end to all hatred, a spiritual awakening for everyone, a solution to pollution, and for me—maybe just a few little trinkets. You know what I—You choose."

The Inscription: "Lauren—Is this the perfect card for you or what?! Hope you have a great 1993. Looking forward to spending more of it with you. Love, Tom & Kathleen"

That little girl on the card was really an amazing reflection of me as an adolescent, beginning at age thirteen. I did absolutely love science throughout my childhood, and the little insatiably curious scientist was still very much present, but beginning at age thirteen, Lauren, the little outraged activist, began to emerge. I was beginning to develop a very strong intellectual and emotional orientation toward integrity, peace, economic equality and social justice. I was outraged by discrimination, and by oppression of all kinds.

You see, the little girl who was so greatly loved by her mother and grandmother, the extremely curious little kid with the amazing inner life, the kid who had enough intellectual curiosity and imagination to wonder whether a whole other universe existed on a blade of grass, that kid, when outside the safe cocoon of her family, community and school, lived within the larger society as a second-class citizen. Throughout my elementary school years, until I was nearly eleven years old, I saw the ugly symbols of, and lived in the reality of, racial segregation every day.[7] The "White Only" (in other cities and states "Whites Only") signs were **everywhere.**

Images of segregation:
https://www.youtube.com/watch?v=c-7eNRB2_0Q

7 The 1896 Plessy v. Ferguson Supreme Court decision that established segregation, required that all public facilities for Americans of Color and European Americans be separate but equal. In reality, they were **always** separate, but they were **never** equal.

I couldn't drink from the same water fountains from which white kids drank. I couldn't use the same restrooms they used. In some places, there were three restrooms, "Men, Women and Colored". I couldn't eat with my parents at the same restaurants at which white kids ate with their parents.[8]

We couldn't go to Pontchartrain Beach (the city's formerly "White Only" amusement park that was right on Lake Pontchartrain and Lakeshore Drive, a five-minute drive from our home in Pontchartrain Park), which I really wanted to do, to ride what seemed to me to be the most amazing roller coaster in the world.

The "White Only" Pontchartrain Beach

Our separate, much smaller and utterly unequal amusement park was Lincoln Beach, located on what seemed to me as a child, a very long distance down Haynes Blvd., which had no public transportation.

8 The two African American restaurants that my family went to, Dooky Chase and Levata's Oyster House, like all of the city's other black eating establishments, had incredible food, so fortunately, we were not at a "food disadvantage" by eating at segregated restaurants. It may have been the only way in which segregation did not result in a social and economic hardship for us.

The "Colored" Lincoln Beach

https://www.nola.com/300/article_4756e82a-0432-5bab-a9f8-a4c831ad4c7f.html

When my family went to "the Lakefront"[9] for Fourth of July, Memorial Day or Labor Day family picnics, we, along with all of the city's other African-American residents,[10] had to try to find a spot between Seabrook and Franklin Avenues, which I would guess is perhaps a fifth to a quarter of the entire Lakefront Drive area. The entire remainder of the lakefront, from Franklin Avenue all the way out to its end at the Southern Yacht Club, was "White Only".

Early one summer afternoon in the early 60's, my extended family, after arriving at Mandeville Louisiana's Fontainebleau State Park for a family picnic, nearly left after about 45 minutes of riding around looking for the park's Colored section. Fortunately, we eventually did find it, and had our picnic. But if looks could kill, those we received from the European American patrons while we rode through the white only section, would surely have made **that** day, our **last** day.

We couldn't go into the Howard Johnson's ice cream parlor on the corner of Congress Drive and Chef Menteur Highway that we passed every single day on the way home from school to have any of the twenty-eight flavors of ice cream that were so prominently and colorfully displayed in its front window. When we went to the train station to get my great uncle Marshall who lived in New York City and came down by train to visit us every summer, we had to sit in the station's "Colored" section, which was perhaps one-third of the whole station. The entire rest of Union Station was the "White Only" seating area.

My mother and I went grocery shopping at the Gentilly Schwegmann's supermarket every other Saturday, which was billed, at the time, as "The Largest Supermarket in the World." On the inside, it literally went on for as far as my eyes could see. It was in terms of size, the 1960's precursor to Costco. When

9 New Orleanians refer to Lakeshore Drive, a long, very pleasant avenue that runs along Lake Pontchartrain, the city's northern border, as, "the Lakefront". For its entire length, the lake is on one side of Lakeshore Drive, and a very nice picnic area is on the other.

10 I shall use the terms "African American" and "Black", and the terms "European American" and "White" interchangeably.

Mama and I stopped at its long, L-shaped lunch counter at the front of the store for a sandwich and soda, we weren't allowed to sit and eat our meal at the large front section with the nice counter stools. We had to go around to the shorter side of the "L", a much smaller side counter where there were no stools. African American customers had to order lunch on that side and then either stand at the short counter while eating, or sit on the adjacent staircase. My mother and I never did either. In retrospect, I believe that the indignity of doing so was probably simply far too much for my mother. We bought our sandwich and soda and then left. I'll never forget the visual of White People sitting comfortably on the front counter stools eating their lunch, and Black People either standing at the small side counter or sitting on the nearby tile staircase—essentially, on the floor, eating theirs. There were sometimes so many people sitting on those steps that they'd be half-way up the entire staircase, always with a passageway on the right side as you looked up. Walking along the passageway were White People who were going to and from the second-floor business offices.

In the front section of the store were two water fountains, each on either side of a large, white round, floor-to-ceiling support column. Down one side, in big, bold, black, capital letters, the word, "W-H-I-T-E" was painted. Down the other, "C-O-L-O-R-E-D." The "white fountain" was tall, silver, metal, and cold. Ours was low, white, porcelain and hot. Judging from the frost that accumulated so quickly on the mouthpiece, the "white fountain" had a strong, steady stream of icy cold water. Ours, a trickle of warm.

When my mother took me to the Shrine Circus at the Municipal Auditorium, we had to sit so high up in the auditorium's Colored section, the "nosebleed" seats, that it was virtually impossible to see the action taking place on the stage floor below. It was the same segregated Municipal Auditorium in which Lemar Jr. and his friends attended concerts of their favorite groups. The Coasters, the Platters, and the Drifters were Lemar Jr.'s three favorites.

He and his friends sat up in the segregated balcony high above all the White teens in the orchestra seats below them, as they **all** watched the African American performers on the stage.

My parents couldn't listen to jazz in any of the French Quarter jazz clubs, the same clubs in which Black musicians were performing for "White Only" audiences.

We watched the Mardi Gras parades on either Claiborne Avenue or Canal Street. While Jim Crow laws didn't prohibit us from being there, it was known that St. Charles Avenue, the "uptown" section of New Orleans, was the area where the city's White residents watched the parades. We watched them along Canal Street. It was a kind of de facto segregation.

My mother absolutely loved musicals. I grew up with the 33rpm soundtracks of the Broadway productions of The Sound of Music, The King and I, My Fair Lady, and South Pacific among others. I don't know whether any of them were performed in New Orleans at that time, but had they been, we wouldn't have been able to see them since they would most certainly have been performed at the Saenger or the Loew's Theatres or some other "White Only" venue.

In addition to Lemar Jr.'s Ray Charles, Temptations, Coasters, Drifters, Platters, and Sam Cooke albums, Lambert's Earth Wind and Fire, Miles Davis, Eddie Harris, Wes Montgomery, Dave Brubeck, and Chicago albums, and the music I liked, the Supremes, Simon and Garfunkel, Stevie Wonder, the Mamas and the Papas, The Fifth Dimension, Dionne Warwick, the Beatles, the Shirelles and John Denver, I also grew up listening to the orchestral music which my mother loved. I have in my garage to this day, in vinyl, her favorites—Dvorak's New World Symphony; Rimsky Korsakov's Scheherazade; and her three absolute favorites, Finlandia, Swedish Rhapsody, and Handel's Messiah. At Christmas, I listened over and over and over again to my mother's album, The Glorious Sounds of Christmas by the Philadelphia Orchestra, Eugene Ormandy conducting, with the Temple University Concert Choir.

Mama loved orchestral music so much that she wanted to instill a love for it in me. Her plan—go to Werlein's Music Store on Canal Street to buy me a piano (the only place of any reputation to buy a piano in the city), and send me to piano lessons. I enjoyed studying piano, and did well in my lessons.[11]

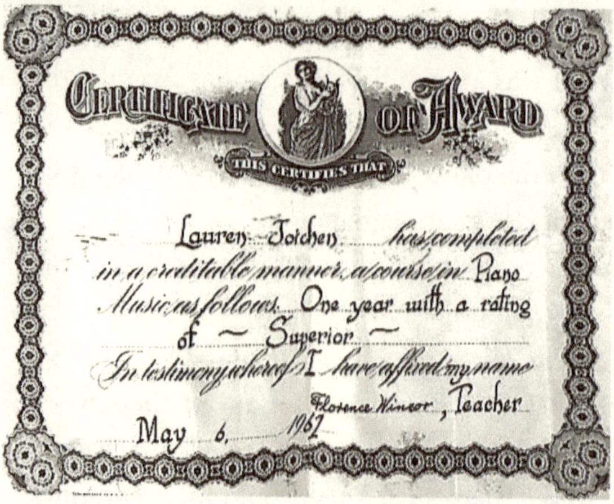
Certificate of Award
This certifies that
Lauren Joichen has completed in a creditable manner a course in Piano Music as follows: One year with a rating of ~ Superior ~
In testimony whereof I have affixed my name
Florence Wincor, Teacher
May 6, 1962

My Piano Lessons Certificate

When my mother attended my piano recitals, she always had a beautiful bouquet of flowers that, after my performance, she handed to me with a big smile and hug, saying through her tears, "I'm so proud of you." At my last recital Mama attended, after I had played my piece and was standing before the piano at the front of the stage bowing my head to the right and left in response to the audience's applause, she quickly walked up the middle aisle of the auditorium to the elevated stage and handed me my bouquet right there and then. As I leaned down to take the flowers from her, as always, she said through her tears, "Laurie, I'm so proud of you."

After my lessons began, nearly every time my mother went shopping, she bought me yet another album of piano music. My

11 I still have many of my childhood mementos because my mother, thinking that I might enjoy looking at them at some point as an adult, saved them all for me in a little box that lived on the top shelf of my closet. I am happy that I still have my day camp certificates and so many other of my childhood keepsakes that I was able to include in this book.

favorites, which remain in my collection today, are The Exciting Pianos of Ferrante and Teicher; My Favorite Chopin, performed by Van Cliburn; and my all-time favorite, Rachmaninoff's Piano Concerto No. 2 in C Minor, performed by Taylor Edwards with the Royal Festival Orchestra. I don't know whether any of those orchestras ever performed in New Orleans at that time, but if they had, they too would have been performed at "White Only" theaters.

Me at 13 Dressed for My First Piano Recital

My mother took me to see the Disney movies of the 1960s—Mary Poppins, One Hundred and One Dalmatians, Lady and the Tramp, and Chitty Chitty Bang Bang are the ones I remember. She took me to every Sidney Poitier movie that came to the theater—Lilies of the Field, To Sir with Love, A Patch of Blue, Guess Who's Coming to Dinner, and In the Heat of the Night. She took me to the biblical movies she loved—The Greatest Story Ever Told, The Ten Commandments and King of Kings, and to the James Bond films she enjoyed—From Russia with Love, Goldfinger and Dr. No. When she did, we went either to one of the city's five "Colored" movie theaters, the Claiborne, the Carver, the Gallo, the Famous and the Caffin, or to one of its segregated theaters, the Circle and the RKO Orpheum, where we sat upstairs in the

"Colored" section. There were even separate concession stands in the segregated theaters, one for White and one for Colored.

In addition to the city's Colored and segregated movie theaters, there, were, of course, also some that were "White Only", the Saenger Orleans and the Joy on Canal Street, the Fox on Elysian Fields Avenue, the Tiger on Franklin Avenue, and the one closest to our house, the Gentilly Art on Gentilly Boulevard.

I saw no Black salespeople or cashiers in department stores, drug stores, grocery stores, or furniture stores—no stores. I saw us only sweeping and mopping their floors. I saw only White men as politicians. The President, Vice-President, Senators, and Representatives on both the Federal and State levels were all White men, and on the local level, the politicians were also only White men. On television, as news reporters, news anchors, meteorologists, and sportscasters, I also saw only White men. People who looked like my family were clearly not in charge.

Even the city's **cemeteries** were segregated, as they were all over the South. The descendants of the same people who lived with European Americans in their plantation homes, waiting on them "hand and foot" from the moment they woke up in the morning until the moment they went to bed at night, the descendants of the same people who during slavery, cleaned their homes, cooked their food and cared for their children, the descendants of the same African American women who, during slavery, breastfed their children, the descendants of those same people were not good enough to have their remains buried in the same cemeteries as the descendants of the European Americans.

MY REACTION TO SEGREGATION

During those, my childhood years, I was struck by the absolute unfairness of segregation. It was extremely difficult for me to understand why we—my brothers, my parents, my grandparents, cousins, aunts and uncles, all my friends, because of how we looked, because of the physical characteristics with which we were born, were being treated, every day of our lives, as second-class citizens. My thought was, "But White People were born white just like we were born brown. (Children think in colors, not in categories, such as black and white.) They didn't choose to be born white and we didn't choose to be born brown. It's not fair."

Years later, as an adult, I realized that in addition to being morally bankrupt, segregation was also tremendously financially unjust. Throughout the entire time that we were forced to live as second-class citizens in a segregated society, in what was essentially an American apartheid, we paid not a single penny less for our goods and services, and not a cent less in taxes. No "discrimination adjustment" was made for us. Apparently, lawmakers didn't opine, "Well, since they're **getting** less, we really should **charge** them less. It may hurt us a bit financially, but it's well worth it to not have our children go to school with them, to not sit next to them at the movies or see them in our amusement parks, to not have to eat with them, use the bathroom with them, share water fountains with them, and sit next to them on the buses."

If any such discussions based on a fairness argument did occur among lawmakers, those who advocated for such a two-tiered economic structure, lost. The reality was that while being required by law to sit in only the back of the bus, we paid **the exact same fare** as White riders who rode in the front. While either standing or sitting on the stairs adjacent to the side section of Schwegmann's lunch counter, we paid the exact same price for our sandwiches and sodas as the White patrons who sat at the nice counter stools in the front. While being consigned to the smaller section of

Fontainebleau State Park with its inferior picnic area and inadequate restroom facilities, our parents paid **the exact same state income taxes** for the park's maintenance as did the state's White citizens. In all the stores in which we weren't allowed to try on clothes, hats and shoes, or to return them if they didn't fit, we paid **the exact same price for and sales tax on** that **clothing**. My parents and all of the city's other African American residents who were fortunate enough to be able to buy a home, paid **the exact same real estate taxes** on their homes as White home owners paid on theirs. They paid **the exact same Federal income taxes** on their salaries. Math has never been my strong suit, but one needn't be a math whiz to realize that it would have been a tremendous economic benefit to African American families and communities if, as an acknowledgement of the crippling discrimination under which, by law, we were forced to endure in every aspect of our lives when in public, they would have charged us 33, 25, 20, 15 or even 10 percent less for goods and services or paid even 10 percent less in income, sales, and property taxes. It was a benefit that tragically, we were denied. We paid the same for everything. We paid...to be humiliated—publicly.[12]

---

12 Among the most memorable conversations I ever had about the racial discrimination that I experienced during my earliest years of life was that which I had about five years ago with a White, European man who was my friend for a few years. He was from Romania and had grown up in his country under communism. I will never forget my friend's reaction to my story, to my telling him that if he and his parents had been able to visit the United States during that time, and had they come to New Orleans during their visit, they would have been able to go to amusement parks, restaurants, theaters, movie houses and many other places that my parents and I would have been prohibited from entering; that my parents and I would not have been able to drink from the same water fountains as he and his parents; that we wouldn't have been able to use the same restrooms that he and his parents used; that we would have had to sit behind them on public service buses; that he and I would not have been able to attend the same school; that our families would likely not have been able to live in the same neighborhood, and that all of those things, the water fountains, restrooms, lunch counters, everything that we had, would have been vastly inferior to everything that they had. As he looked at me in pure amazement, my friend responded, "Lauren, in Romania, we didn't know anything about this. All we knew was that the United States was the land of freedom, and we all wanted to come here. I can't believe that your own country would treat you and your parents and other Black Americans like that. I can't believe that I, a foreigner, could have come here and been treated better than you and your parents, **you, who are Americans**. It was different, but kind of like me growing up in communism. You had no freedom. Lauren, you and me, we're human beings. We're human beings. There's no difference. I'm sorry, Lauren." And as through his thick Romanian accent, he uttered that last sentence, my friend, a large, fit, muscular blonde-haired, blue-eyed man of over six feet, wiped tears from his eyes.

In retrospect, I realize that the utter injustice of segregation could very well have scarred me as a child. But because my mother told me that segregation was wrong, that the people who believed in it were wrong in that belief, and that we were on the right side, the just side, the moral side of the issue, not only did segregation not affect my self-esteem, it actually provided me an emotional template through which I and everyone I knew and loved, were fighting a valiant battle of right against wrong, of justice against injustice, of good against evil. I felt good being on the "right" side, the side, I thought, of the people who were intelligent and mature, the side that was therefore ultimately destined to win. As a child, I was totally unaware that that very struggle of what I thought of as good against evil, was providing me with a very early backdrop against which I was already beginning to develop as a value, the goal of living a conscious, examined life of principle.[13]

SEGREGATION: MY BUFFER AGAINST IT

WHAT I HAVE DESCRIBED IN MUCH ABBREVIATED FASHION IS THAT both the time at and place in which I was born resulted in my experiencing the ugliness of segregation as a part of my introduction to life. It is ironic that in a different way, I was born during America's golden age. It was our golden economic age, a time during which millions of us whose parents, like mine, had been raised in poverty during the depression, became our families' first generation to grow up middle class. There had been middle class African American families during the decades after emancipation and preceding the 1950's, primarily those of

13 I have been struck, in many conversations with my wife, Barbara, by how different her childhood was in southern New Jersey during the 1950's and 60's. She and her family are also African American and as a child, her parents took her and her siblings to events from which, because of segregation, we were totally shut out. Her mom took them to see the Rockettes at Radio City Music Hall. They had Sunday outings to Baskin Robbins. They visited the Philadelphia Museum of Art, rode on all the rides in Atlantic City, and could use the public library that was nearest to their home. Barbara listens to the stories of my childhood under segregation with nothing but pure amazement. She was aware of the existence of segregation, of course, but had never before heard actual stories of what it was like to actually live in it every day and of what happened, initially when it ended. My stories have been a real eye opener for Barbara.

attorneys, physicians, ministers and business owners, but they were by far the exception. Primarily as a result of the legacy of slavery, every generation of African-Americans during that period was significantly poorer than European Americans. We were, in the 50's, the first generation of Black kids whose parents were not primarily lawyers, doctors, clergy and entrepreneurs, to grow up middle class in any appreciable numbers.

We were Baby Boomers who grew up in the post-World War II economy. Many of our fathers were veterans of the war, making a college education through the G.I Bill possible for some of them.[14] Our parents, members of The Greatest Generation, were able to purchase their homes with either FHA (Federal Housing Administration) or VA (Veterans Administration) loans. Certain kinds of government jobs were becoming available on a limited basis to People of Color for the first time at the Federal, state and municipal levels. It was a time at which a couple such as my parents, a public-school secretary and a mailman, could afford to buy a suburban home and a nice car and live comfortably.[15] While it was a time of crippling discrimination against People of Color, still, Pontchartrain Park, the African American community in which I grew up, was a total product of America's economic golden age.[16] It

14 After the war, however, at least one million African American World War II veterans were denied benefits under the GI Bill on the basis of race.
How the GI Bill's Promise Was Denied to a Million Black WWII Veterans—HISTORY

15 While at that time some Federal government jobs were slowly becoming available to African Americans, jobs as city police officers, firefighters and employees in Federal, state and city agencies were still largely not available to us. The segregated public school system and the U.S. Post Office, in which my mother and father worked respectively when we moved to the Park, were perhaps the two employers that, beginning in the 50's, most contributed to the existence of an African American middle class. My grandparents' generation supported their families principally by working as janitors, domestics in private homes, laborers, hotel maids (as was Gramzie when she was young), bellmen, truck drivers (as was Gramps, my father's father), and river front workers (as did Gramzie's brothers, my great uncles William and Paul, and her sister, my great aunt Celie).

16 Knowing that my parents had both more education (high school diplomas) and more employment opportunities than my grandparents, and that my generation lived much more comfortably than my parents did when they were children, I thought, as a child and young adult, that I was simply witnessing the progressive march of history, society merely becoming more intelligent, and thus, less prejudiced. I never dreamed that in reality, those of us who are Baby Boomers had actually won the birth lottery. I never thought that for the generation after us, it would be harder to afford a college education, harder to find meaningful employment in one's chosen field, harder to purchase a home, harder to be in the middle class. We had no way

was one of the very first, and indeed, I believe that it was **the** first planned, suburban community for African Americans. Growing up in Pontchartrain Park was for me, a **powerful** buffer against the totally racially segregated society in which I was growing up.

Aerial View of Pontchartrain Park before Construction of the Homes

The New Subdivision Sign [17]
City Archives New Orleans Public Library
Louisiana Division

of knowing that we had actually been born during a brief window in time during which we had tremendous opportunities that a generation later, may not exist for our children.

17 The sign was later changed to "Pontchartrain Park"

Pontchartrain Park, my childhood neighborhood, was dedicated on January 31, 1955.

Dedication of Pontchartrain Park, January 31, 1955
City Archives New Orleans Public Library
Louisiana Division

The Park was like "Black Leave It to Beaver Land." We were all two-parent families. I don't remember a single family going through a divorce the entire time I was growing up there, from the time I was two until I left after graduating from college, when I was twenty. With the exception of one family that moved to California in the mid '60's, I don't even remember any families moving out of the Park. We were an extremely stable community of Black families—the Woods', the Gougises, the Glapions, the Allens, the Vickmans, the Dejoies, the Aguillards, the Nelsons, the Bushes, the Kennedys, the Gardners, the Merrimans, the Durrels, the Villavasos, the Coulliets, the Permillions, the LeBlancs, the Pierces, the Blanchards, Uncle Ikee and his family, who lived four blocks from us, and so many others.[18]

My understanding is that we were the second family to move into "The Park," as it was widely known throughout the New Or-

18 I was an older teenager when I learned that one of my friends was from a blended family. I'll refer to them as the Smiths. I learned that Mrs. Smith had been married prior to being married to Mr. Smith, and that my friend's two older brothers had a different last name and a different father from herself and her younger brother. I was totally surprised by that information and realized that the Smiths were the most atypical of any family that I knew in my entire neighborhood.

leans "Colored" community. Our moving day was Thanksgiving Day, 1955. Indeed, after looking at the architectural plans for the entire community, my parents bought our home after seeing the plans before it was actually built. Gramzie told me that every Saturday morning while the house was being built, my mother would pick up her younger sister, my Aunt Verlie, drive out to our lot, and very excitedly look at the progress that had been made in the construction the prior week. On Thanksgiving Day of 1955 when we moved in. Lemar Jr. was twelve, Lambert was eight and I was two.

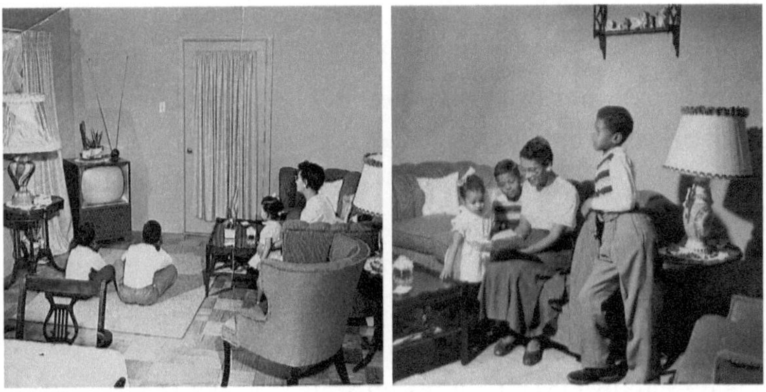

My Mother, Lemar Jr., Lambert and me at home in the Living Room—1955

In the middle of the community was an 18-hole golf course with two large lagoons and a clubhouse for golfers.The larger lagoon we called "Nanny Goat Island." In the earliest days of the community, it was wooded and actually had goats living on it that were clearly visible from the golf course. The popular story among us kids that there was a rickety old shack in the middle of the woods with a little old man living in it, intrigued my imagination to no end.

The Club House The Golf Course
City Archives New Orleans Public Library
Louisiana Division

Pontchartrain Park was a neighborhood of back yards filled with various colors, kinds and sizes of gym sets and round, plastic, two and three ring inflatable kids pools. At the back of the community was Lake Pontchartrain, tennis courts, basketball courts, picnic grounds, a baseball field for the kids in the community, and right beside the baseball field, a baseball stadium, the lights of which are visible in the above "New Subdivision Sign" photo. There were two playgrounds with swings, sliding boards, merry-go-rounds, see-saws and monkey bars.

Children Playing at 1 of Pontchartrain Park's 2 Playgrounds
City Archives New Orleans Public Library
Louisiana Division

Pontchartrain Park had an elementary school, Coghill, (named after African American educator and civil leader Mary Dora

Coghill https://en.wikipedia.org/wiki/Mary_Dora_Coghill) that Lorna attended from kindergarten through 6th grade, and even an accredited university, Southern University in New Orleans, (https://en.wikipedia.org/wiki/Southern_University_at_New_Orleans).

It seemed that almost every family, including ours, had a dog.[19] Saturday mornings were filled with the sound of lawnmowers from every direction, the overpowering smell of freshly cut St. Augustine grass, and dozens of men walking along the golf course, including my father. Apparently, though, it took him a while after we moved to the Park, to warm up to the game. I heard my mother once say that for the first year or so that we were in our new home, my father regularly made the following comment about the golfers, "Look at those fools. Out there doing all that walking in the hot sun chasing a little white ball around." His change of heart about the game apparently happened not too long thereafter because I don't remember my father ever not being a golfer, and an avid one at that, and judging from the three trophies that he was awarded by the Pontchartrain Park Golf Club, Daddy was pretty decent on the course.[20]

19 Our dog was Duke, a big, black and brown German Shepherd who looked very much like Rin Tin Tin, the famous German Shephard star of the 1950s TV Show of the same name. Lambert was especially close to Duke. Every Christmas morning, Mama had a stocking under our Christmas tree for Duke filled with doggie treats.

20 In the dining room of the house, my father taught me how to both putt and swing. I loved playing with his little green, plastic electric putting machine that spat the ball back to the putter, but I never did catch the golf "bug". He was much more successful, though, with Lemar Jr. and Lambert, who are, to this day, absolute golf fanatics. As for me, I play a pretty mean game of mini golf.

My Father Receiving a Trophy from the Pontchartrain Park Golf Club

In its earliest days, Pontchartrain Park had a governing board on which my mother served. The Board was followed in time by the Pontchartrain Park Improvement Association, of which she was the secretary. She was also the editor of the early editions of the community newspaper, the Pontchartrain Park Patriot, and an organizer of the House of the Month Club. [21]

21 Homes in the community were judged each month for the beauty of their front lawn and landscaping. The house judged **most** beautiful, was awarded the "Pontchartrain Park House of the Month" front lawn sign.

http://photos.nola.com/tpphotos/2011/11/175pontchartrain.html

Pontchartrain Park Improvement Association Directors' Meeting Nov. 3, 1957: From left: F.T. Bechet; C.W. Acox; Mrs. J.B. Vickman; H.S. Dorsey, chairman; Mr. Permillion, president; Mrs. Selina Joichin; Rev. A.A. Jones, Chaplain.

I remember that on one occasion, members of the Improvement Association met with the manager of the "all white" Gentilly Arts Movie Theater, requesting that they set aside one day per week on which we could see movies there, a kind of "Negro Night." I don't know whether the Association was successful, but because I have no memory of having ever gone to the Gentilly Arts, I doubt that it was.

I have in my possession to this day, the inch-and-a-half thick binder of notes that my mother took at all of those Pontchartrain Park Improvement Association meetings, and as such, am acutely aware that I am sitting on an absolute gold mine of history.

On New York Circle, the little cul-de-sac in which my family lived, there were our next-door neighbors on the corner, Mr. and Mrs. Morial and their kids Julie and Marc, [22] then my family at

22 Mr. Morial later served two terms as the first black mayor of New Orleans. In the Fall of 1977 when he was elected to his first term, he spoke at the University of Pennsylvania where his son, Marc, and I were both students and quite coincidentally, next door neighbors again in the W.E.B. Du Bois residential living facility, "the black dorm." The first thing Mr. Morial said to me when I went up to greet him after his remarks was, "Laurie Joichin. Look at you, all grown up, and working on your doctorate. Young lady, your mother would be **so** proud of you. If Selina could see you now." I called my father the next day and told him about that exchange. After his initial surprise, "You saw Dutch?!" (Mr. Morial's nickname, which he was called by

5019 New York Circle, and on the other side Mr. and Mrs. Acox and their son, Clarence Junior. Next to the Acoxes were Mr. and Mrs. Wharton and their seven kids. Next door to the Whartons were Dr. and Mrs. Burgeron, and next to them, Mr. and Mrs. Carr and their daughters Shelly, and much later, Stacy. Next to the Carrs were Mr. and Mrs. Hayes and their daughter and then on the other corner of the circle were Mr. and Mrs. Doucette and their five kids, Gaynelle, Lloyd Junior, Terri, Michelle and their youngest son, Dion.

On DeBore Drive, just outside of the circle, were Mr. and Mrs. Rubion and their kids Barbara and Lemar Jr.'s best friend, Lil Pat (Mr. Rubion was Patrick Sr., i.e., "Big Pat" to the adults), and Mr. and Mrs. Sneed and their four daughters Gwen, Roz, Deb and Karen. Around the corner on Congress Drive in the gorgeous big, white, sprawling house on the hill, were Dr. and Mrs. Adams and their daughter Carolyn.

Lemar Jr., Lambert and Me in Front of Our Parents' New 1959 Ford Fairlane 500

many of his peers), he responded with his customary "Uh huh." it was uttered this time with a chuckle. I knew that he delighted to hear Mr. Morial's comment about my mother. Years later, Marc (currently the Executive Director of the National Urban League) also served two terms as mayor of New Orleans.

There were two churches in Pontchartrain Park. In "the new section," as we called it, built in the 60's on the other side of the golf course, was Holy Cross Lutheran Church. On our side was the church my family attended, Bethany Methodist Church.[23] Bethany was chartered in 1957, two years after Pontchartrain Park opened. Before Bethany was built, ours was one of the homes in which church service was held on a rotating basis. My mother was one of Bethany's founding members, the lead soprano of its Sanctuary Choir, Chair of its Pastor-Parish Relations Committee, and a member of its Bi-Racial Dialogue Group, the Methodist Women's Guild, and the Building Committee. As Chair of the Pastor-Parish Relations Committee, she was successful in leading the effort to keep our minister, Reverend Kennedy, at Bethany when church officials were going to re-assign him to another church. As a member of the Building Committee, she worked tirelessly on getting the new sanctuary built. To say that my mother truly loved Bethany would be an understatement of mammoth proportions. My mother was totally committed to Bethany. It was exceptionally close to her heart. She had a profound and abiding religious faith. My mother's deep-seated faith in God was one of the pivotal foundations of her life. I'm sure that Gramzie, also a woman of deep faith, was her model.

23 After the 1968 merger of the Methodist Church with the Evangelical United Brethren Church, the names of both churches were changed to the United Methodist Church, after which Bethany became Bethany United Methodist Church. In researching the history of the Methodist Church as an adult, I was surprised by that merger because I had always thought of the Methodist Church (especially in comparison to Catholicism, New Orleans' predominant religion) as enlightened, modern and liberal, anything but evangelical, which in my mind was synonymous with fundamentalist, or orthodox.

My Mother with the Methodist Women's Guild
(Third from Right, Front Row, in White Suit)

We were a real community. The way in which our parents in the circle came together to beautify their homes typifies the munificent neighborhood spirit they all shared. They decided, at some point, that in addition to cutting their lawns, they also wanted to edge them. Consequently, they held a meeting and decided that they'd all pitch in toward the cost of an electric edger. I can still see that edger in my mind's eye. It was red and three-wheeled and at our house most of the time. I was probably about eight when I finally stopped being afraid of the sparks that flew when its steel blade nipped the sidewalk. We shared that edger for years.

Every year on Halloween night, it seemed that there were at least ten thousand kids out trick-or-treating, all in costumes. At Christmas, I don't remember a single house not being beautifully decorated. On Christmas morning, the neighborhood lawns and sidewalks were filled with kids playing with wooden croquet sets, tin kaleidoscopes, a myriad of board games, plastic bowling pins and balls, kid-sized golf sets, dolls, and matchbox cars, while the streets were overrun with traffic jams of kids on skates, shiny new bicycles, and even one surrey with a fringe on top.

There was the jingle of the ice cream truck (that I still remember and can hum even today), that passed through the neighborhood every summer evening without fail, the sound of bicycle bells, metal skates on cement, girls jumping rope and playing hop scotch, boys playing football, and kids practicing drums, flutes, clarinets, trumpets, and pianos.

It was from my perspective as a child, a world of Schwinn bicycles, of metal skates with metal keys, of the Etch-A-Sketch, of Give-A-Show Projectors, Pogo Sticks, Snow Cone Machines, of Slinkies, Silly Putty, Pick-Up Stix, Jumping Beans, Play-Doh, plastic bowling balls with plastic pins, finger painting, Crazy Clock (Crazy Clock Game. - YouTube) and a variety of other kids board games, and the wonders of the View Master's astounding 3-D pictures. It was a time, years before Sesame Street's cultural diversity, of Captain Kangaroo and Mr. Green Jeans, Shari Lewis and Lamb Chop, Howdy Doody, and Bozo the Clown. My favorite cartoons were Casper the Friendly Ghost, the Flintstones, the Jetsons, Mighty Mouse, Gumby and Pokey, Popeye, and Rocky & Bullwinkle with its cast of characters, Sherman, Mr. Peabody, Nell, Dudley Do-Right, Oil Can Harry and the Fractured Fairy Tales. Dick Tracy, Annie, Beetle Bailey and Blondie were "required" reading every Sunday morning as soon as the Sunday morning paper hit the front door. I only read four comic book series: Superman, Popeye, the Archie series, and the Betty and Veronica series, but I'm sure I read hundreds of them.[24]

These were the pre-FM days. Radio was only AM, and in New Orleans, the four most popular stations for our generation were WBOK and WYLD, which played "black kids' music", and WNOE and WTIX, which played "white kids' music". I liked and listened to all four.

For television, we had the three major networks. In New Orleans, they were Channel 4, WWL (CBS), Channel 6, WDSU (NBC), and Channel 8, WVUE (ABC). Channel 12, WYES (PBS),

24 I had no interest in The Hulk, Batman, the Avengers and any other superhero comic books because it seemed that the characters did nothing but fight all the time. They were just too violent.

and Channel 26 (WGNO) came along much later. Remote controls and channel surfing were purely the stuff of sci fi.

My two favorite TV shows, both science fiction, The Twilight Zone and The Outer Limits, were scaring the life out of me and every other kid I knew. Leonard Bernstein's Sunday afternoon Young People's Concerts, the television airing of The Sound of Music and the Wizard of Oz that happened around Christmas, and the Easter season television airing of Peter Pan with Mary Martin were never missed.[25] Mama and I always watched them together. If you grew up in New Orleans, mad scientist Morgus the Magnificent and his sidekick Chopsley were compulsory Saturday night viewing, and Mr. Bingle was a daily visitor during the Christmas season.

The three-month summer vacation from school felt like three years, and summer was a time of hand suckers, pink, blue and white coconut pralines, and nickel huck-a-bucks (sweet frozen cups). It was also a time of S & H Green Stamps and of the milk man who delivered fresh milk in glass bottles with cardboard tops right to your front door. We had Sugar Smacks, and the "Snap, Crackle and Pop" of Sugar Pops for breakfast, and snacked on Sugar Daddy suckers after school. Tony the Tiger was telling us to put Sugar Frosted Flakes in our stomachs, and Esso was telling us to put a tiger in our tank. It was the time of mimeograph machines with their amazing smelling ink and frost-covered, silver metal ice trays with handles so cold they stuck to your fingers. Tab and Tang (the latter of which went into space with American Astronaut John Glenn) were terrific, both Bosco and Brylcreem were "boss," and people who brushed their teeth with Pepsodent wondered where the yellow went! I dreamed of seeing the USA in a (convertible) Chevrolet. When adults talked about "the war", everybody knew without question that it was World War II. Music

25 When I think about that Peter Pan production now, I find the portrayal of its Indigenous characters enormously disconcerting. Both its stereotypes and the use of the term, "Red Skin," while shocking by **current** standards of cultural appropriateness, were, unfortunately, quite commonplace when the production was done in the early 1960's.

was on 45's and 33's and even a few of your parents' heavy old 78's were still around. These and many other memories of growing up in Pontchartrain Park will remain with me forever. They are as clear for me today as if it all happened yesterday. My memories of and very fond feelings about growing up in Pontchartrain Park are shared by so many of us kids who grew up there, as well as by our parents who lived there for many years as adults[26]. Growing up in Pontchartrain Park provided me and all of us kids, a powerful buffer against the evil of segregation.[27]

OUR PARENTS AS OUR INSPIRATION

Pontchartrain Park was a community of African-American adults who were remarkable role models of grace, maturity and exquisite dignity in the face of the incredible daily indignities of segregation. Many of our parents were active members of the New Orleans NAACP and the New Orleans Urban League. As Lambert and I have said in our numerous conversations about the adults who were in our lives during our childhood, they were extremely "civic-minded."

Our parents had inspiring dignity. I **never** heard either my mother or Gramzie utter a single curse word—never, **not once**. Our mothers even used the word, "expecting". I never heard the word, "pregnant", and we kids weren't supposed to use it. "Pregnant", as it turns out, was a bad word. Even though they were all on a friendly, first name basis with each other, in talking to us kids about another adult, our parents referred to their peers by their title and last name— "I spoke to Mrs. Saunders this morning and she said she'd be happy to give you a ride to school in the morn-

26 It still hurts that today, eighteen years after Hurricane Katrina, Pontchartrain Park has still not fully recovered from it. Today, The Park looks absolutely nothing like the community in which I grew up. In pictures taken shortly after the storm, only the very tops of roofs could be seen. My family's home, 5019 New York Circle, was totally destroyed, and now, a different home occupies the lot. Uncle Ikee's home, just a couple of blocks away, was also totally destroyed by Katrina.

27 Pontchartrain Park - How a new subdivision built in New Orleans in the mid 1950's during the height of segregation brought momentous changes to the life of a black family – AGOTT (tribes.org)

ings with Terry and Kenneth", or, "Mr. Williams said that he'll be taking the Cub Scouts on a field trip next month."

Our parents referred to us as young ladies and young men. It may have been the little boy standing up in the front row of the kids' movies Mama showed at our church on Saturday nights to raise money for the building of the new sanctuary, whom she addressed as follows, "Young man! Young man! Sit down in front please." It may have been the teenager who, when my mother stopped at a stop sign on her way home from work one evening, opened the front passenger door of her car, grabbed her purse from the seat and ran. The kid made the mistake of running into a dead-end alley and unbelievably, my mother ran after him. When his back was against the alley's back wall, and he was clutching my mother's purse and looking right at her, she said to him, "Young man, I'm sure your mother doesn't know that you're out here doing these kinds of things. Now you can have the money that's in my bag, but I need my purse back." The kid then dropped my mother's purse and dashed past her, out of the alley. It may have been any of the girls at church who'd done something particularly nice on a given Sunday, about whom she'd say, "She's such a nice young lady."

Although we lived in the midst of a racist, segregated society, racism manifested in New Orleans in such a way that we were spared the emotional pain of seeing our parents be personally deferential to European Americans. We never saw them drop their eyes in the presence of, step off a sidewalk for, or say "Yes, Sir" and "Yes, Ma'am" to them. Perhaps it was a function of being in a large city as opposed to a rural area where, for African Americans, not engaging in such personal indignities was often a matter of life and death. Instead, as children, we watched our parents work responsibly at their jobs as secretaries, teachers and school principals, as mailmen, high school coaches and guidance counselors, as elementary school nurses, and in a few cases, doctors and lawyers.

My mother had a career first as a secretary (using the term of the day), and later an Administrative Assistant, which she very much enjoyed. I watched her go to work every day in a professional dress, matching earrings and necklace and coordinating pumps and purse. I admired how professional my mother looked every day and wanted to emulate her professionalism when I grew up. Had her early life circumstances been different, however, she would have gone to college as she planned and wanted so badly to do. Her father, my Grandpa Jim, told her very late in her process of preparing to attend Southern University in Baton Rouge that he didn't have the money to send her. My Aunt Johnnie believes that if my mother **had** graduated from college, she would most likely have majored in Business Education with the intention of going into elementary and secondary educational administration, with classroom teaching as a back-up because that is exactly what my mother advised Johnnie to do when she entered college.[28] When Grandpa Jim told Mama that he didn't have the money to send her to college, she was devastated, but as an alternative, immediately enrolled in Straight Business School in New Orleans, from which she graduated.

As for my father's career, he told me several years after he retired, that he'd always hated his job in the Post Office, a fact that I had never before known. He loved science, medicine particularly, and wanted to be a doctor. Daddy was actually a freshman at Southern University when he was drafted for "The War."

In the midst of the tremendously racist society that was 1950's and 60's New Orleans, our parents taught us that violence was not only immoral, it was also unproductive (and thus a tremendous waste of precious time) because it was always and ultimate-

28 My Aunt Johnnie didn't want to go to college. She admired my mother tremendously, and wanted to be a "secretary" just like her big sister, "Nina." Mama, however, was very clear that Johnnie should go to college and coordinated all of the details that made it happen. I was too young to remember, but I can imagine the pride Mama must have felt at her baby sister's college graduation. And Gramzie, who worked as a hotel maid for years? She must have been simply overflowing with pride to see her youngest earn a college degree in Business Education with a minor in English. My Aunt Johnnie retired from the New Orleans Public School System after thirty-five years as a teacher of Business Education.

ly doomed to fail. They taught us that it was non-violence that would change the world. They taught us that all people are created equal, and that we must never hate White People. They taught us that there were many thousands of White Americans of conscience and integrity who, often putting their own personal safety at grave risk, both supported and actively participated in the Civil Rights Movement. They taught us that we should not hate those who hated us, for they were simply unaware of who we are. Our parents told us that in being blind to the image of God in which **we** were created, they were also blind to the same image of God in which **they** were created. They taught us that love is infinitely more powerful than hate and that it is love that in the final analysis, without fail, always wins.

But perhaps more than any others, there were two immeasurably valuable lessons that our parents gave us. The first, and unquestionably the most important, was that we were immensely loved, that we were wonderful, smart, good, and talented kids, and that no one was better than us, no matter what societal messages we received about the inferiority of blackness. The second message, which they dutifully drilled into us, was that if we "applied" ourselves. "You have to 'apply' yourself," was one of my mother's most used admonitions to us whenever we didn't perform our best at something. She told us that if we did well in school and worked hard, we could both do anything and be anything we wanted and thus that there was nothing that we couldn't accomplish, crippling discrimination notwithstanding.[29]

Our parents' lessons of both self-respect and that we weren't inferior to anybody were never more clearly illustrated than on

29 In retrospect, I suspect that our parents may not have actually believed that. They were very well aware that if as adults, we faced the same level of racism with which they were living their adult lives, there were many opportunities that would be totally unavailable to us. But in their love for us, their intention was to encourage us, to build our developing self-esteem. My guess is that as our parents encouraged us, they deeply hoped and fervently prayed that their promise to us would not be, as it was for them, a dream deferred, but would, instead, be our adult reality. I learned as an adult that some black parents told their children that they had to be twice as good as a white person to get half as far. The intention, I imagine, was to both prepare their children for the reality of American society as it was, and to motivate them to work very hard.

the day a handful of White golfers showed up at the Pontchartrain Park golf clubhouse attempting to pay their fee and play a round of golf on the course. Mr. Lassiter, the Clubhouse proprietor, reminded the men that segregation was the law, that the law went both ways, that the Park's golf course was for Black golfers, and that theirs were the City Park and Audubon Park courses, uptown. He then very politely turned the men away. The White golfers protested, but Mr. Lassiter stood his ground until they left.[30]

We watched our parents during the Civil Rights Movement as, despite any resulting personal inconvenience, they courageously took a stand against discrimination by, among other things, participating in boycotts of stores that engaged in racially discriminatory employment practices.[31] We watched them coordinate community and civic meetings that were organized around issues of discrimination. We watched them as active members of church committees fighting segregation and other forms of discrimination. We observed them battle evil outside of our community, while internally, we watched them simultaneously coach our little league teams, direct our summer camps, lead our scout troops and attend with so much pride, our recitals and ballet concerts. We watched our parents be amazing examples of both strength and tenderness, compassion and wisdom.

We, their children, are the infinitely blessed beneficiaries of all of those indescribably inspiring messages. We are the beneficiaries of watching our parents in the 50's and 60's not just **teach** us all of those lessons, but indeed **live** them all. I cannot describe in words the tremendous wisdom, strength and dignity with which our parents responded to racism and segregation. One would had to have experienced them at that time to truly understand their

---

30 I am aware of that story only because my father came home that day and beaming with pride, told my mother and me of the incident.

31 In order to shop during the long Civil Right Era boycotts of Gentilly stores, our parents drove all the way to the sections of the city in which they had grown up. Every Saturday for well over a year, my mother drove up to the Circle Food Store in the city's Seventh Ward where she and my father grew up, to do our grocery shopping, passing up the Gentilly Schwegmann's, which, on Chef Menteur Highway, was five minutes outside of the Park, but which was being boycotted for racially discriminatory hiring and firing practices.

poise, their self-respect and, in turn, the compelling impact which their example had on us, their kids.

MY MOTHER AS MY INSPIRATION

While the adults in our community were role models for all of the neighborhood kids, **my mother** was, without question, **my** most powerful role model. She was a community activist who gave from her heart, always attempting to meaningfully contribute to Bethany, her church, Pontchartrain Park, her community, and the United States, her country. In addition to being an extremely active member of Bethany, Secretary of the Pontchartrain Park Improvement Association, and editor of the early editions of *The Pontchartrain Park Patriot*, my mother was both a member and an employee of the New Orleans Urban League, and was deeply committed to its goals of economic opportunity for African Americans. It was her deep compassion for others that compelled her activism. Gramzie was an astonishingly compassionate person and she clearly instilled that same level of compassion in my mother.

My mother was also the Organizer-In-Chief of our entire extended family. She took care of all of Gramzie's needs. She informed Uncle Ikee about Pontchartrain Park and encouraged him to consider purchasing a home there, which he did in 1956. Uncle Ikee owned his home until Hurricane Katrina destroyed it fifty-one years later. She got my Aunt Johnnie into and through college and helped both my aunts, Verlie and Johnnie, find homes and jobs. When Uncle Ikee lost his wife, my Aunt Gerlie, leaving him with two very young boys, my cousins Gerard and Drexel, my mother stepped in, cooking for them and helping with the boys every day until Uncle Ikee remarried. My mother organized our family gatherings and, in every other sense, "was there" for **all** of us—Gramzie, her (Mama's) siblings and their children—and of course, us, her own family.

Family was **extremely** important to my mother. She went from her job to either Gramzie's or my Aunt Verlie's for lunch almost every day. My Aunt Verlie and my mother were very close and Verlie shared with me once that she always enjoyed having lunch with my mother on those days, just the two of them, in Verlie's kitchen. Mama's surprise wedding gift to my Aunt Johnnie epitomizes the many ways in which she demonstrated her love to all of us. Several days before my Aunt Johnnie's wedding, Aunt Johnnie and her fiancé, with the help of several family members and friends, brought all of their new furniture and other belongings to the home in which they were going to live. There were so many wedding details that required taking care of, however, that the newlyweds had no time before the wedding to unpack and actually settle into their new home. Therefore, when Aunt Johnnie and her new husband arrived at the house very late on their wedding night, they expected to find it just as they'd left it a couple of days earlier, filled with boxes and bags, and their made-up bed as the only semblance of order. When the newlyweds opened the front door of their home on that night, however, to their utter amazement, all the furniture had been arranged, all the curtains hung, pictures were on the walls, rugs on the floors, all their clothes were unpacked and neatly folded in their drawers, their shoes and hanging clothes were neatly arranged in the closets, canned foods were neatly placed in the kitchen cabinets, and the refrigerator and freezer were full. In her astonishment, the moment she opened the door of her new home, Aunt Johnnie knew that she was witnessing her big sister Nina's loving fingerprint. It was my mother's very same loving fingerprint that touched us all. My mother was the pillar of our family, a leader in our community and the center of my world.

Among the most important lessons that my mother taught me, Lemar Jr., and Lambert was that just as no one was better than **us**, and **we** were no better than anyone else. My mother always taught us that we should never either believe or behave as if we were better than other people because we lived in Pontchartrain Park, and that "having a little more than other children" didn't mean we were any better than other children. Mama believed that lesson with all her heart and wanted to be sure that we did as well. I have clear memories of my mother expressing deep and sincere concern about people who were poor not only in the United States, but indeed around the world. Perhaps it was having grown up very poor during the depression that caused her to feel so deeply for those in need. My mother taught us that **all** people had equal worth and equal value and that we were **all** children of God.

SCHOOL AS A REFUGE

I WAS REMINDED OF THAT MESSAGE EVERY DAY AT SCHOOL. FOR A reason explained later, from kindergarten through sixth grade where elementary school ended, I attended Robert R. Moton Elementary, which was in the heart of the Desire Project, one of the city's largest public housing developments. For several years after it opened in 1949, and throughout the time I attended school there, 1957-'64, the Desire was for working class African Americans, a pretty nice place to live. Compared to the often badly dilapidated wooden houses in which many of the city's African American residents had lived after emancipation through the years of the depression, the Desire Project may indeed have been considered a very nice place to live. When I began attending Moton, all the buildings, sidewalks and streets were relatively new, less than ten years old, and they looked it. Some of the residents had landscaped the building in which they lived. The apartments were large and sunny. There was no stigma to living in the projects then. They were just the places where people who were low wage earners lived. Its residents were the maids and bellmen of the French Quarter hotels. They were the custodians of downtown office buildings. They were the "lunch ladies" and janitors in the

African American public schools. In the projects, in those days, there were no teenagers hanging out all night, no sound of police sirens, no gunshots. There were no gangs. There was simply the sound of hundreds of kids playing outside whenever school was out—hopscotch, football, jump rope, and with dolls, marbles, hula hoops, jacks, yoyos, tops and kites.

I knew what the Desire sounded like after school because Gramzie lived there at that time and my mother dropped me off with her every day both before and after school. Mama moved Gramzie to the Desire not long after it opened. A year or two prior, a number of Gramzie's relatives had moved into and thoroughly taken over her house in the Seventh Ward. Not liking that situation one bit, my mother told Gramzie about a nice new housing development where she thought Gramzie and her two younger daughters, my aunts Verlie and Johnnie, would be comfortable. Gramzie looked at the apartment and at the development itself, and after some initial reluctance and subsequent persuasion, finally agreed to move in. Gramzie lived in the Desire until I was in eighth grade when again, Mama moved her because the Desire was just beginning to "get rough" at that time. Gramzie's Desire Project address, 3351 Desire Parkway, Apartment A, and her phone number, Whitehall (WH) 3-5804, will remain with me for the rest of my life. Sadly, after Gramzie moved out, over time, the Desire Project became widely known as the most violent, crime-ridden project in the city.

I'm quite amused, thinking back now, about the reason I attended Moton. By the time I was three, I asked every day when I was going to be able to attend school. I mean I really wanted to go to school...and I really bugged my mother about it. I wanted to go to school so badly, in fact, that for Christmas, when I was three, I got a miniature school desk (we called it a peg table at that time) so that I could pretend that I was in school. My mother was one of the two secretaries at Moton. The school principal, Mrs. Anna B.

Henry was her supervisor, and (despite their different roles at work) her good friend. When I turned four, in order to stop my daily, "I wanna go to school!" protests, my mother asked Mrs. Henry if I could just sit in with the kindergarten class at Moton. The plan was for me to then officially enroll in kindergarten the following year at Valena C. Jones Elementary, that my parents, my Uncle Ikee, my aunts Verlie and Johnnie, and Lemar Jr. and Lambert had all attended. Mrs. Henry agreed and my mother got a permit from the School Board for me to attend Moton since it was not the school, which based upon my zip code, I was supposed to attend. Because I was born in August, I was in kindergarten the entire school year. As it turned out, my kindergarten teacher, Mrs. Bertrand, told my mother at the end of the year that I had done very well in the classroom, both socially and academically, and that it would therefore be a real shame for me to have to spend an entire year repeating kindergarten. She suggested, although I'd just be turning five, that I be put into first grade as a test, just to see if I was academically ready for it and was able to keep up. If it turned out that I couldn't, I'd then go back to kindergarten. Apparently, I did just fine in Ms. Napoleon's first grade class because I never saw the inside of Mrs. Bertrand's kindergarten classroom again.[32]

---

32 Since I began kindergarten at four, and first grade at five, throughout my entire educational experience, from kindergarten through my Master's Degree program, I was almost always the youngest person among my schoolmates and friends. It is probably fortunate, for that reason, that I never had an interest in typical teenage and college student activities, such as going to parties and clubs.

By the end of first grade, I had all my friends and knew many of the teachers at Moton—it was my third home (my parents' home was my first, and Gramzie's apartment was my second) and I loved it. Moton was a beautiful new school in which all of the classrooms had an entire wall of glass, which we finger painted and decorated for every holiday. There were lots of maps and world globes, books, puzzles and games in the classrooms, and even a big goldfish pond outside of the school library.[33] The teachers, all my mom's friends, were dedicated to making sure that we received a good education, despite and perhaps because of the fact that our school was in the project. Indeed, Mrs. Henry was so dedicated to the kids, that for our kindergarten graduation, we wore satin caps and gowns in Moton's orange and white school colors, and marched to "Pomp and Circumstance." Having discovered through conversations with junior high schoolmates who'd attended other elementary schools that none of them graduated from kindergarten in caps and gowns, I asked my mother sometime during my early teen years, why we had caps and gowns at Moton's kindergarten graduation. She explained to me that Mrs. Henry knew that many of my classmates, simply because of the circumstances of their birth, might well not finish high school and that she (Mrs. Henry) wanted the kids to be able to remember that they did wear a cap and gown, at least once in their lives.

Moton was, of course, all black, all the kids, all the teachers, the cafeteria workers, the custodians, the principal, Mrs. Henry, and the two secretaries, my mother and Mrs. Height. I **loved** Moton. We worked hard in class every day, and had lots of homework every night. I got a terrific education at Moton. I was fascinated by

33 I suspect that as is true of dedicated teachers today, Moton's teachers may have used some of their personal funds to supplement whatever the school district provided for our classrooms to buy many of the teaching aids we used in class, especially at that time during which African American schools were grossly inadequately funded in comparison to those attended by the city's European American children. Even our textbooks were second-hand, made obvious by the fact that the table on the inside front cover in which White students, over ten years, had entered their name and the date on which they received the book, was already full. A table was then pasted to the inside **back** cover of the books that we then began filling in with our names and dates in order for us to use the books for another ten years.

everything I was learning in geography, in history, and, of course, in science, my absolute favorite subject. In retrospect, in view of my later experiences with colorism in junior high and racism in senior high school that I'll describe later, I was very fortunate to have experienced all of elementary school—to have lived the first ten years of my life—without experiencing either. Nobody asked to feel my hair. I didn't get asked how chitterlings are cooked. The tan that I returned to school with after a summer vacation of playing outside all day didn't surprise anyone. I didn't come back to school to, "You're so brown! I didn't know **you** could tan!" In all of my classrooms, and in my Brownie and Girl Scout troops, I was just another kid in the class and in the troop. I was able to just be a kid.

Me in Third Grade as Cinderella's Fairy Godmother in Moton's Annual School Play

I felt so loved and so safe during my years at Moton because my mother dropped me off at Gramzie's house every morning before going to work at Moton. Then, when I was four and began school at Moton, my aunt Verlie, who then lived with Gramzie, combed my hair, dressed me and walked me to school when it was time. After school, I went to my mother's office and played in the space under her desk until it was time for me to go home. When I was a little older, I walked to Gramzie's after school in order to play with my friends, the children of Gramzie's neighbors, until Mama picked me up. Because I attended the same school at which my mother worked and because I was with Gramzie both before and after school everyday, I was never physically very far away from either of them, whether I was at home or at school. The result was that I felt my mother and grandmother's love and protection at all times, **wherever** I was.

One of the best things to have ever happened in what was my entire life at that point, occurred the summer after I completed fourth grade. My parents, in their late thirties by then, were going to have a mid-life surprise—and it was indeed quite a surprise! Of course, "expecting" was the only word I heard when the adults discussed it. "Your mother's 'expecting' again!" I was almost nine when my little sister, Lorna, came into the world that summer. Mama and Mrs. Henry, Moton's principal and Mama's boss, were such good friends that Mama asked Mrs. Henry to be Lorna's godmother, to which she very happily agreed. Our family of five, was now a family of six.

Mama, Daddy & the Four of Us

Mama now had a second little girl to adore...and adore her she did. Shortly after Lorna was born, my mother once said to me, "Well, Laurie, after you've left home and gone away to college, I'll still have my little Lorna with me." Even though we were nearly nine years apart in age, I was **elated** to have a baby sister and I loved her dearly. "Mama and Her Shadow" were now "The Three Musketeers." It was the summer of 1962.

Laurie and Lorna in 1963 and 1964

I played a lot and learned well during my years at Moton. One of my most valuable experiences there, however, was that of having fully enforced my mother's lesson that all human beings are equal. I saw and learned through my own lived experience that the children that I went to school with at Moton, the kids who lived in the project, those kids who had far fewer material comforts than I did, were just like me. I saw that they were no different from me and from my friends in Pontchartrain Park. I saw that it didn't matter if you were poor. You were still a human being with the same feelings and the same dreams as other people. I saw it every day in my school friends who wanted to grow up to be nurses and teachers, doctors, police officers and firefighters. I saw that while they had far fewer material comforts than we did, many of the apartments in the project in which my friends from school lived were just as clean and just as neat as was my and many of my friends' homes who lived in Pontchartrain Park.[34]

The harsh reality for Moton's kids**,** however, was that simply because of an accident of their birth, i.e., because of the economic circumstances into which they just happened to have been born, the likelihood that they would be able to pursue their dreams was much smaller than it was for the kids who lived in the Park, racism notwithstanding.[35] That being so, I'm sure that some of Moton's kids did go on to complete high school and college and that some may even have graduated from graduate, medical and law school. I'm confident of that because there were some very smart kids at Moton—**very** smart. I had very good grades, but one of my classmates, Gwendolyn Hamilton, in addition to having grades that were equivalent to mine in every other subject, also did well in

34 Most of my friends at Moton, as I remember, did not have their fathers in their home. At the time, a man's presence in the home automatically disqualified the family from living in public housing and receiving other benefits that were available to low-income families. The harsh reality for such families, however, was that their husband/father's low-wage salary as, for example, a janitor or a bellman, was simply not enough to fully support the family. The father was, therefore, forced to leave his family in order for the family to receive the benefits required to live. I remember many of my friends at Moton talking about how their mother and siblings went to a relative's home over the weekend during which they spent the two days with their father. Men dared not visit their families in their public housing apartment because, if "caught," the family would be promptly thrown out of their apartment and all their public benefits would cease. Such a system, one that forced African American men out of their homes, i.e., that prohibited them, by agency regulation from living with their families, brings to mind the centuries-long practice, during slavery, of the intentional separation of Black families. It was done by "selling" a person to another plantation owner. The "sale" of a person away from their family was often done for profit. At other times, it was done as punishment for the infraction of some rule or another. It is because families were so often torn apart during slavery that the very first thing that many African Americans did immediately after emancipation was search for loved ones who had been "sold."

35 Even as a child, I was able to understand that the financial disadvantage that my school friends faced because of an "**economic** accident of their birth," was as happenstance and, in my mind, as unfair, as was the discrimination that we all faced (regardless of our economic differences) because of a "**racial** accident of birth."

arithmetic, my academic nemesis. That advantage made Gwendolyn, overall, a better student than me. For that reason, at the end of fifth grade, Gwendolyn got the gold Citizenship Award for Girls and I got the silver...and Gwendolyn was a kid from the project. Gwendolyn, along with my friend Glenda, brother and sister Gentry and Kimberly Stevens, and my friend Joseph Rose were only a few of many really smart kids that lived in the Desire Project. They needed opportunity. Those kids were just kids. They just needed a chance.[36]

My mother never told me to not talk about our home and our neighborhood with my friends at school, but I knew, intuitively, that I shouldn't. I knew not to talk about my long Santa list every Christmas, that I always got every item on the list every year, and that I made a beeline from my bed to the Christmas tree every Christmas morning to see all the toys that were waiting for me. I knew not to talk about my favorite toy, my marionette puppet show with its stage, curtains, and all its puppets, which must've been rather expensive. I knew not to talk about my room with its

36 I recently heard it said on a radio show that many European Americans do not see African American children as children, that they do not attribute to them the innocence of childhood. Rather, they see Black children as just small Black people, with the same mental and emotional attributes that in their stereotypes, they attribute to Black adults. The October 2022 incident of a White New Jersey man who called non-emergency police in response to a little Black girl, who in compliance with a state campaign in which residents were asked to kill a species of invasive bugs that harm trees, was being a good citizen and spraying for the bug outside her home. The words of the caller (who was the little girl's across-the-street neighbor) were recorded on the telephone line of the dispatcher who received his call: "There's a little Black woman walkin' and sprayin' stuff on the sidewalk and trees.....I don't know what the hell she's doin'. It scares me though." The man was unable to see a nine-year old child **as** a child. In his eyes, she was a small Black adult, "a little Black woman." 'Am I in Trouble?': Neighbor Calls Police on 9-Year-Old Black Girl Spraying for Bugs - YouTube

Even as we learned about the utter unfairness of society, all my friends and I (both in Pontchartrain Park and the Desire Project) had every bit as much of childhood's wonderful innocence and naivety as White children. The knowledge that many White People do not **see** Black children as children is therefore heart-rending for me. I'm sure that European Americans who adopt African American children, as well as those who have Bi-racial biological children who are African American in appearance, are fully aware of the innocence of **all** children.

As a side-note, I find it extremely interesting that while as a general, sexist norm, men are not supposed to show and certainly not admit fear, White men's both experience and verbal expression of their fear of Black People is generally not only understood, but also acceptably expressed. Fear as a common psychological/emotional response that many White Americans have of Black Americans, as well as the consequences of that fear, are discussed in detail in *On Race and Racism Humanity's Bottom Line*

white French provincial furniture and canopy top bed. I knew not to mention all my stuffed animals that lived on my bed, or going to see Disney movies with my mother. I knew not to mention that one of my favorite things was to watch old Fred Astaire and Ginger Rogers movies at home with my mother. Mama loved watching them dance. "Just look at that. They're so graceful," she'd always say. I knew not to mention the fact that every year, the night before Easter, Mama and I dyed and tattooed all of the Easter eggs for our Easter baskets, or to talk about the big pink, green and yellow basket full of candy that I (and my father and brothers) woke up to every Easter Sunday. I knew not to mention the two sets of encyclopedias, Colliers and World Book, and the accompanying set of children's books in the living room that I enjoyed reading. At school, I didn't talk about our complete 1959 six record set of The Golden Record Library's recordings, "A Musical Heritage for Young America," which included "The Treasury of Great Classic Fairy Tales" that I listened to incessantly, and my absolute favorite, "The Instruments of the Orchestra." I didn't talk about my family's traditions of seafood, potato salad and green peas almost every Friday night, donuts and chocolate milk every Saturday morning, and a big breakfast of grits, eggs, bacon, biscuits and pineapple juice every Sunday morning. I knew that my friends at school, in all likelihood, neither did, nor had, many of those things, and instinctively, I knew not to mention that I did. I didn't want to make my friends feel bad. I feel incredibly fortunate that I learned so early in life that not only are there no superior and inferior people based upon race, there are also none based upon class. Living in Pontchartrain Park while attending school in the Desire Project taught me that lesson in a very deep and profound way, very early in my life. It taught me not only compassion for those who are financially less fortunate than I, but also respect.

I attended Moton for seven years, from kindergarten through sixth grade, the end of elementary school. I completed sixth grade and graduated from Moton Elementary in 1964, when I was ten. At the graduation ceremony, I was awarded the Girls' Silver Citizenship Award.[37] Receiving the award meant a lot to me because I thought that it made my mother proud, which, more than anything else, I **always** wanted to do.

Girls' Silver Citizenship Award

Looking back on my seven years at Robert R. Moton Elementary School, what is clear is that like Pontchartrain Park, it was for me, a powerful refuge from the reality of the larger segregated society in which I was growing up. Attending Moton, a segregated school in which I was just a kid, not "a Black kid", during my first, my formative, my most impressionable years of life, was for me, a blessing.

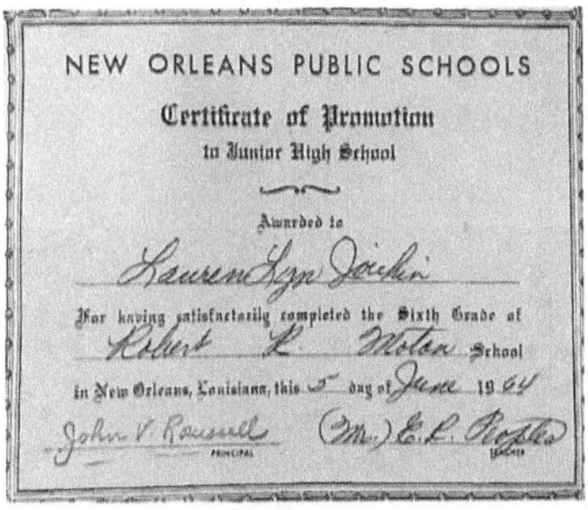

NEW ORLEANS PUBLIC SCHOOLS

Certificate of Promotion

to Junior High School

Awarded to

For having satisfactorily completed the Sixth Grade of

Robert R. Moton School

in New Orleans, Louisiana, this 5 day of June 1964

PRINCIPAL TEACHER

My Certificate of Promotion from Elementary to Junior High School

37 Upon graduating from sixth grade, the academically first, second, and third ranked girl and the academically first, second, and third ranked boy of my elementary school were awarded the gold, silver, and bronze citizenship awards, respectively. I received the silver award for girls. My classmate, Gwendolyn Hamilton, who was always better than me in arithmetic, received the gold.

THE END OF SEGREGATION - IT WAS HARD

SEGREGATION ENDED WITH PRESIDENT JOHNSON'S SIGNING OF THE Civil Rights Act on July 2, 1964, one month after I graduated from Moton.[38] My grandparents were in their 60's, my parents, their early 40's. Lemar Jr. was 20, Lambert, 16, I was ten, and Lorna hadn't quite turned two. We watched the news report of the signing of the Act on the nightly news. I remember that night as if it were last night. I had seen the adults in my life share what as a child I experienced as very real and profound collective **fear** during the Cuban Missile Crisis when I was nine. I had seen them share a collective **grief** when President Kennedy, (whom I knew all of the adults respected, admired, and thought was a very good president) was assassinated when I was ten[39]. I had never**,** however, seen them share a collective **elation**. That is exactly what happened the day the Civil Rights Act of 1964 was passed. I was almost eleven.

That night, following the news that we had gotten earlier in the day of the passage of the Act, the house phone rang "off the hook." Gramzie, Uncle Ikee, my aunts Verlie and Johnnie, the neighbors, my mother's friends from Bethany, and my parents' other friends from the community, were all calling. I wanted to know what was going on, why all of the adults were so happy. I asked my mother what the law said and why the grown-ups were so excited. "Well, Laurie," she said to me, "You know the twenty-eight flavors of ice cream you've been wanting to try at Howard

38 Among other things, the Act prohibited segregation in all public accommodations.

39 The day President Kennedy was killed was the most horrible day of my life to that point. I was in sixth grade. He died at 12:30 p.m. Central Time, the time zone in which I lived. We were at school, at lunch. When we returned to class, our teacher told us that the president had just died. Even as kids, we were all stunned and saddened. The principal made an announcement over the school's public address system that because of what had just happened, we were being sent home early. That evening, the adults, who were also shocked, were extremely upset. I remember that there was much crying that evening, by both women and men. President Kennedy's assassination was so poignant for me, and among my most powerful childhood memories not only because it was in and of itself so traumatizing, but also because in addition to seeing the national coverage of the event, our local news outlets covered it for months. Lee Harvey Oswald, the president's assassin, was a native New Orleanian, and his activities in the city within the months both shortly before and after the assassination were the subject of a huge investigation in the city, the coverage of which was on the local news every evening for months.

Johnson's?" "Yeah," I said in great anticipation of what might be coming. "Well," she continued, "This new law says that we can go there now. We can go to the Howard Johnson's ice cream parlor now." "And we can eat the twenty-eight flavors of ice cream?" I asked with even more anticipation. "Well," my mother said smiling, "We'll take them one at a time, but yes, we can go to Howard Johnson's, sit at the counter and have ice cream now." I responded with one word, "Wow." I was particularly excited about the prospect of going to Howard Johnson's ice cream parlor because among my favorite toys was the Howard Johnson's soda fountain/ice cream play set. During segregation, while playing with my toy, I imagined that I was at the ice cream parlor while being prohibited from being there in reality.

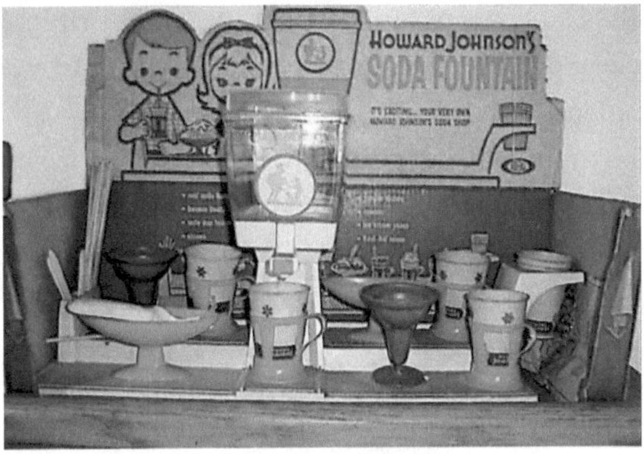

Howard Johnson's Soda Fountain Toy

My mother continued, "And now we can go to Pontchartrain Beach and ride that big roller coaster you see all the time and that you've been wanting to ride." She went on to explain that the law said that we could now get a hamburger at Royal Castle if we wanted to, and eat lunch at Morrison's Cafeteria, and that when my Girl Scout troop went to City Park, we could now ride the kiddie train around the park. She explained that the train was no longer "white only", i.e., just for white children. I'll never forget thinking at that moment, "This one law is doing all of that?! That's a powerful law." It was an evening I'll never forget.

Within days, I also saw that at Schwegmann's supermarket, Mama and I no longer had to drink water from the warm, low, white, porcelain "Colored" fountain from which warm, and depending upon the weather, sometimes hot water was dispensed. We could now drink from the cold, tall, silver, metal fountain, the one on the side of the column on which the soon-to-be-gone letters, "W-H-I-T-E" were painted, from which icy cold water was dispensed. Within those same few days, I also learned that my mother and I could now use the "Ladies Room", and that the third or "Colored" lavatory of the familiar three restroom line-up, "Men", "Women" and "Colored," would soon be gone. The adults in my life could now go to a French Quarter club to listen to jazz. African American families could now go to the Gentilly Maison Blanche Department Store restaurant for dinner. It seemed to my ten-year-old consciousness that the entire **world** was changing, and indeed…it was.[40]

But the process of integrating what had since the end of slavery been a completely racially segregated society was not easy. It was hard. For me as a child, it was often frightening. From birth until the end of my tenth year, which was also the end of elementary school for me, my sole experience of racism had not been personal. It had been comprised solely of my exposure to segregation, a phenomenon which, while very much a **part** of my world, was also, in a very real sense, **outside** of it, outside, that is, of the immediate world of my family, neighbors, church, teachers

40 Just as the many existing "slave narratives" chronicle the lives of formerly enslaved people of African descent in the United States, and similarly, as the first-hand accounts of African Americans who fled the South during The Great Migration were masterfully recorded in Isabelle Wilkerson's *The Warmth of Other Suns*, our stories, the stories of those of us who experienced segregation, need to be likewise chronicled. We who were born in the middle of the post-World War II baby boom (1946 to '64) are the last to remember segregation. My younger sister, born in the last two years of the Baby Boom, does not remember it. She and her late Baby Boomer contemporaries were just too young when it ended. Those of us in my age group, who are the last to have those memories, are, of course, in the autumn of our lives. My sincere hope is that a gifted author with the passion to do so, will record and publish our stories of having grown up in American apartheid. No less than the nightmare of slavery, and the desperation of those who fled during the Great Migration, it is a tragic legacy well-worth recording.

and friends, the world which, by far, both most mattered to and influenced me.

The end of segregation occasioned my first **personal** experience with racism. I graduated from Moton Elementary in June 1964, the month before the Civil Rights Act became law. Three months later, in September, I entered seventh grade at Rivers Frederick Junior High School, just two months after the passage of the Act. For the first time, I had to ride public service buses to school. Among the many public accommodations that the law required to be integrated immediately were city buses. Prior to the passage of the law, African Americans were required to sit in the back of the bus behind a tin sign that was attached to the top of the seat located adjacent to the back door of the bus. After riding all their lives in the front of the bus, with us seated in the smaller back section (and often standing back there even when seats were available in the front), it must have been visually quite shocking to white New Orleanians to see us suddenly, and for the very first time, sitting in the front of the bus. It must have been especially jarring to them in those instances in which either we sat next to them, or a lack of seats in the front required them to stand. They would never dream of sitting in an available seat in the back of the bus.

I was one of about thirty kids from Pontchartrain Park who rode three city buses every day to and from Rivers Frederick Junior High School—the Congress to the Broad to the Elysian Fields bus. The morning commute was fine because our neighbor, Mr. Sanders, gave me and his own two kids, Terri and Kenneth, both of whom also attended Frederick, a ride to the Elysian Fields bus stop, resulting in our having to ride only the Elysian Fields bus in the morning, which wasn't a problem. After school, in the afternoon, the Elysian Fields and the Congresses buses were also fine. But that afternoon crosstown ride on the Broad Street bus that we took between the Elysian Fields and the Congress buses was horrendous. When the 3:15 bell rang, ending the school day, the thirty or so of us walked to the Elysian Fields bus stop. As we did, all I could do was think with sheer dread, about what was soon coming—the unmerciful harassment and abuse we received on the Broad bus, every single day, from the older and much larger White boys from Cor Jesu Senior High. After the Elysian Fields bus ride, we'd board the Broad bus at the corner of Elysian Fields and Gentilly Avenues, and because of the new law, sit anywhere there was a seat. The Cor Jesu boys got on at the next Gentilly Avenue stop, and seeing us sitting in the front of the bus, would get angry, and then lean over and yell any number of hate-filled epithets and messages in our ears. The one I remember most clearly, was, "Lil niggah, you think you good as a White man now just 'cause you can sit in the front of the bus?! Is that what you think? Huh? You'll **never** be good as a White man no matter **what** the damn president says! You **still** nothin' but a monkey! Get up and give a White man his seat, niggah!" We sat there stoically, as 12, 13, and 14 year olds, looking straight ahead, terrified on the inside but blank-faced and as still as posts on the outside. Some of the White boys, while yelling in our ears, would also thump our boys on their heads with either their hands or their books. That would lead, inevitably, every day, to physical fights, right there on the bus, between the White and the Black boys. When it started, we girls would take our boys' books and run to the back of the bus. The consistent and inevitable result was that our junior high school boys, who were younger and therefore considerably smaller than the Cor Jesu senior high school boys, would exit the bus with bloody noses and black eyes, every day. It was absolutely terrifying to both watch and to be so physically close to. The white bus driver (there were only white bus drivers in those days), never intervened, not once.

I believe the White Cor Jesu boys thought that if they intimidated us enough, we'd just give up and run to the back of the bus. But those white kids didn't know our parents. They didn't know us.

The lenses through which they saw us were so clouded that they could not see who we were. They had absolutely no idea that the dignity that our parents had instilled in us would not allow us to sit in the back of the bus anymore. As very young people, we **sat** our ground. Even though the girls ran to the back once the fighting started, we always began the ride sitting in the front. I realized as an adult looking back on that time, that the act of sitting in the front of the bus every day, knowing full well what was coming, was my and my schoolmates' small bit of activism during the Civil Rights Movement. I feel particular pride in my 12, 13, and 14 year old male schoolmates, however, because at the moment at which they defiantly took their seats in the front of the bus, they knew that they were the ones who were going to take the brunt of the White boys' onslaught. As I look back on that experience now, I think of it as our junior high school multi-month Rosa Parks movement.

By the end of the school year, some nine months later, the White boys had finally stopped harassing us. Most white passengers on city buses had gotten used to integrated seating by then. Only a few were still either jumping up and standing the second one of us sat next to them, or scooting all the way over to be sure nothing of theirs was touching anything of ours. It was a tremendous relief when the daily harassment and abuse by the Cor Jesu boys finally ended. That horrible afternoon Broad Street bus ride made seventh grade treacherous. I was eleven.

It wasn't, however, only the integration of the city buses that was tough. Integration didn't come easily to New Orleans in **any** context. For some time after the passage of the Civil Rights Act, there were small outbreaks of violence across the city. One of the results of that violence I remember most vividly was that rather than integrate its pools at Pontchartrain Beach, Audubon Park and City Park, the city closed them in order to prevent the likely violence between Black and White residents (fueled, I believe, primarily by White residents) that would likely have occurred in the water.

Our parents also experienced the discomfort of the early days of integration. I remember seeing the utterly icy and often downright hostile looks on the majority of the white patrons' faces the first time we went into any formerly "White Only" establishment. Our parents saw them as well. As adults, they experienced the discomfort of going into formerly "White Only" restaurants, restrooms, and clothing store fitting rooms, of sitting in the formerly "White Only" section of the train station, bus station and airport, and being in a myriad of other early integration situations. I heard adult conversations, for example, about being refused service in restaurants, sitting there sometimes for more than an hour, being totally ignored.

That very thing happened to my father one night in what had always been a "White Only" steakhouse on Chef Menteur Highway that he'd passed every day for years on his way to and from work. He decided to eat at the restaurant one night, just because now, after integration, he could. After the waiter ignored my father for close to a half hour, he left, but only long enough to go outside, use a pay phone and call a few of his buddies. Fifteen minutes later, when there were ten Black men sitting in that little steakhouse, the wait staff "jumped to it," bringing my father and his friends their steaks and drinks without missing a beat. That was only one example (probably among many others, of which I remain unaware to this day) of our parents' courage and quiet grace during that difficult time.

Still, it felt to me that we, the kids, as young students who were integrating the schools, were on our own "front line" during the early days of integration because we dealt with the often-extreme reaction from so many of our European American peers every day. I heard of vicious fights between the Black and the White kids that were taking place every day, and that occurred for months at some schools - Durham Junior High, and Kennedy Senior High, among the worst.[41]

Of course it is well-documented that African American college students were also on the front lines during the early days of desegregation. I was personally inspired by my Aunt Johnnie who was a student in the early 1960's at Southern University in Baton Rouge, Louisiana, an Historically Black University among the country's 100-plus Historically Black Colleges and Universities, HBCUs. My aunt marched in student demonstrations at the downtown Baton Rouge Woolworth's Department Store, which Southern's students organized in response to the store's segregated lunch counter. The Southern University students named their movement, "5,000 Strong." My aunt told us that they marched every day, and that nearly all of the university's students participated in it. Aunt Johnnie told us that because when they left campus, she and her fellow students never knew whether they were going to survive another day, they began their daily marches by walking from the campus to a local church to pray. She said that she and her fellow students fully understood the danger of their activities, but that they were totally willing to die for their convictions. After prayer, the students continued by walking from the church all the way to the downtown Woolworth's. Upon arrival, carrying signs, and either silently or while singing freedom songs, they walked around the store for hours. On one of her visits home during that

41 The story of Ruby Bridges is perhaps the best-known account of an African American student's life during that time. It describes Ms. Bridges' experience as a little first grader at New Orleans' historically all-white William Frantz Elementary School. The parents of many of Frantz's European American students withdrew their children from the school because one African American student, Ruby, had enrolled. For the rest of that entire academic year, Ruby was the only child in her classroom. She was taught, every day, by her courageous European American first grade teacher, Mrs. Barbara Henry. Frantz Elementary and Moton Elementary were just a couple of miles away. Ruby was having her experience of being the only Black child, and indeed the only child in her class while very nearby, I was having my very different experience of being a Black child in a Black school, and the emotional freedom that accompanied it. Ms. Bridges tells her story in her book, Through My Eyes.
http://www.barnesandnoble.com/s/through-my-eyes-ruby-bridges?store=allproducts&keyword=through+my+eyes+ruby+bridges

The Narrated Story of Ruby Bridges (for children)
http://www.youtube.com/watch?v=dYM-72AftEo

time, my Aunt Johnnie told us that she and her fellow students had been tear gassed during a recent demonstration, and that they regularly faced big angry, frothy, barking police dogs, and water streams from city fire hoses that could knock a horse over. Her experiences seemed to perfectly mirror all of the images of civil rights sit-ins and demonstrations that were being televised nearly every night on the national news. Gramzie and Mama were simultaneously both extremely proud of Aunt Johnnie, and dreadfully frightened for her safety—but I remember their fear far more than their pride. Although my Aunt Johnnie reported feeling that her life and the lives of all of her fellow student demonstrators were potentially at risk each time they demonstrated, she said that fortunately, she had had only one brush with actual physical danger. It was an experience during which she and other students ran and jumped over a fence to escape police dogs. In the end, Woolworth's did indeed integrate its lunch counter.

As for our parents, because most of them worked primarily in environments that were either all or predominantly African American, didn't spend a lot of time around White People during the week. They also drove cars and thus didn't ride city buses as we did. Our grandparents were retired by then. Since, however, our parents lived with the indignities of segregation well into adulthood, and our grandparents almost their entire lives, they had paid their dues and then some, dues they never owed; dues which over the course of my parents' lives, deprived each of them on at least one occasion, of well-earned promotions on their jobs.

[Upon leaving the public school system, my mother's first job was with the Veterans Administration, becoming the agency's first African American secretary in the city. She ultimately left that job because a young European American woman half her age who had been promoted over her, and to whom she began reporting, spoke to her in a manner that was both mean and patronizing, a situation that was intolerable for her. Thankfully, after my mother left the Federal government, she took a job, her last job, which she truly loved, with the New Orleans Urban League. My father, in testing for a supervisory position with the Post Office, had on one occasion, earned among the highest scores in the city, and on a second, had the highest score of all applicants. On that occasion, knowing that they could not legally deprive my father of a supervisory position, the Post Office administration offered him a supervisor's job in Houma, Louisiana, nearly 50 miles from the city, at a time during which there were no freeways.]

Those "dues" made it only fair for our parents, their peers, and our grandparents to have been spared what turned out to be the utterly insane daily indignities of ending segregation that we, their children, endured every day. I am very well aware, however, that the city's African American adults who worked in jobs as maids, porters, and bellmen in city hotels, as janitors in downtown office buildings, as dishwashers in restaurants, and in a myriad of other low-wage jobs, indeed experienced those indignities on a daily basis, both on their jobs and while riding city buses. They were the adults who worked every day in the presence of European Americans, many of whom may have been very angry about the passage of the Civil Rights Act and who, through their personal demeanor, may have, on a daily basis, taken out that anger on them.

It was just six weeks shy of my 11th birthday when segregation ended. I cannot imagine living as an adult in its debilitating indignity. My parents, however, did just that. They were in their early forties when it ended. My grandparents, in their sixties, lived in it for the majority of their entire lives. I so wish I could give back to my parents and grandparents all of those years of their lives to live in dignity and freedom. Tragically, I cannot. No one can. For them, justice delayed truly **was** justice denied. With the passage of the Civil Rights Act of 1964, segregation ended. It took 99 years, nearly a full century after the end of slavery in 1865, for it to happen, and even then, it was not easy. It was hard.

FACING ONE OF RACISM'S MOST PAINFUL LEGACIES – COLORISM

UNFORTUNATELY, AT THE SAME TIME THAT I HAD, ON CITY BUSSES, MY first personal experience with **racism**, I also had my first personal experience with **colorism**, the discrimination that People of Color engage in against each other based upon the darkness or lightness of our skin. Colorism is very clearly described by the old adage that I, and I suspect millions of other African Americans of my generation, learned in childhood, "If you're light, you're alright. If you're brown, stick around. But if you're black, get back."[42] Historically, that message has created a human hierarchy **within** groups of color (based upon and reflecting the same racial hierarchy of the entire human race), with light-skinned people at the top, medium brown-skinned people in the middle, and dark brown-skinned people at the bottom. Colorism has wreaked indescribable emotional and psychological pain and suffering within groups of color and within those groups, in **families.**

I attended Rivers Frederick Junior High for seventh and eighth grades, and it was there that I had my first experience of colorism. I was, of course, **aware** of colorism before I started junior high school. It would have been impossible to have lived in New Orleans for eleven years without at least **knowing** about colorism, but prior to going to junior high school, it hadn't actually affected me. It was during my seventh and eighth grade years at Frederick that I saw colorism "up close" for the first time.

Frederick was in the Seventh Ward of New Orleans. The residents of the Seventh Ward at that time, and indeed until Hurri-

42 As a child growing up in New Orleans, I knew many light-skinned, straight-haired African Americans, some of whom thought of and referred to themselves as "Creole." The majority of Creoles married and taught their children to marry only other Creoles in order to "keep the light skin and straight hair in the family." Many thought of themselves as being superior to the city's other African American residents. Still others considered themselves to be a different race entirely—the Creole race.

cane Katrina hit, were not exclusively, but certainly overwhelmingly Creole—very light-skinned African Americans who often had green or blue eyes and very straight, sometimes light-colored hair. The Seventh Ward was almost a kind of mini "color city" within the city, and Frederick was in the heart of the Seventh Ward. During my two years there, I observed that some of the teachers (not the majority, fortunately, but not a small minority either), all of whom were African American, were more comfortable with, and therefore noticeably warmer toward, the light-skinned Creole kids. As for the students, some of the dark brown-skinned and light brown-skinned kids disliked each other automatically on the basis of skin color. The first time I saw Rogers and Hammerstein's "West Side Story," the fights between the Puerto Rican Sharks and the Irish/Italian/Polish Jets reminded me of the rival between the dark and light-skinned kids at Frederick. I never saw any **violence** between them, but you could cut the **tension** between them with a knife. Not only was there absolutely no socialization between the two groups of kids, there was also a kind of system of de facto segregation between them in which they separated into friends groups, sports teams, and lunch cliques.[43]

I was neither light nor dark-skinned. With skin that was medium brown, I was in the middle. Even my hair was in the middle. It was neither straight nor napped.[44] It was fuzzy, but it was long. The

---

43 I had thought for years that colorism was unique to the New Orleans African American community. I eventually learned, however, that colorism is and historically has been present in African American communities across the United States. In conducting several months of training at Howard University in the mid-1990's, the first time I walked down the hall to the President's office, I noticed immediately that the pictures of most of the past presidents that lined the wall leading to his office were not only male, which was no surprise, but also unmistakably light-skinned. Colorism among African Americans is the subject of Spike Lee's 1988 film, "School Daze", set at an African American university. At the end of the film, one of the characters, utterly frustrated by the colorism that plagued the school, stood in the middle of one of the campus quads, both hands in the air, and yelled at the very top of his lungs to all within shouting distance, "Wake Up!"

44 The term "nappy" in reference to African hair has become a pejorative, connoting "bad" hair. For that reason, I have used the term "napped" to describe African hair. Our hair is not curly in the traditional understanding of that word. Rather, it is napped in the same sense that Berber rugs are napped. Thus, I use the term "napped" as just a factual, neutral descriptor of African hair.

former was bad. The latter, good. I felt as if I was in a really weird kind of color/hair limbo. I longed for my life at Moton.

The whole "color thing" was very painful to me because like most African American families, mine has members who are at both ends and also in the middle of the range of human skin color. Gramzie had thirteen grandchildren, four from Uncle Ikee, four from my mother, three from Aunt Verlie and two from Aunt Johnnie. Our skin colors run the entire gamut of the human complexion spectrum, and Gramzie loved all of us, all thirteen of us, the same. With all of our complexion diversity, we never played the color card in my family. Never.[45]

But colorism ran deep in New Orleans. For decades, it was the strict practice of certain African American sororities and fraternities to admit as members, only those whose skin was of a "certain" hue. In some, membership was open to those whose skin was a bit darker, but only **if** they had "good," i.e., straight hair. For many years, the Autocrat Club, a New Orleans social club for African American men, informally excluded black men who were not light-skinned. Entrance depended upon whether you could pass a test widely-known by African Americans of my and preceding generations—the Brown Paper Bag Test. If your skin was **lighter** than a paper bag, you were allowed admission. If it was **darker**, you were not, unless, of course, you had "good" hair.[46]

I was at Rivers Frederick from September 1964 until June 1966. I found the colorism that I experienced there particularly painful because of the reality of my mother and grandmother's lives. Gramzie had dark brown skin, African hair, African facial

45 My Aunt Johnnie shared with me when I became an adult that my mother bought her a beautiful red coat to take with her to college, but because she (Aunt Johnnie, who was considerably darker in complexion than my mother) had heard over her entire life that dark brown skinned people were not supposed to wear certain colors, red among them, because they accentuated their "darkness," she was too embarrassed to wear it. My mother talked to her younger sister and told her that she did not want her to feel that way, that she should absolutely not be ashamed of her color and that the coat looked beautiful on her. Aunt Johnnie wore that red coat with pride throughout her college years. Colorism touched us all.

46 I discuss the issue of African Americans and our socialization to think of our napped, African hair as bad and straight, European hair as good, as well as the psychological and emotional impact of that socialization, in *On Race and Racism: Humanity's Bottom Line.*

features and apparently (judging strictly from appearance, which is absolutely not a reliable indicator) none of the European American genes that millions of African Americans possess as the result of the rape of thousands upon thousands of African American women by their European American enslavers during the long legacy of American slavery. Gramzie didn't appear to be "mixed" with anything. She had the appearance of a beautiful African woman. Mama looked very different. Indeed, one might look at the two of them and not even believe that they were mother and daughter. Mama was very light-skinned and had European facial features and very straight black hair.

Gramzie had always told us that my mother looked like one of her great aunts, a very old picture of whom she had shown me since I was little. The woman in the picture, however, while very light-skinned with straight hair, didn't look anything like my mother. As a child though, I accepted without question what Gramzie told me. I didn't know until I was eighteen, the real reason why there was no resemblance between my mother and the woman in the picture.

In February of 1924, Gramzie was a very young woman who worked as a maid cleaning rooms in the New Orleans Jung Hotel. Although she was only eighteen, she was already married to Jim Gray. "Grandpa Jim" had the same complexion, hair texture and type of facial features as Gramzie. He looked like an African man.

One of Gramzie's work days at the hotel in early February of 1924, began, I'm sure, like any other. She had no way of knowing that after that day, her life would be forever changed. At some point during what was otherwise probably quite a routine work day, one of the white patrons "had his way with her," and nine months later, my mother was the result. Those are literally all the details I know. It was the kind of thing that adults just didn't talk about with children.

My father was the one who told me the story. It happened during a conversation one Saturday night during which he was quite sloshed. In response to a question I had just asked about Grandpa Jim, my father looked at me and said, "Laurie, now...you know your Grandpa Jim isn't your real grandpa, right?" "Huh? Grandpa Jim not my real grandpa?," I replied in utter surprise. "Think about it, Laurie. How could a woman like your Gramzie and a man like your Grandpa Jim get together and make a baby that looks like your Mama? What happened is that your Gramzie was a young girl working at the Jung Hotel and one day, one of the white patrons had his way with her, and that's how your Mama came to be." To say that I was shocked in that moment would be a total understatement. I was at a complete loss for words. After several seconds, perhaps a full minute, I managed to ask two questions—whether Gramzie told Grandpa Jim what happened before Mama was born, and if so, how he responded. In response, my father told me that he didn't know whether Gramzie had told Grandpa Jim what happened before my mother was born, but went on to say that whether or not she told him at the time, my mother's appearance at birth must've made it obvious to him that he wasn't her biological father. The last thing he said about the matter was that Grandpa Jim loved my mother dearly nonetheless, and raised her as his own. He explained that Grandpa Jim trusted Gramzie completely, and understood that what had happened to her happened to a lot of young African American women and girls at that time, especially those who worked in hotels and private homes.

My father didn't decide to tell me that story because he thought that at eighteen, I was old enough to know. The conversation happened quite accidentally. If it hadn't happened during one of our "enhanced" talks (that happened only after he'd been drinking), I may never have known the truth about my mother's conception. That was the only conversation that my father and

I ever had about the matter, and I don't even know whether he remembered the next day that the conversation even happened. I never once asked Gramzie about it.

Gramzie

Mama

Grandpa Jim

Although at the time I didn't know the actual story of my mother's conception, I understood even as a child of about ten, why she cried so much when she and I watched at home in the living room, the original 1934 version of the movie, "Imitation of Life." The film centered on the relationship of an African American mother and daughter. In the plot, the very light-skinned daughter passed for white and in so doing, totally denied her dark brown-skinned mother. Even though Mama never did and never would have done such a thing to Gramzie, I knew exactly why the movie's plot moved her so deeply. I knew that on some fundamental level, the characters reminded her of Gramzie and her. Sitting there in the living room watching the movie with my mother, I just put my arms around her, patted her back, and tried, in my child-like way, to comfort her.

In addition to Mama and Gramzie, my parents were also dark and light-skinned. Unlike many African American New Orleanians who shared her physical appearance, my mother didn't marry a man who looked like her in an attempt to have children with light skin and straight hair. My father had dark brown skin and African hair.

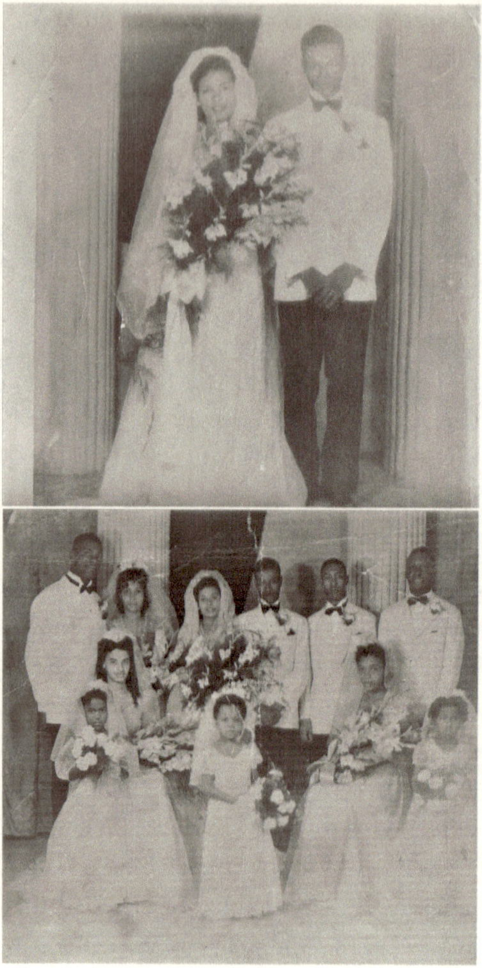

My Parents' Wedding Pictures

Witnessing and deeply feeling, as I did, the immense love between Gramzie and Mama, and loving them both as much as I did (my love for them was as deep and as intense as their love for me), combined with the fact that my father was dark brown-skinned, I found the colorism at Frederick immensely disturbing. Just as with racism, I had the insight, even at that young age, to clearly see both the insanity and the inhumanity of colorism. I knew that as African Americans, we were doing to each other the very same thing that European Americans had historically done and were continuing to do, to all of us, and I hated it.

CHAPTER TWO

HIGH SCHOOL: THE ACADEMY OF THE HOLY ANGELS

MY FIRST EXPERIENCE OF PERSONAL RACISM

Two weeks after my 13th birthday in September 1966, I began my freshman year at The Academy of the Holy Angels High School, AHA or "Holy Angels," as it was often called, an all-girls Catholic high school. Even though we were not Catholic, my mother, thinking that I would get a better education in a Catholic school than in a New Orleans public high school, upon my completion of 8th grade at Rivers Frederick Junior High, enrolled me at Holy Angels.

Prior to beginning high school at Holy Angels, my only experience of racism had been through the institution of segregation,and the harassment that my junior high school classmates and I faced immediately after it ended—being badgered every day by

White, senior high school boys while riding home on the newly integrated city buses. With the exception of Gramzie's dear friend, Miss Maymi, and her two grown kids, Don and Marion, who were like family, up to that point in my life, I had had no personal interactions with European Americans. My experience of racism at Holy Angels was my first encounter with racism from people who knew me. I think of it as my first experience of **personal** racism.

The vast majority of the roughly 550 girls at Holy Angels were European American and they were not at all used to attending school with African American kids. They weren't, I suspect, used to being in the company of African Americans in any context. The Civil Rights Act of 1964, which integrated all public accommodations, had been the law of the land for only two years, so having to share the school restrooms with us, having to share the gym showers with us, drinking from the same school water fountains that we did, eating with us in the cafeteria, and sitting next to us in class were all relatively new to them. Additionally, it didn't help that there were fewer than 20 African American students in the entire student body. Specifically, with the exception of one senior, four or five sophomores and roughly ten of us freshmen who were African-American, the entire student body of Holy Angels was white.

My experience of racism at Holy Angels began immediately. I had just turned only thirteen when I began high school there, but I had a very clear understanding of the racism that I was experiencing. One explanation that my mother gave me when I was very young was that White people who treated us badly were simply behaving consistently with the way they had been taught their entire lives to behave toward us, and that they behaved that way because they really didn't know us. They knew only what they were taught to think and to believe about us. They didn't know that we were in actuality totally different from their stereotypes of us. They didn't know what they didn't know...but they certainly **thought** they knew. Those words were front-and-center in my mind as I experienced the coldness of some of my white schoolmates every day. I knew that for many of them, we were in all likelihood, the very first African-Americans they had ever experienced in any significant way. That understanding, however, while useful to me on an intellectual level, didn't make the daily emotional experience of being in what felt like a generally frosty atmosphere one bit more comfortable.

At the beginning of the school year, each freshman was assigned, by lottery, to a senior who was to be her "Big Sister" for the first two weeks of school. The "Big Sister, Little Sister" program was AHA's freshman orientation with a bit of very light "hazing" thrown in. The hazing was simply having to take orders from your big sister—to bring her lunch to her or carry her books to her next class, for example. Suffice it to say that my big sister, who was not the one African-American in the senior class, was far less than happy to have wound up paired with me as her "little sister." I could tell by the way she looked at and spoke to me on the first day of our pairing that she actually wanted to have nothing to do with me. Her very first order on day one of the orientation was for me to come to school the next day with my hair in braids all over my head, a big ribbon at the end of each, every one a different color. I refused! I was thirteen and quite little and my big sister was seventeen or eighteen and quite large, but the dignity that my mother had instilled in me, even at that tender age, made such an instruction utterly unthinkable for me. I never told Mama about that "assignment" because I knew how deeply it would hurt her. I also have absolutely no doubt that she would not have allowed me to comply with it. That was the only order my big sister ever managed to give me because I literally hid from her for the remainder of the two weeks of freshman orientation. In comparing notes with the nine or so other black kids in my class, I discovered that they had somewhat normal experiences with their big sisters.

Mine was the worst. It was just the luck of the draw, and it was horrible.

But one of my earliest experiences with racism shortly after I began high school came not from my schoolmates, but from students of Nicholls High School, a public high school that was a few blocks down St. Claude Avenue from Holy Angels. One morning early in my freshman year, I rode the Louisa to the Galvez bus and walked the four or five blocks down St. Claude Avenue from the Galvez bus stop to school. On that walk, I had to pass in front of Nicholls, which had been all-white before integration, and which may still have been at that time, or at least predominantly so. That was one of the most harrowing walks of my young life. As I walked in front of the school, a group of twenty or thirty White students, while yelling "Niggah!" and "Niggah girl", broke soda bottles on the sidewalk and threw the glass fragments at my legs. I had never been as frightened in my entire life, not even riding the Broad Avenue bus home from Frederick, but just as I did on the bus, I did not and knew that I could not show it. With my heart thumping in my chest at what felt like ten times its normal rate, I just kept walking and showed no fear. I somehow escaped that nightmare essentially unharmed, with just a few small bloody nicks on my calves. Luckily, I had tissues with me and before arriving at school, was able to clean up the little bits of blood that were streaming down my legs. Later that evening when I told my mother what happened, she was appalled, frightened and very worried. She told me to **never** walk in front of that school again and instead, to start taking the St. Claude Avenue bus the few blocks from Galvez Street to school. I did from then on. That first half of my freshman year at Holy Angels was by far the most uncomfortable.

What I received from many of my white peers wasn't outright hostility. It wasn't overt racism. To my knowledge, no one ever called me or any of my African American classmates by any racial epithets. It was more subtle than that. It was more "coolness", being given a cold shoulder, than anything else. It was a kind of physical and emotional distancing, and I felt it strongly. It was being related to everyday by some of my white schoolmates as undesirable and less intelligent. It was also being asked questions about African Americans by some of my classmates that were clearly based on racial stereotypes. A number of the questions that some (but certainly not all) of my white classmates asked me demonstrated that they held several traditional, well-known stereotypes about African Americans. Among them were that we like the same kind of music, have rhythm and are excellent dancers, that we like and eat only "soul food", that we live in poverty, and that we don't know who our fathers are. Essentially, the questions my classmates asked demonstrated that they viewed African Americans as extremely shallow and one-dimensional. Essentially, we were not real people to them. It was nauseating. What I found most troubling about the stereotypes, however, even more than their content, was that in the minds of those who held them, they applied in equal measure to **all** Black people. We all like the same music. We all have rhythm. We all like and eat only soul food. We all live in poverty, and none of us know who our fathers are. Having to interact with those stereotypes "close up and personal" for the first time in my life was a shock to my thirteen-year-old emotional system.[47] To Lauren, the young science nut, such a belief system seemed both utterly senseless and irrational. I knew that those stereotypes were utterly false because they were so untrue of my family and of every black family I knew, and because of the community in which I had grown up, I knew a lot of black families.[48] To Lauren, the

47 Not too much later on, I learned about other entrenched stereotypes that millions of White Americans hold of Black Americans—that we are dumb, have low morals, are criminally-inclined, sexually promiscuous, and lazy. The pain of knowing that those characteristics are closely associated with any entire group of people, much less the group of people to whom you belong, can simply not be fully understood without experiencing it.

48 I fully acknowledge the many African American neighborhoods across the country in which the majority of residents live in poverty, and in which there is a high rate of teen pregnancies and single-parent families. One thing I know for sure, however, is that the people in those communities are as inherently intelligent, as inherently creative, and as inherently gifted as all other people, and that whatever level of crime and other social dysfunction exists in the communities in which they live, is the result of not genetics, not their African heritage, but **is**, rather,, the product of centuries of racism.

young, highly sensitive person, the stereotypes were deeply hurtful, and felt enormously unfair.

All of that said, some of AHA's white students, fortunately, were, from the beginning, very kind and warm. I remember their names and can see their faces to this day. One in particular, Janis J., who sat behind me in Sister Mary Margaret's freshman homeroom class, became a friend. As the year progressed, a sizable number of white students became more comfortable with, and thus friendlier toward us. I suspect that it was their daily experience with us, seeing us come to school every day with our uniforms as crisply ironed and our saddle oxfords as clean and shiny as theirs. It was watching us come to school with completed homework every day, and seeing us raise our hands in class, correctly answering questions every day. In essence, it was their **experience** of us every day as just normal people, ordinary kids living with our parents and siblings just as they did, that demonstrated to them in a way that only regular exposure to the unknown, different "other" can, that we were not unintelligent, that we were not lazy, that we were not the misbehaving black demons that they had been taught we were.

As for our teachers, the nuns, a few of the older ones, two or three at most, while not in any way hostile toward us, seemed to be noticeably uncomfortable with us. All of the other sisters, however, were fine, and several were really quite nice. Two in particular, Sister Mary Dominic Savio, my tenth-grade biology teacher, and Sister Mary Rose Elizabeth, my senior homeroom and English teacher, were actually very sweet to me.

Needless to say, I didn't become involved in any extra-curricular activities at Holy Angels. The one activity I did try was outside of school. It was Junior Achievement, a national program with a focus on entrepreneurship and preparing young people for the business world. Its goal was to teach kids the skills necessary to become financially literate and empowered.[49]

I had absolutely no interest in either business or entrepreneurship, none; but, the Junior Achievement representative who pitched the program to the AHA student body was so charismatic, and his presentation so exciting, that I decided to try it. In the program, students were organized into units that were called "companies." Each company had a name, and approximately eight-to-ten or so kids. My company was "Interbank." The companies made a product of some kind, developed a marketing strategy for it, and then sold stock in the company. The more of its product a company sold, the more valuable was its stock. I was so excited about starting with my company. I looked forward to brainstorming what product we'd make, to the imagination required in designing and figuring out how to make it, and to the ingenuity of developing a sales approach and marketing strategy for it. It wasn't the business aspect of the program that interested me. It was the creativity required. It all seemed as if it would be so much creative fun.

The very first thing I noticed at my company's initial meeting was that I was the only African-American kid in the company. I tried my best to offer my suggestions. I wanted to be a good team member, and I knew I had great ideas. Two months later, I quit the Junior Achievement program. None, not one, of the other kids in my company would talk to me. I got the silent treatment the entire

---

49 I have often wondered what extracurricular activities I may have pursued had I attended a black high school. I am by nature (i.e., by MBTI temperament Myers–Briggs Type Indicator - Wikipedia an introvert, and in part because I was a year ahead in school, was also socially a bit less mature than the majority of my peers, perhaps making it likely that I wouldn't have become involved in many activities. Student government may have held some interest for me, however, and my love of writing may have resulted in my writing for the school newspaper. While I'm not at all a poet, I actually placed third in a poetry writing contest in high school. I lost the poem many years ago and remember only that it was a social commentary on the political and social state of the nation at that time. I still have my third-place trophy!

two months. I remember that there were two kids who wanted to be nice to me—a girl and a boy. I could tell because they'd smile kindly at me when no one else was looking. I understood, though, that they were under tremendous unspoken peer pressure to not acknowledge me and I felt bad for them. At the end of those two months, I was hurt and extremely disappointed that I was not going to have the Junior Achievement experience. My mother was hurt and disappointed for me.

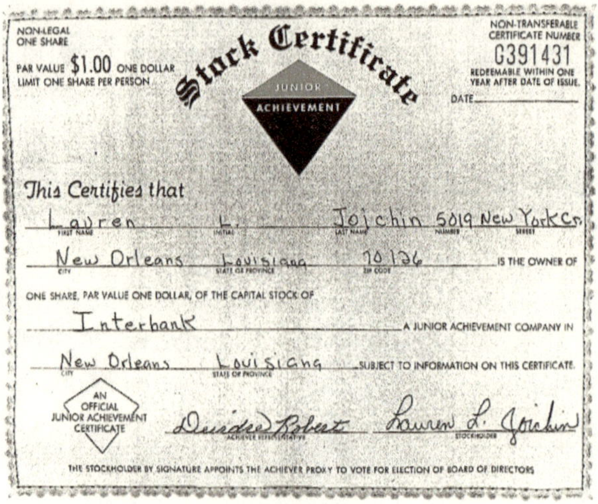
NON-LEGAL
ONE SHARE
PAR VALUE $1.00 ONE DOLLAR
LIMIT ONE SHARE PER PERSON

Stock Certificate

JUNIOR
ACHIEVEMENT

NON-TRANSFERABLE
CERTIFICATE NUMBER
G391431
REDEEMABLE WITHIN ONE
YEAR AFTER DATE OF ISSUE.
DATE

This Certifies that
Lauren (FIRST NAME) L. (INITIAL) Joichin (LAST NAME) 5019 (NUMBER) New York Cr. (STREET)
New Orleans (CITY) Louisiana (STATE OR PROVINCE) 70126 (ZIP CODE) IS THE OWNER OF
ONE SHARE, PAR VALUE ONE DOLLAR, OF THE CAPITAL STOCK OF
Interbank A JUNIOR ACHIEVEMENT COMPANY IN
New Orleans (CITY) Louisiana (STATE OR PROVINCE) SUBJECT TO INFORMATION ON THIS CERTIFICATE.

AN OFFICIAL JUNIOR ACHIEVEMENT CERTIFICATE

Deirdre Robert (ACHIEVER REPRESENTATIVE) Lauren L. Joichin (STOCKHOLDER)

THE STOCKHOLDER BY SIGNATURE APPOINTS THE ACHIEVER PROXY TO VOTE FOR ELECTION OF BOARD OF DIRECTORS

My Junior Achievement Stock Certificate

While the racism that I experienced in high school was a definite deterrent to my becoming involved in extracurricular activities, it did not deter me from doing my very best academically. As was the case before I even began kindergarten, I still loved learning, and worked hard in all of my classes. To this day, in my box of childhood and adolescent mementos, I still have my two class notebooks of which I was particularly proud....those from my biology and geometry courses with their illustrations that I meticulously drew.

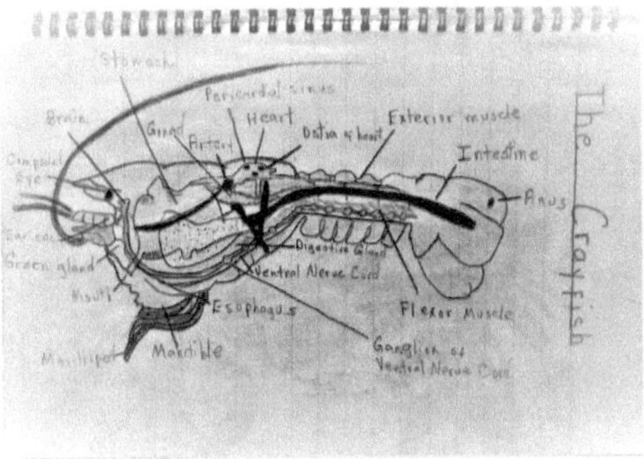

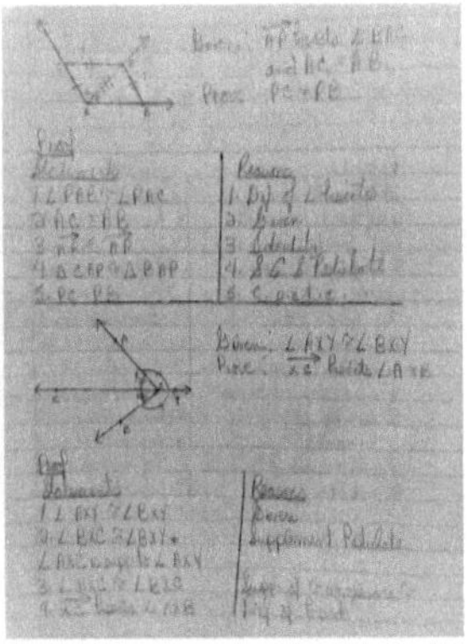

Illustrations from my 10th Grade Biology and Geometry Notebooks

RACISM AND THE CIVIL RIGHTS MOVEMENT: THEIR INDELIBLE IMPACT

DURING MY CHILDHOOD AND ADOLESCENT YEARS, I WAS VERY strongly influenced by two things. The first was my personal experience with racism, i.e., the racial discrimination that we experienced during segregation, and the racial harassment that we experienced after segregation. It was the discrimination that I both personally experienced and that I witnessed other African Americans experience—the "White Only" American apartheid society of my earliest years, the harassment that my Rivers Frederick classmates and I experienced from the Cor Jesu High School boys on the city bus, the verbal and physical abuse I experienced from the Nicholls High students, the alienation that I felt at Holy Angels, the experience of being ignored in my Junior Achievement company, and my many other experiences with racism that I've chosen to not even chronicle here. All of those experiences imprinted upon me a keen, finely-tuned, razor sharp awareness of what we, as human beings, are capable of doing to each other when we are unaware of our equal humanity. The experience of acquiring that awareness was bitter. It had a sharp, painful, cutting edge; one that **no** child deserves. That said,

I wouldn't exchange my experiences for the world, for I'd be a very different person today without the understanding and the wisdom that they afforded me. Most significantly, my experiences gave me both an intellectual awareness and an emotional sensitivity that left me with a dogged determination to do something with my life that I hoped would be profoundly important in increasing both understanding and compassion in the world. Essentially, I wanted to help humanity to evolve, to mature.[50]

The other factor that affected me profoundly during my adolescence was that of having been a child during the heyday of the Civil Rights Movement. I was especially moved by Dr. King's speeches. I believed very deeply and sincerely in his message of non-violence. I believed that just as you fight fire with water, you fight hatred with love. I thought that it was utterly foolish to try to fight fire with more fire, and hatred with more hatred. The thought of doing so was utterly irrational to me. Predictably, then, in my early teens, another side of me, which was quite different from Lauren the junior scientist, began developing—Lauren the passionate Civil Rights activist. In addition to wanting to address racial stereotypes themselves, I began to feel a deep need to address the injustice that **resulted** from the stereotypes. My first encounter with daily, personal racism at Holy Angels caused Lauren, the inquisitive junior scientist, to wonder how people could hold such false, negative thoughts, such awful stereotypes that were so deeply entrenched about people whom they didn't even know As a result, I became fascinated with the process of how stereotypes develop. I began to want to do something about them. I wanted to

50 Growing up during the heyday of the Civil Rights Movement, and being a young woman in my early 20's during the height of the second wave of the women's movement and the birth of the LGBTQ, and environmental movements, and living in cities, at the time, Philadelphia, New York City, and Washington, DC, in which I was able to be actively involved in the movements, had a significant impact on my consciousness. I thought of them all as movements for the growth and improvement of humanity, movements to make humanity more conscious and more compassionate. Those movements, occurring when they did in my life, were tremendous influences in my life.

help people to either avoid or grow beyond them. It was the birth of my desire to open minds and soften hearts.[51]

But it was Dr. King's speeches that were **most** moving for me. When hearing them, I was both old enough and aware enough for both Dr. King's **words** and the remarkably compelling, poetic eloquence with which he **delivered** his words, to often be literally moved to tears. I knew that Dr. King was engaged in a just movement because I and all those whom I knew and loved were living the injustice that that movement was designed to address. His speeches about the power of love and non-violence went straight to my heart, deeply touching me. His "Drum Major Instinct" https://www.youtube.com/watch?v=BcuifZJdyaY sermon is my favorite, by far, of all of his sermons and speeches.

I was fourteen, and in my sophomore year at AHA on April 4, 1968, the day Dr. King was assassinated. My mother, Lorna and I were in the car and almost home at the end of the day when the radio announcer read the statement. Reverend Martin Luther King, Jr. had been shot and killed in Memphis. In that instant, my mother cried out in sheer anguish, "Oh my God, Dr. King is dead!"

When we got home, what followed was yet another evening during which our phone rang incessantly with family members and many of my parents' friends calling well into the night. This time though, it wasn't elation that they were sharing. It was disbelief and painful, intense sorrow. I hadn't seen the adults in my life so terribly shaken and anguished since the day, nearly five years earlier, when President Kennedy had been assassinated. On the night of Dr. King's death, my heart and that of every person I

51 The "Up with People" young people's movement of the 1960's, with its message of universal brother/sisterhood, spoke beautifully to my adolescent wishes for a fairer, more compassionate world. Although by today's standards, the choir of the "Up with People" group was not very racially diverse, (there was only one African American on the album cover, who was on the back cover, and although there may have been, I don't remember seeing any other People-of-Color in the choir), it was more diverse than any other group I had seen up to that point. My mother bought me the "Up with People" album, https://upwithpeople.org/discover/our-legacy/; https://www.youtube.com/watch?v=HkNfmwjaNic that I loved and listened to over and over again. I still have the album to this day.

knew, was **heavy** with grief. It was one month before the end of my sophomore year of high school, and was, up to that point, the saddest day of my entire fourteen years.

On the day of Dr. King's funeral, I sat on the floor, inches from our den television, with my little portable reel-to-reel tape recorder, taping as much of the service as I had blank tape to accommodate. I knew that I was witnessing history and I wanted to save it. I still have that little reel-to-reel, as well as the tapes on which I recorded the ceremony. The tape recorder, unfortunately, hasn't worked in decades.

Exactly two months and two days later, on June 6,1968, Bobby Kennedy, whom I profoundly admired, was assassinated. It felt to me that Bobby Kennedy exuded true compassion for the poor from every fiber of his being. My fourteen-year-old heart was devastated for the second time within a span of two months.[52]

52 It was for that reason that I was extremely disappointed when I learned years later as an adult, that as Attorney General, Bobby Kennedy, even though he may have done so reluctantly, ordered the FBI to wiretap Dr. King's telephones.

CHAPTER THREE

LAUREN THE YOUNG ACTIVIST EMERGES

I became a young activist in the summer of 1969. My mother was, at that time, the Administrative Assistant to Mr. Larry Cager, the Acting Executive Director of the New Orleans Urban League.[53] As such, she assisted in the coordination of the League's summer voter registration drives, the objective of which was to get African Americans registered to vote. The program's "boots on the ground" were high school students. From the moment my mother told me about the program, I wanted in. The students worked under the direction of an Urban League staff member. That summer, it was Mrs. Oretha Haley, Oretha Castle Haley—Wikipedia a long-time local civil rights activist whom over the course of the summer I grew to greatly admire, and for whom New Orleans' Oretha Castle Haley Boulevard is now named. We

53 Mr. Clarence Barney was the League's Executive Director, but was away pursuing his Master's Degree in Texas during the summer of '69.

were essentially volunteers, receiving only a very small stipend for bus fair and lunch. It was the summer before my senior year at Holy Angels. I was fifteen.

The Urban League's voter registration drive that summer was my very first experience doing grass roots "activist" work, and I enjoyed it immensely. I knew how important it was to vote. My parents were always interested in both what was going on politically in the country, and in current events. The three local newspapers, the Times Picayune (the morning paper), the States Item (the evening paper), and the Louisiana Weekly (the local African American paper), were all delivered to the house, and my parents read them. I saw both my parents vote in what I'm sure was every election, national, state and local. I knew that they took both voting and their Democratic politics very seriously. Additionally, although it hadn't been a part of any history class curriculum in school, I had read on my own that African-American men had gained the right to vote in 1870 with the passage of the fifteenth amendment, but that women, no women, including white women, were allowed vote until 1920, a full fifty years after black men received the right. I learned that the women's vote came about only in response to the suffrage movement, without which, women may not have gained the right to vote for another several decades. I remember Dr. King speaking about how African-Americans' constitutional right to vote was being trampled on in many places in the South through the use of bogus and totally illegal poll taxes, literacy tests and Ku Klux Klan intimidation tactics. I learned what civil rights voter registration activists had gone through only a few years earlier in other places in the South, and that James Chaney, Andrew Goodman and Michael Schwerner, all three in their early twenties, had actually been murdered by the Klan for doing exactly what we were doing that summer---helping African Americans register to vote.[54]

54 I was not taught **any** of this history in school. It was the beginning of my understanding of just how utterly incomplete was the American History that my and all preceding generations had been taught in school. In *On Race and Racism: Humanity's Bottom Line*, I provide some of the missing pieces of the history of American racism that were not taught to my generation of Americans, and sadly, may still largely not be taught today.

As I volunteered in the Urban League's voter registration drive that summer of 1969, all of that history, as well my knowledge of what civil rights voter registration activists had gone through only a few years earlier, came vividly alive for me. I thought about James Chaney, Andrew Goodman and Michael Schwerner, who, when they were killed, were not much older than we were at that time. I found completely gratifying, however, the process of knocking on doors, talking to people about the importance of registering to vote, and on the spot, scheduling a ride for them to the registration location, knowing that another volunteer was waiting for them there, ready to walk them through the registration process, at the end of which there would be one more African-American who was registered to vote. It was only four years after the passage of the historic Voting Rights Act of 1965 giving all Americans the right to vote without being discriminated against on the basis of race.[55]

I desperately wanted two things. First, I wanted fairness. I wanted justice for people who had been discriminated against for so long. I wanted us to be genuinely regarded and, in every way, treated, as the full human beings that we are with all of the accompanying dignity and equality thereby required. I wanted all people to understand on a deep level, that we are all equally human. Second, even though I was a young teenager, I wanted European-Americans to experience their lives from a place of far greater emotional maturity. I wanted them to at least glimpse the unimaginable possibilities that existed for their lives, how they would feel

55 As a fifteen-year-old volunteer in a 1969 summer voter registration drive, I could have never imagined that in 2013, nearly fifty years after the passage of the Voting Rights Act, our nation's highest court would gut Section 5, the strongest section of the Act, as it did in its landmark Shelby County v. Holder decision. As a result of that ruling, Americans of Color once again face horrible and quite obvious attempts to both suppress our vote through a variety of means, and to intimidate us into not voting at all. It is almost unbelievable to me that we are yet again fighting that same old, tired, weary battle, the battle for the right to vote. There is a common saying within the community of civil rights activists that seems to be just accepted as true; "Every generation has to win its freedom anew." That apparent acceptance of having to fight similar battles all over again in every generation makes me both extremely uncomfortable and very sad, and yet, I know that it is indeed the reality. With each successive battle, however, I tell myself, "Just as the bob of a pendulum oscillates back and forth several times before the swinging stops and it finally settles into a nice strong, stable mid-point, this too, in time, shall pass. I know not when, but this too, this battle for full human rights, will end."

in their hearts, and thus how they would behave, were they capable of truly experiencing African Americans and all other People of Color as their sisters and brothers in the family of humanity. Essentially, I wanted for our entire species, both the intellectual and the emotional freedom that I knew was possible for us if we truly understood and deeply felt that we are all equal. I knew that I wanted to do something significant in my life to make that emotional freedom our reality. I felt intensely that the work of helping our species to mature beyond racism and all other forms of prejudice was the work of The Creator. Doing social justice work that encompassed those goals truly felt like a spiritual calling. Reverend Kennedy's many sermons I had grown up hearing every Sunday solidified that conviction.

The experience of working in the New Orleans Urban League's voter registration drive as a high school student that summer was the beginning of what became my lifelong attempt to make the world a fairer, more just place that reflected what I deeply believed was a higher, Divinely-inspired human consciousness.

CHAPTER FOUR

MY WHOLE WORLD CRASHES

A DEVASTATING LOSS AND THE END OF MY CHILDHOOD

So there I was during the summer of 1969, the summer before my senior year of high school, a happy, very seriously committed fifteen-year-old voter registration volunteer. Wednesday, July 2nd of that summer was my parents' twenty-sixth wedding anniversary. The next day, Thursday, July 3rd, my entire world was turned upside down, inside out, and knocked completely out of its orbit when suddenly and completely unexpectedly, Mama died shortly after midnight, three days after having a routine and very minor female surgery. She was forty-four years old and in the prime of her enormously vibrant and active life when suddenly and without warning, she was gone from **my** life, and from all of our lives. My entire world had crashed and it was the end of my childhood.

There are no words to describe the anguish I experienced when my mother died. I could write an entire book about how losing one's mother in adolescence impacts teenage girls, but suffice it to say that my mother was the center of my entire universe and neither my love for her nor the pain that I felt when she died can ever be fully expressed in words. My mother lived an extremely rich and full life, a life of conscience. She was the organizer-in-chief of our entire extended family, and was greatly respected and admired as a leader in Pontchartrain Park, Bethany Church, and at the New Orleans Urban League. Her life was characterized by a deep love for her family, commitment to her community, compassion for others, especially those less fortunate, generosity of spirit, and civic engagement. There was **no one on Earth** whom I deeply loved, respected, and admired more than my mother.

Two days after Mama died, on the morning of Saturday, July 5th, to my utter surprise, Sister Mary Monica, the principal of Holy Angels, and two other nuns (I don't remember who they were) came to the house to visit with me. I could clearly see their sorrow, compassion, and concern. I was sincerely touched by their kindness, and especially their concern for me, which was visibly quite genuine. That afternoon, the proofs of my cap and gown pictures arrived in the mail. Seeing them ripped my heart in two. My only thought as I looked at the photos through uncontrolled tears was, "Mama would've been so proud. Mama would've been so proud of me." The pain felt as if it had saturated every cell of my body.

My mother's funeral was the next day, the morning of Sunday, July 6th. I wore all white to the service. Reverend Kennedy officiated. He was so emotional that he could hardly get through the service. I sat with my father and two older brothers in the first row on the left side of the center aisle of the church, no more than four feet from my mother's casket.[56] Throughout the entire service, my father, who was sitting on my right, had his left arm around me, rubbing and patting my upper arm.

The next morning, Monday, July 7th, was the short service at Bethany prior to the internment. When the service was over, crying inconsolably, I got up from my chair, walked up to my mother's casket, and with both my arms stretched over it, laid my torso on top of the casket, kissed it, and laid the right side of my face on it. I did not move until my father got up from his chair and pulled me away, having to use a degree of force to do so.

Within a half hour after the service, we were at the cemetery. That was when the finality of my mother's death hit me hardest. The day after she died, it struck me that she would have to be buried, the thought of which destroyed me. In my nearly sixteen-year-old mind, as long as my mother's body was still "here," her death wasn't quite real. Actually burying her body, i.e., putting it in a tomb, made it real in a way that it somehow hadn't been before. To this day, I remember as clearly as if it were yesterday, my indescribable pain of standing in front of the tomb in which my mother's casket had been placed, looking at the casket, knowing that her body was inside it, and that within minutes, the tomb's heavy stone front square was going to be put into place, permanently sealing in her body. I have **never** in all the years of my life since that moment, experienced **anything** as painful.

My parents had known each other their entire lives. They grew up together on the same block of the 7th ward, on LaHarpe Street, indeed as next-door neighbors. They attended Valena C. Jones Elementary and McDonogh 35 High Schools together, and married each other at 18 and 19 years old. In the blink of an eye, my parents' relationship of over forty years and their marriage of

56 My Aunts Verlie and Johnnie thought that Lorna, who was three weeks away from her seventh birthday, was too young to attend the funeral. Gramzie also did not attend. My aunts were seriously concerned that because of Gramzie's health, a heart condition among several others, attending my mother's funeral may have put her at grave risk. Lorna was with Gramzie during the service. While Lorna was spared the emotional trauma of my mother's funeral, in retrospect, I believe that her not attending it deprived her of necessary closure.

twenty-six years had ended. My father was a forty-five-year-old widower, and Lemar Jr., Lambert, Lorna and I were motherless.

It was three weeks before Lorna's seventh birthday, and six weeks before my sixteenth. Lorna was going into second grade at Coghill Elementary, and I was headed into my senior year at Holy Angels, a depressed, emotional wreck. It was in part, the suddenness of it all. On Sunday morning, June 29th, 1969, my mother was, as she had always been on Sunday mornings, at church, in front, singing lead soprano in the choir. One week later, on Sunday, July 6th, she was again in front of Bethany, but this time, in a casket.

My mother's siblings, Uncle Ikee and my Aunts Verlie and Johnnie were crushed. Uncle Ikee deeply loved his younger sister, Selina, and Aunt Verlie and Aunt Johnnie loved and admired their big sister, "Nina," to no end. Uncle Ikee spent the entire night Mama died walking around his back yard until the sun came up the following morning. Sometime in the late 1990's, more than twenty-five years after my mother died, I interviewed my Aunt Verlie about our family history, recording more than two hours of conversation with her. Talking about Mama, my Aunt Verlie said, "Nina was my sister, and I love her and I still miss her."

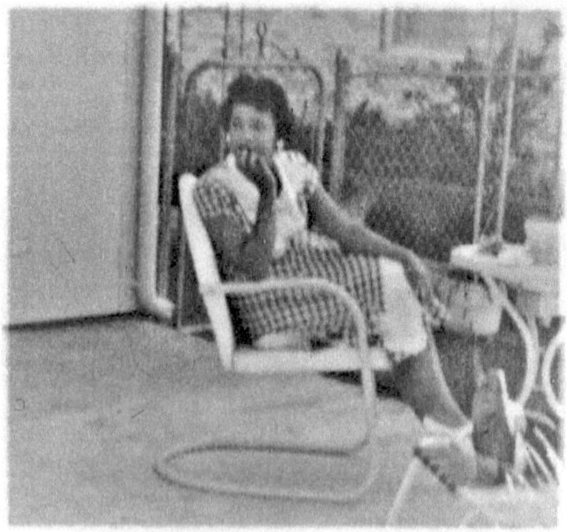

My Mother on Uncle Ikee's Patio at a Family Gathering

But it was **Gramzie** for whom, by far, my heart ached most. Her grief seemed to be an infinite, bottomless pit of profound anguish. She had lost her eldest daughter, her beloved Selina. It absolutely tortured me that Gramzie was hurting so severely and that there was absolutely nothing I could do to help her. I did, however, step into my mother's shoes after she was gone, and took care of all of Gramzie's needs—cashed her sixty-five-dollar Social Security check, paid her monthly rent, did her grocery shopping and picked up her medications from the pharmacy. Doing all those things for Gramzie, however, did absolutely nothing for my feeling of absolute helplessness, because I couldn't take away her indescribable pain. My hurt over Mama's loss was compounded by the pain that I saw Gramzie experience. My mother's sudden, shocking death was a tragedy for my entire family.

Two weeks after the funeral, Lambert, who was twenty-one and in the Air Force, was shipped off to Clark Air Force Base in Manila, Philippines for the last of his four years of service, and Lemar Jr., at twenty-five, left to begin basic training in the Army. Six months later, he was shipped off to a Vietnamese jungle. Because Lemar Jr. and Lambert left so soon after my mother died and were then so far away from home for so long, I wasn't able to really witness their immediate grief. And Lorna? She was just **so** young. My father had explained to her that Mama had died, but she didn't really understand what that meant. She didn't understand the finality of death. She was just too young. For two weeks or so after Mama died, she'd ask every time the doorbell rang, "Is that Mama?" Her question devastated my father. After a couple of weeks, when the doorbell rang, she no longer asked. Lorna's experience (as was **all** of ours) was that Mama was in her life one minute, and gone the next.

One night shortly after Lemar Jr. and Lambert left, my father sat me down on the living room couch to talk to me about his "plan." He would go to work, of course, do the food shopping (or "make groceries" as we say in New Orleans), cook—which he did very well, and do the laundry. I'd go to school, naturally, keep the house clean and take care of Lorna. With both our hearts ailing with severe pain, the two of us followed Daddy's plan and it worked. We went on, as we had to, and on a practical level, did ok.[57]

SHOCK AND SADNESS: THE COMMUNITY GRIEVES

My mother's death sent shock waves through the entire Pontchartrain Park Community. From the beginning, she was without question, one of its pillars, and was truly loved by the **entire** community. The notice of her death published the next month in the *Pontchartrain Park Patriot* read in part:

> August, 1969
>
> Residents of Pontchartrain Park were saddened last month in the announcement of the sudden death of Mrs. Selina Joichin. Mrs. Joichin was a tireless community worker. She had served on numerous boards in both civic organizations and Bethany Church. She leaves to mourn...a host of relatives and friends and the entire community of Pontchartrain Park.

Mama was adored as well by our minister, Reverend Kennedy, and our entire Bethany church family. Upon her death, the members of Bethany's Bi-Racial Dialogue Group, of which she was a member, wrote the following letter to Reverend Kennedy:

57 It never occurred to me that going from a two- to a one-income family, as we did after Mama died, may have had a dramatic impact on our standard of living. The reality, however, is that it did not. My father, on his U.S. Letter Carrier annual salary of $18,000, was able to pay our $75.00 monthly mortgage, all of our other household expenses, my senior year tuition at Holy Angels, and later, my college tuition and books. He was even able to buy me a little used Toyota Corolla during my senior year of college.

July 21, 1969
The Rev. Edward A. Kennedy, Jr.:

When we first came together as a Bi-Racial Dialogue Group almost a year ago, none of us knew just what to expect. We shared a common hope, however, that through an open and honest sharing of ideas and feelings, we would each gain a better understanding of ourselves and a deeper appreciation of one another as persons. We believed then, as we do now, that this kind of understanding is desperately needed in the face of the racial distrust and tension which burdens our land.

One member of our group who contributed immeasurably to its success was Mrs. Lemar L. Joichin. Selina brought so many things—she brought a warm and cheerful personality; she brought ideas and insights which grew out of her work with the Urban League; she brought a religious conviction which few experience in concern for other people as individuals and for her community. In all of these ways she enriched the lives of those of us who were privileged to know her.

In token of our gratitude for that privilege, we desire to have some small share in the future of Bethany Methodist Church which meant so much to her. It is our understanding that the music room in the new (church) building will be dedicated to Mrs. Joichin. If possible, we hope that the enclosed check can be applied to the purchase of some item for that room. We hope that this gift will in some small way express our appreciation for what Selina meant to us.

After her death, Bethany's choir room was indeed dedicated to my mother's memory. She was the choir's lead soprano. A bronze plaque with an engraved dedication to her was placed above its entrance. Beside the door, a picture of my mother was hung. Quite fittingly, in the photograph, she was outside of Bethany, with her choir robe folded over her right arm.[58]

Photograph of My Mother that Hung at the Entrance of Bethany's Choir Room for 35 Years

My mother's dedication plaque and picture hung outside of Bethany's choir room for thirty-five years. They were there until 2005 when Hurricane Katrina damaged Bethany severely, destroying them. The church was rebuilt, but without my mother's plaque and photo outside the choir room door. By then, too much time had passed. Too few of her contemporaries were still at Bethany for there to be an effort to replace them.

58 Many years later, Uncle Ikee told me that it was he who had hung Mama's picture beside the entrance of Bethany's choir room. Uncle Ikee was not a member of Bethany, or of any church, but he knew how very much Bethany meant to my mother, and was proud of the plaque that hung over the choir room door in her memory. The photo shows her outside of Bethany's first little sanctuary. Tragically, Mama did not live to see the new sanctuary after working tirelessly on the church's Building Committee for several years to raise funds for its construction. It was consecrated on December 28, 1969, approximately six months after her death.

My mother truly did have a **beautiful** soprano voice that was no less than operatic in strength. Before Bethany was founded, she was a member of the choir of LaHarpe Street Methodist Church, her childhood church that was directly across the street from the houses in which she and my father grew up as neighbors.

My Mother (7th from right) with Other Members of the LaHarpe Street Methodist Church Choir

The week after Mama died, we received the following letter, addressed to "Joichin Family":

> We thought that you would like to know the persons who have made contributions to Bethany United Methodist Church as of this date, in memory of your wife and mother, Mrs. Selina G. Joichin.
>
> [A list of all the contributors' names and the amount of their contributions followed.]
>
> Clarence W. Acox,
> Financial Secretary

My mother was very deeply committed to the goals of the Urban League—improving the lives of African Americans through economic equality and opportunity, and was genuinely loved at her job at the League. Within days of her death, the New Orleans Urban League forwarded the following letter to the house:

> To: The Family of the Late Selina Joichin
> c/o Urban League of Greater New Orleans
> 1821 Orleans Avenue
> New Orleans, Louisiana 70116
>
> Dear Friends:
>
> The shocking news of the loss of your beloved Selina reached our office this morning.
>
> All of the Members of the Administrative and Clerical Council of the National Urban League are deeply grieved over her death.
>
> We remember her as the vivacious, efficient Administrative Assistant of the New Orleans Urban League who did so much last year to make our stay during the (national) conference memorable.
>
> We share your sorrow and mourn your loss.
>
> Sincerely,
> Theresa M. Moss, President
> Administrative & Clerical Council
> National Urban League

At the behest of her boss, Mr. Larry Cager, the Acting Executive Director of the New Orleans Urban League at the time of her death, the 1969 Conference of the National Urban League was dedicated to her memory.

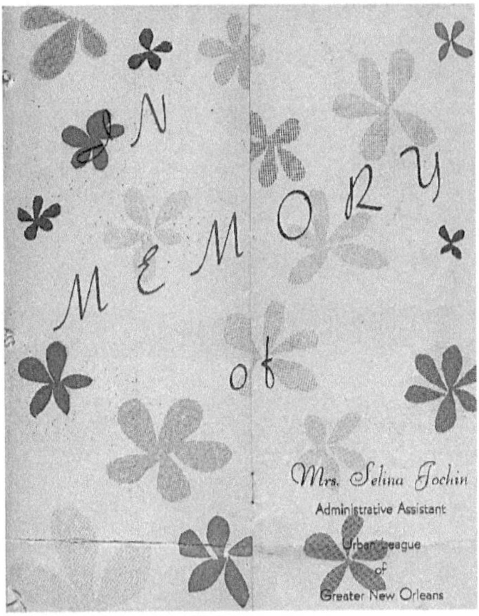

Program of the 1969 National Urban League
Conference in Washington, DC.

Dedicated to My Mother

The 1970 Annual Report of the New Orleans Urban League was also dedicated to my Mama's memory. The dedication, which appears on the report's inside front cover, includes a poem which Father Eugene McManus, a New Orleans Urban League staff member and my mother's colleague and friend, wrote for her. The dedication reads:

THE 1970 ANNUAL REPORT IS DEDICATED TO MRS. SELINA G. JOICHIN. PRIOR TO HER UNTIMELY DEATH LAST YEAR, SHE EXEMPLIFIED THE BEST IN URBAN LEAGUE COMMITMENT AND COMPETENCY DURING HER THREE YEARS OF SERVICE AS ADMINISTRATIVE ASSISTANT. HER HOPE FOR THE TRUE AMERICA, CONCERN FOR THE DISADVANTAGED, DEDICATION TO EXCELLENCE, AND PRIDE IN BLACKNESS EMBODIED THE ESSENCE OF URBAN LEAGUE PURPOSE AND HER MEMORY CONTINUES TO INSPIRE US ALL.

THE NEW ORLEANS URBAN LEAGUE

Selina

Brightly, life engulfed her heart
and danced her to the joy of living,
hoping, dreaming,
laughing, giving . . .

Deeply, suffering grieved her soul
and stirred her to a sense of doing,
prodding, working,
pushing, moving . . .

Gently, dusk enshrined her eyes
and cloaked her in its sable grace,
Black and lovely - -
God's gift to every race.

Eugene P. McManus, S.S.J.

1970 New Orleans Urban League Annual Report
Dedicated to My Mother

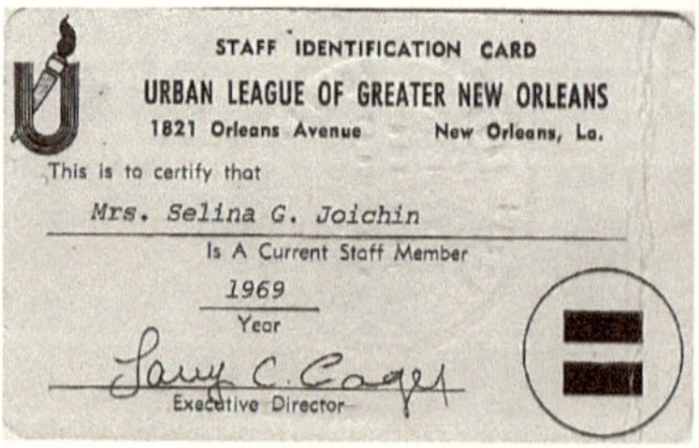
STAFF IDENTIFICATION CARD
URBAN LEAGUE OF GREATER NEW ORLEANS
1821 Orleans Avenue New Orleans, La.
This is to certify that
Mrs. Selina G. Joichin
Is A Current Staff Member
1969
Year
Executive Director

ADDRESS: 5019 New York Circle
HOME TELEPHONE: 288-5234
SOCIAL SECURITY NO. [redacted]
SIGNATURE

My Mother's Urban League Staff Identification Card

Anyone who knew my mother knew that she was not only highly respected for her activism, she was also genuinely loved for her sincerity, her warmth and her deep-seated compassion for those less fortunate. Mr. John Pecoul, New Orleans Urban League

Housing Director, was one of many who were well aware of that. Mr. Pecoul wrote on the inside cover of the sympathy card that he sent to my father:

> Dear Mr. Joichin:
>
> We were shocked and saddened to hear about Selina. Being with her was like being in the sunshine. We extend our deepest sympathies to you.

Ms. Gloria Bartley, one of the young women with whom my mother worked at the Urban League, had feelings of such endearment toward Mama, that on Mother's Day of 1969, Mama's last Mother's Day, Gloria sent her the biggest, most beautiful bouquet of flowers I had ever seen. Two weeks after my mother's funeral, Gloria called me at home saying that she wanted to take me to dinner. Over the meal, she shared her profound grief with me. She told me that the week after Mama died, she went to see Mama's doctor and said the following to him, "Doctor, this was supposed to be a routine, very minor surgery. Now Mrs. Joichin is gone. How could this have happened?" Gloria said that the doctor responded, "It's just one of those things that happens sometimes that we don't understand." I was deeply moved that Gloria had done that. A few years later, after she married and had a son, Gloria gave birth to a baby girl. She named her Selina.

Mama died only five years after the passage of the Civil Rights Act of 1964, i.e., after only five years of no longer having to use separate and highly unequal public facilities. She had, in other words, only five years of freedom. I'd have given both my arms to have been able to change that for her.

On July 3, 1994, the **twenty-fifth** anniversary of my mother's death, I was in New Orleans visiting family. I hadn't planned to be there on that specific date; it just happened that it was a convenient time for me to make the trip. July 3rd that year was a Sunday. I attended church at Bethany that morning. To my utter surprise, the printed program for the service had a full-page dedication to my mother, which included two pictures of her, the dates of her birth and death, and the following words:

> Remembering Mrs. Selina G. Joichin on the anniversary of her death. Selina Joichin was a devoted member of Bethany. She became a member of Bethany during its infancy. During her time at Bethany, Selina served as a member of the Sanctuary Choir. Selina had a beautiful voice and used it to praise God.
>
> While serving as Chairperson of the Pastor-Parish Relations Committee in 1966, she was among the persons who were instrumental in having our then pastor, Rev. Edward A. Kennedy, Jr., continue in service at Bethany.
>
> Mrs. Joichin was an Executive Secretary of the Urban League. She used her skills to serve Bethany as secretary...without remuneration until the time of her passing.
>
> The choir room was named the Selina Joichin Choir Room, in her memory. Many persons, members and friends gave donations to the church in her memory to help defray the cost of furnishing the choir room.
>
> There is a photograph of Mrs. Joichin on the wall outside the choir room. We who knew Selina Joichin thank God for having her pass this way on her Christian journey. We shall always remember her with love.

My Mother as a Young Woman

The week after my mother's death, with all of my grief and pain, I continued my volunteer work with the New Orleans Urban League's summer voter registration drive. I knew that completing my service in the drive would have made her proud, and more than anything else, that is what I wanted to do. Six weeks later, on August 15th, I had my sixteenth birthday, and the voter registration drive ended the following week.

A few days later, the summer ended and the school year began. Within days of the start of school, I received my Certificate of Appreciation for participating in the drive. I had always enjoyed receiving such certificates because of the feeling of accomplishment that they gave me. My certificate acknowledging my completion of my volunteer duties in the drive would have been particularly meaningful to me, both because my mother was a staff member at the League and because of the significance that voter registration work held for me. Indeed, under normal circumstances, I might have hung the certificate on a wall in my room. In my emotional state of deep, deep grief, however, upon receiving it, I felt nothing. I just placed it in the little box of childhood keepsakes that my mother had kept for me on my closet shelf.

URBAN LEAGUE OF GREATER NEW ORLEANS

This Certificate of meritorious service is awarded to

Lauren Joichin

in deep appreciation of his-her participation in the urban affairs project of the Urban League of Greater New Orleans during the summer of 1969, and for his-her uncompromising devotion to the cause of freedom, justice and self-determination for the black community of the city of New Orleans, on this the 13 *day of* September, *1969, at the city of New Orleans, Louisiana.*

Larry C. Cager
Interim Executive Director

(Mrs.) Oretha Haley
Urban Affairs Project Director

My New Orleans Urban League Voter Registration Project Certificate

I BECAME A TEENAGE MOM

AT SIXTEEN, I WAS A HIGH SCHOOL SENIOR AND THE TEENAGE MOTHER of a seven-year-old. Despite my youth and my depression, Mama's example of a powerfully loving mother left me strong enough to be aware that it was crucial for Lorna to have a happy childhood, and I wanted, to the extent that I was able, to give her that. I was painfully aware that I couldn't bring my mother back to her, but I wanted her, in every other way, to have everything I had as a child.

I took my responsibility to step into my mother's shoes and become Lorna's mother extremely seriously. Because I loved her so much, and because I knew how important it was, I wanted, and tried to every extent that I possibly could, to give her a happy childhood as I had. From the first of the four nights that my mother was in the hospital prior to her death until Lorna was old enough to do it herself, I took total care of her. Every night, I brushed her teeth, bathed her, put her pajamas on her, and tucked her into bed with a kiss. In the morning, before she went to school, I ironed her school clothes, then woke her, washed her face, brushed her teeth, combed her hair, dressed her, made sure she ate breakfast, and had the quarter for her lunch that my father left on his dresser for her every morning. In the first year after our mother died, during my senior year of high school, I dropped her off at school every morning before going to school myself, and picked her up in the afternoon. My father cooked every evening (which he did very well) and I dished up Lorna's dinner, ate my dinner with her, and made sure she ate hers. Whenever we weren't at school, Lorna and I were **always** together. Just as when I was little and I was my mother's little shadow, Lorna had now become mine.

For all of Lorna's birthdays, including her seventh birthday three weeks after Mama died, I gave her the same kind of big birthday party that my mother had given all of us, every year.

I bought her costume and took her trick-or-treating every Halloween. I made sure that she woke up to a big Easter basket every Easter morning.

Just as my mother had watched the kids' television specials of the time with me, I also watched them with Lorna—Rogers and Hammerstein's 1965 production of Cinderella and Fred Wolf and Harry Nilsson's absolutely wonderful 1971 animation, "The Point," are the ones I remember.

Just as my mother had also watched the kids' holiday TV shows with me, I also watched them with Lorna—the 1964 animated TV Christmas special, "Rudolph the Red-Nosed Reindeer," the 1965 "Charlie Brown Christmas Special," the 1966 "Grinch that Stole Christmas," and the 1969 "Frosty the Snowman" animated Christmas shows.

Every Christmas, I played Christmas Carols in the house and put up a Christmas tree for Lorna. My father gave me the money for her toys, and just as my mother had done for us, I went from store to store, getting every single item on her Santa list, then brought them all to Gramzie's where I very carefully hid them until Christmas Eve. Then, on Christmas Eve night, I set out Santa's cookies and milk on the dining room table with her, gave her a bath, told her that Santa would be coming later in the night, and then tucked her into bed. She always went to bed **very** excited. Then, after she was soundly asleep, I'd drive up to Gramzie's, pick up her toys, go home and lay them all out under the tree, looking forward to seeing her utter delight the next morning.[59]

I taught Lorna all the things about proper decorum that my mother, in her most gentle loving way, had taught me, among them, to speak in "correct" English, to not be "loud and common" in public, to be polite and say, "yes, please" and "no, thank you", to chew with her mouth closed, to cover her mouth when she yawned, to not sit on public toilets and to let her lips touch only the water when drinking from public water fountains.

But far more importantly, I attempted to give Lorna the same emotional template in her formative years that I had received in mine—the same simultaneous warmth and strength of character that my mother had so exquisitely modeled for me. I also wanted to give Lorna a spiritual base for her life, so I took her to church with me for as long as I attended.[60] I remember telling her once before my seventeenth birthday to always remember that God loved her much, much more than any human being did. I tried to teach Lorna all the lessons that my mother had taught me about respecting **all** people, regardless of their class, their race, their complexion, their religion, their disability, or any other characteristic that we human beings use to divide ourselves. I tried to teach her the compassion that I learned from nearly sixteen years of watching Mama and Gramzie in the world.

---

59 Christmas was **so** special for me when I was a child. It was an absolutely magical time. Needless to say, the first Christmas after my mother died was extremely difficult for me. Additionally, I was sixteen, so, the childhood wonder of the season had long since faded. Consequently, but for Lorna, Christmas at 5019 New York Circle would not have come during those years.

60 For reasons explained in my spiritual memoir, I stopped attending church two years after my mother died, when I was eighteen and a sophomore in college. One of my greatest regrets is that when I stopped attending church, I did not have Lorna continue with Sunday School. I wish that she had grown up in Bethany as I had.

I loved Lorna **tremendously**, and because tragically, she doesn't remember my mother and knew only me as her surrogate mother, she also loved me—very much. For that reason, Lorna and I bonded in a way that I believe resulted in our being closer than most sisters. I was her caregiver, her mother, really, and she was my little girl. Today, Lorna remembers well attending the ballet lessons in which my mother enrolled her,[61] and all of the material vestiges of Mama's love for her that she had until she graduated from elementary school - her backyard gym set, sand box, merry-go-round, see saw and picnic table, as well as her little girl's room with her white, French provincial furniture, canopy-top bed, kitchen set, mini table and chairs, blackboard, and Show N' Tell video/record player. But it hurts me deeply that Lorna remembers only those physical remnants of my mother's love for her, and has only bits and pieces, mere flashes, really, of minor memories of Mama as a person. She was just too young.

MY SENIOR YEAR OF HIGH SCHOOL IN RETROSPECT

MY SENIOR YEAR AT HOLY ANGELS WAS THE WORST YEAR OF MY LIFE. I was severely grieving my mother's death. During that year, a few of my African American classmates and I exchanged books written by black authors, *The Autobiography of Malcolm X*, Claude Brown's *Manchild in the Promised Land*, James Baldwin's *The Fire Next Time* and Ralph Ellison's *The Invisible Man*, among them. Even in the midst of my personal profound depression during which, overall, I felt emotionally numb, I was able to read them. They were actually a distraction that I desperately needed.

In reading the books, I was able to feel distress in being introduced for the first time (especially in Malcolm X's autobiography) to a world about which I knew next to nothing, the world of northern black urban poverty. The descriptions of the abject economic

61 Seeing all of those beautiful, little African American girls in their tutus, ballet shoes, braids and curls every time Mama and I took Lorna to dance class touched me, even as a teenager.

deprivation, drug dealing, prostitution and violent crime that typified it shocked me. I knew that the Jim Crow laws under which we had so recently lived in the South did not exist in the North, and that the North was where African Americans had historically gone for greater economic opportunities. For those reasons, as a very naive sixteen-year-old, I believed at that time that African Americans who lived in the North faced minimal racial discrimination. Learning that millions of African Americans who lived in the North lived in a state that was actually far worse than that in which my family and every other African American that I knew lived was extremely distressing.

In reading the books, I also became aware of tragic aspects of African American history of which I was formerly totally unaware. It was the beginning of my comprehension of how historic, systemic, societal racism had so detrimentally affected the **economic** status of African Americans. Most impactful to me, however, is that I began to understand for the first time, how both historic and institutional racism had impacted the mental and emotional health, the dignity, the self-confidence, the very self-esteem of African Americans. Ironically, while I felt many emotions in response to growing up under segregation and experiencing the difficulty of integration, righteous indignation, fear, and stalwartness primarily, I never felt anger. Segregation was a societal wrong, it was evil, but my response to it wasn't anger. Figuratively speaking, you don't get angry at the devil. You may fear him, but you don't necessarily get angry at him. What you do feel, is a dogged determination to defeat him. Similarly, my formative years left me not with anger, but with a dogged determination to defeat the evil of racism.

In reading about northern, urban poverty, however, for the first time, I felt angry about racism. I was angry about what I thought was the total injustice of it all. I saw my world as one in which courageous Black People were valiantly and courageously fighting injustice. That world, the world of northern, urban poverty, was one in which millions of Black Americans lived hopeless lives of poverty, and frequently either the victims or perpetrators of crime on other Black People. I began to talk to my classmates about what I was reading, speaking passionately about what I was learning and feeling. It was the utter unfairness that was so striking for me, the unfairness of having one's entire life affected so dramatically, and in such negative ways, simply on the basis of the racial group into which, as an accident of birth, one happened to have been born. I remember my reaction well, "Why do our people have to suffer so much, even in a place like Massachusetts where Malcolm was from? As much as we've suffered down here, why is it no better, and in some respects, much worse up there? I thought the North was better." I felt outrage that apparently there was no place, nowhere in the country where we were regarded and treated as equal. As a child growing up in the Deep South, I thought that it was just in the South that we were dealing with White People who couldn't see us. I was both furious and frustrated to learn that millions of White Americans in the North couldn't see us either, and was horrified by the consequences to our lives of their blindness. Although that was some fifty-four years ago, I remember my emotions clearly.

I graduated from The Academy of the Holy Angels High School in May of 1970, ten months after my Mama died. The ceremony was held in the French Quarter's iconic St. Louis Basilica in Jackson Square. At the end of the ceremony, I marched with my classmates down the cathedral's center aisle to the front door, my eyes overflowing with tears, searching the ceiling from left to right for a glimpse of my mother's smiling face.

I said goodbye to AHA and to my high school years. My still grieving, deeply-wounded heart notwithstanding, it was time for my next chapter.

CHAPTER FIVE

COLLEGE AND MY SAVING GRACE THE LSUNO NAACP COLLEGE CHAPTER

STAYING HOME FOR COLLEGE - MY SECOND HEARTBREAK

Going away for college was, as an adolescent, the thing to which I most looked forward. It felt to me like an incredibly exciting adventure. I really wanted to go away to college. I knew that I'd miss my mother and Gramzie terribly, but I couldn't wait! I thought of college as a major life chapter and a critically important rite of passage. Throughout high school, I had imagined what it would be like. I saw myself in a small liberal arts college in a small college town somewhere in the north, where I very naively assumed that because it was the north, the students would be liberal and non-racist. I thought about experiencing beautiful, colorful Autumns and snowy white winters for the first time in my life. I thought about seeing the kind of scenery I had seen only in calendar pictures as a kid: mountains, forests, streams, and waterfalls. I thought about the new friends I'd make of many different races and cultural backgrounds who had grown up in various parts of the country.[62]

But Lorna was entering third grade and had just turned eight when it was time for me to leave for college. I loved Lorna **deeply**, and there was simply no way I could leave her with my father at such a tender age. Losing my mother was the deepest **pain** of my life, and while not being able to go away to college was the deepest **disappointment** of my life, I could **not** leave Lorna. I never once, after my mother's death, even entertained the idea of leaving her when she was so young. Our two older brothers had to leave for military service shortly after our mother died, so either my father would have taken care of her alone (which he couldn't have done because he had to work), or she would have gone to live with Gramzie, or one of my mother's two younger sisters, my Aunts Verlie and Johnnie. I simply couldn't bear the thought of any of those scenarios. I was deeply aware of how extraordinarily important Lorna's childhood was in her development into a confident, emotionally healthy, mature young woman. I also knew that fully armed with my mother's deep love and magnificent parental example, even at the young age of not quite sixteen, I was able to be a surrogate mom to Lorna in a way that no one else in my family could. By the time I started college, I had been Lorna's surrogate mother for over a year, and by then, she had bonded with me and I with her, so I absolutely could not and did not want her to be without me at such a tender age.

I had done well on the NMSQT (National Merit Scholastic Qualifying Test), which I took in my junior year of high school. As a result, at the beginning of the Fall semester of my senior year, a number of colleges sent me an introductory letter to their univer-

62 As I was growing up in New Orleans, my family didn't travel, and with very few exceptions, I knew only people who had been born and grown up in New Orleans.

sity with an admission application and catalog. Knowing, as I did at that time, that I was going to have to stay home for college to take care of Lorna made receiving all of those materials especially difficult for me.

Doris L., perhaps my best friend in high school, was going away to Barat College in Illinois. A number of my male friends, who were students at St. Augustine, the number one-ranked African American boys' Catholic school in the nation, had done particularly well both in high school and on the standardized tests that high school students took at that time, the NMSQT, PSAT, and SAT, and as a result, had gotten **the** college gold ring. Kevin M. went to Harvard. Michael S. went to Yale. Verlie O. went to Princeton. Eddie J. went to Wesleyan in Middletown, Connecticut.[63] Kern R. went to Claremont College in Claremont, California. Augustus J. went to Clark College in Atlanta. Doris L.—my best friend in high school—went to Barat College in Lake Forest, Illinois. They all left in the fall of 1970. I desperately wanted the opportunity that my friends had, and **I felt left behind!** Losing my mother was my life's first great heartbreak. Not being able to go away to college was my second.

In September 1970, I began undergraduate school at Louisiana State University in New Orleans, LSUNO, and continued to live with my father and Lorna at home in my childhood bedroom. I was still severely grieving Mama's death and, therefore, in my freshman year, did nothing but attend class and go home.

LSUNO - MY BEGINNING AND FINDING THE CHAPTER

LSUNO WAS OVERWHELMINGLY WHITE, BUT TO MY UTTER SURPRISE and delight, and totally unlike my high school experience, I don't remember ever experiencing any racism at the university. It may have resulted from LSUNO's being a large, urban university with

63 Wesleyan was among the universities that sent me an application and catalog. Of all the schools that sent me materials, I liked Wesleyan by far, much more than any of the others. When I learned that Eddie J. was going to Wesleyan, I coveted the experience that I knew he was going to have there.

many students who had attended New Orleans public schools that were probably a lot more racially diverse than AHA's student body. It may have been the result of the fact that integration, required by the Civil Rights Act of 1964, had been the law of the land for six years by then, and over the course of those six years, New Orleans had fully integrated all public facilities. Thus, perhaps my college classmates were by then used to being in the presence of African Americans. Whatever the reason(s), I was relieved and delighted to not be in my classes and around campus-in-general as a highly visible person who was stereotyped because of the color of my skin. At LSUNO, I was able to be just another student.

One of the best things that happened to me during undergraduate school occurred at the beginning of my sophomore year. I found the LSUNO NAACP College Chapter.[64] Finding the College Chapter at the beginning of my second year was the thing that helped me finally begin to emerge from my then two-year depression over the loss of my mother. My first-hand experiences as a child who lived under segregation for nearly the first eleven years of my life left me with a sincere and heartfelt commitment to social justice, and the major social injustice in my world at that time was racism. Joining and becoming an active member of LSUNO's NAACP College Chapter was therefore a "natural" for me. After my freshman year of having a very heavy heart and doing nothing but going to class and returning home, the College Chapter became my home away from home. It was my home at school. Between classes, Chapter members hung out in the Chapter office located in the University Center, the Student Union. Rather than just going to the library and sitting alone between classes, which is what I had done throughout my entire freshman year, I had a place to go between all my classes, and throughout the day. Depending on our class schedules, at least two to six of us would always be in the office together. It was a place where I could not

64 The NAACP at that time, had three components: the Branches, i.e., the adult division, the College Chapters, which of course were university based, and the Youth Councils, the high school division.

only be with friends, but with friends with whom I had a lot in common, and thus felt very comfortable. It felt like a true, small sister/brotherhood. The College Chapter was a tremendous help to me in overcoming my depression over losing my mother. It was, indeed, my life line; my path back to my life, to myself. In finding the College Chapter, I was both making friends and working with them on issues that were especially meaningful to me.

We were a small group with no more than ten or twelve of us active at any one time. Over the three years of my activism with the Chapter, however, there were roughly about twenty of us—Claude, Bobby, John, Margie, Brenda, Lisa, Yada, Lansen, Gilda, Kent, Madeleine, Loretta, Simonette, David, Henry, Larry, Anthony, Hannah, Dwight and me—but we were an **active** little College Chapter. It was the early '70. We all had our huge Afros, and I wore my "Free Angela" button every day.[65] We met every Friday night at a different member's home, planned our activities for the following week, and then played Jeopardy, and occasion, Password, for hours. I was very active in the Chapter, and was elected Secretary months after I became a member. When I told my father that I was the Chapter's new secretary, he smiled and said, "You're following in your mother's footsteps." I was, of course, deeply touched.

Our NAACP College Chapter was extremely active. We had a series of meetings with the university president to discuss LSUNO's very small number of faculty of color. We sponsored "Thanksgiving in the Ghetto," a program in which we provided Thanksgiving dinners to families living in poverty. We sponsored "Easter Kiddie Day," a program in which children who lived in the city's public housing projects came to campus to participate in an Easter egg hunt and other children's games and activities.[66] We raised funds

65 The button was a show of support for Dr. Angela Davis, the African American activist and professor who, in 1970, was wrongly arrested, jailed, and charged with murder. I felt a particular bond with Dr. Davis both because she was a Professor of Philosophy, which I had identified as my personal career goal, and because she was an activist. I thought that after completing my education, I too, would be an activist Professor of Philosophy. I was elated when Dr. Davis was ultimately acquitted of all charges.

66 New Orleans, at the time, had a lot of projects—the Desire Project, the Florida Avenue

for our various programs through "can shakes," during which we stood in front of various grocery stores throughout the city with a soda can in our hands labeled, "NAACP," shaking them and saying over and over again to store patrons as they entered and exited, "Give to the NAACP. Give to the NAACP." We always did pretty well with our can shakes. We were just teenage college students, but we **worked** our little NAACP College Chapter.[67]

Of all of the activities in which we engaged, most memorable for me was our picketing of perhaps a half dozen or so Canal Street stores during the summer of 1972. The targeted stores, as either policy or a matter of practice, hired very few, if any, African Americans. Those stores that did subjected the African American employees to biased disciplinary practices and often fired them unjustly. I don't remember whether the New Orleans NAACP Branch (the local adult division of the NAACP) asked us to do the picketing, but as a College Chapter, after receiving permission from the NAACP National Office in New York (and perhaps after getting a permit from the city to picket—I'm not sure whether a city permit was required at the time), we took it on. For close to eight weeks, every afternoon, in that burning hot New Orleans summer sun and sweltering humidity, we'd meet at an appointed time in front of a particular store, form a circle, hold hands and open with a prayer. We'd then split up to go to our respective assigned stores, in front of which we'd walk in silence, in a circle, for a couple of hours carrying our heavy signs. On some, the inscription on one side read, "Discriminatory Hiring and Firing Practic-

---

Project (which had historically been "all white" and was walking distance from both the Desire Project and William Frantz Elementary School, attended by Ruby Bridges), the St. Bernard Project, the Lafitte Project, the Iberville Project (which was also historically "all white"), the Fisher Homes Project, the Calliope Project, the St. Thomas Project, the Magnolia Project and the Melpomene Project.

67 The BSU, Black Student Union, accused us of being "Uncle Toms" because we were the NAACP, The National Association for the Advancement of Colored People, which was in their minds, an organization of old people who were just not in touch with the contemporary movement for black equality. We paid absolutely no attention to that criticism because it was **we** who were actually doing civil rights work on campus. We had, and we **knew** that we had the support of both the adult New Orleans NAACP Branch and the NAACP National Office in New York, so we were a pretty fearless little band of civil rights activists. Figuratively speaking, we flicked the BSU's criticism off of our shoulders like a fly, and kept on moving!

es," and on the other, "The NAACP Asks You to Please Boycott This Merchant." Afterwards, we'd all meet where we started, put our signs down, and once again in a circle holding hands, sing a few freedom songs, end with a closing prayer, then go home. Some people crossed the picket lines, but many more did not.[68]

I loved those old freedom songs that we sang on the picket line. They moved me. They did so both in the same way, yet also differently from the way the Methodist hymns with which I'd grown up moved me. Both touched my internal chord that was in love with goodness, justice, charity and compassion. My favorites included:

Aint Gonna Let Nobody Turn Me 'Roun

Aint gonna let nobody turn me 'roun, turn me 'roun, turn me roun,
Aint gonna let nobody turn me 'roun,
We're gonna keep on a walkin', keep on a talkin'
Marchin' up to freedom land.

http://www.gospelsonglyrics.org/songs/aint_gonna_let_nobody_turn_me_around.html

We Shall Not Be Moved

We shall not, we shall not be moved.
We shall not, we shall not be moved,
Just like a tree that's planted by the water,
We shall not be moved.

http://www.youtube.com/watch?v=4WXSI6PcjkE

Oh Freedom

Ooooh freedom, Ooooh freedom
Oh freedom over me, over me
And before I be a slave, I'll be buried in my grave
And go home to my Lord and be free.

68 I was not a kid who kept secrets from her parents, but my participation in the demonstrations was a secret for me. I did not tell my father about my participation in them for fear that (out of concern for my safety), he would've forbidden me from participating. Fortunately, my father never did find out about his daughter, college student Lauren, the young civil rights picketer.

http://www.youtube.com/watch?v=yHmUPqI6w9g
At times, we'd sing the anthem of the Civil Rights Movement itself.

We Shall Overcome
We shall overcome, we shall overcome,
We shall overcome someday.
Ooooh deep in my heart, I do believe
We shall overcome someday.

http://www.youtube.com/watch?v=bKDVNSpsBZE
http://www.youtube.com/watch?v=130J-FdZDtY

We marched in front of those stores, in those circles, in the hot New Orleans sun for weeks until their management agreed to meet and talk. Members of the city's adult NAACP Branch attended those meetings and were successful in reaching a fair compromise on every issue with every store. Before long, the number of black cashiers and sales people in the stores was quite noticeable.

Our Summer 1972 Pickets of Downtown New Orleans Stores

That year, 1972, our faculty advisor, Dr. Joseph Logsdon (who was a European American professor in the History Department, originally from Boston, probably in his mid-forties at that time, married with two pre-teenage daughters, and just a down-to-earth, salt-of-the-earth, compassionate, sincere, decent, and good human being) received from the NAACP National Office, the second-place award for **Advisor** of the Year, and our LSUNO College Chapter received the national award for being **Chapter** of the Year, i.e., the most active Chapter in the country. Dr. Logsdon deserved it, and so did we![69]

Later that Fall, I was honored to have been selected to receive the university's third annual Martin Luther King, Jr. Memorial Award in recognition of my work with the Chapter. The letter informing me of the award was dated November 10th, my mother's birthday. As I read the date and then the body of the letter, I simultaneously cried and hoped that she was proud of me.

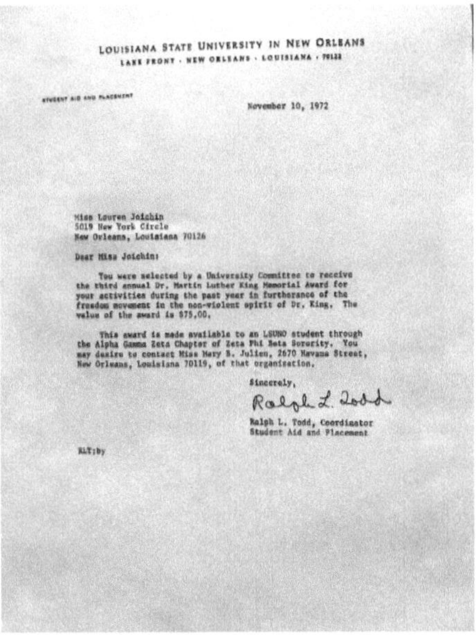

LOUISIANA STATE UNIVERSITY IN NEW ORLEANS
LAKE FRONT · NEW ORLEANS · LOUISIANA · 70122

STUDENT AID AND PLACEMENT

November 10, 1972

Miss Lauren Joichin
5019 New York Circle
New Orleans, Louisiana 70126

Dear Miss Joichin:

You were selected by a University Committee to receive the third annual Dr. Martin Luther King Memorial Award for your activities during the past year in furtherance of the freedom movement in the non-violent spirit of Dr. King. The value of the award is $75.00.

This award is made available to an LSUNO student through the Alpha Gamma Zeta Chapter of Zeta Phi Beta Sorority. You may desire to contact Miss Mary B. Julien, 2670 Havana Street, New Orleans, Louisiana 70119, of that organization.

Sincerely,

Ralph L. Todd

Ralph L. Todd, Coordinator
Student Aid and Placement

RLT:by

Letter Informing Me of My Selection as the Recipient of the Dr. Martin Luther King Memorial Award

69 I believe that our Chapter received the award the following year as well.

Months later, with yet another picket, we worked on getting a monument to the Battle of Liberty Place, i.e., to white supremacy, taken down from the city's downtown tourist area.[70] One of the original inscriptions on the monument read:

"McEnery and Penn, having been elected governor and lieutenant-governor by the white people, were duly installed by this overthrow of carpetbag government, ousting the usurpers, Governor Kellogg (white) and Lieutenant-Governor Antoine (colored). United States troops took over the state government and reinstated the usurpers but the national election of November 1876 recognized white supremacy in the South and gave us our state."[71]

We picketed the monument during the Spring semester of 1973. The following year, in 1974, because of our efforts, the New Orleans City Council added the following inscription to the monument:

Although the "Battle of Liberty Place" and this monument are important parts of the New Orleans history, the sentiments in favor of white supremacy expressed thereon are contrary to the philosophy and beliefs of present-day New Orleans.

Our 1973 Picket of the Battle of Liberty Place
Memorial to White Supremacy

70 https://en.wikipedia.org/wiki/Battle_of_Liberty_Place_Monument

71 In 1933, some of the monument's initial inscriptions were removed, and replaced with one that stated in part: "In honor of those Americans on both sides who died in the Battle of Liberty Place."

Sadly, the monument was not removed for another thirty-four years, in 2007, when monuments to the confederacy were being taken down throughout the country, and even then, amid great controversy and threats of violence.

We were activists not only in the city of New Orleans, but also on campus. We met with the Chancellor (the title, at that time, of the University President), Dr. Hitt, about hiring more African American faculty and staff. We invited Dr. Hitt to our Negro History Week (later changed, nationally, to Black History Month) activities. One such activity was a forum that the Chapter organized for the discussion of a proposed merger of LSUNO and SUNO, Southern University in New Orleans - the New Orleans branch of Southern University in Baton Rouge, one of the nation's top Historically Black Colleges and Universities. Dr. Hitt turned down our invitation, but for a very valid reason that I and the other Chapter members totally understood.

LOUISIANA STATE UNIVERSITY IN NEW ORLEANS

LAKE FRONT • NEW ORLEANS • LOUISIANA • 70122

OFFICE OF THE CHANCELLOR

February 5, 1973

Miss Lauren Lyn Joichin
Chairlady
LSUNO - NAACP
5019 New York Drive
New Orleans, Louisiana 70126

Dear Miss Joichin:

This afternoon I received your letter of February 1, informing me of your plans for Negro History Week, and inviting me to participate in a forum on higher education in Louisiana focusing upon the proposed merger of SUNO and LSUNO. The question of such a merger is certainly a timely one for discussion during Negro History Week, and I hope that you are successful in attracting the possible participants you have listed. As Chancellor of LSUNO, however, I feel that I must decline.

Just a few days ago I was approached by The Driftwood for a statement on this subject, and I replied that at the present moment I thought it inappropriate for me to involve myself in this debate. Whatever I might say would be widely interpreted as an official LSU position on the matter, and such a position can be established only by the Board of Supervisors. My suggestion is that you invite some member of our faculty who is free to speak his opinions without the restrictions that would encumber an administrative officer. Such names as Dr. Raphael Cassimere, Jr., Dr. Joseph Logsdon, and Dr. Paul L. Sanford come readily to mind.

Please be assured of my wish to cooperate with you and with the LSUNO - NAACP in any way that I can, and of my sincere regret in having to make this particular decision.

Very truly yours,

Homer L. Hitt

HOMER L. HITT
Chancellor

Letter from University Chancellor

The following year, 1974, Lorna graduated from Coghill Elementary and I graduated from UNO (The University of New Orleans) with a bachelor's degree in Philosophy.[72] In the beginning of the Fall of that year, Lorna moved to Washington, D.C. to live with Lemar Jr. and his family so that I could start a Master's Degree Program in Philosophy at The University of Connecticut (UCONN). I had major misgivings about separating from Lorna.

72 The name of the university was changed from Louisiana State University in New Orleans to The University of New Orleans months before I graduated.

She was, after all, turning only 12, and was about to start Junior High School. We had a long talk about it, however, during which she assured me that while she would miss me very much, after having spent the summer with Lemar Jr. and his family, she was looking forward to being with them again, and was excited about living and going to school in Washington. I was excited about living in a small New England college town and beginning my new life, my life as a graduate student at The University of Connecticut.[73]

73 Lorna and I never lived together again after I went to graduate school. Just before beginning ninth grade, she returned to New Orleans after two years in Washington, and lived at home with our father. When she did, I flew home and took her on a tour of several high schools in order for her to choose the one she wanted to attend. During her high school years, I brought her up to the East Coast a couple of times to visit with me. Just as my mother had done for me the summer before my junior year of high school, I told Lorna the summer before her junior year, to take a typing course and a driver's ed course because I knew how important it was for her to gain those skills before going to college. Before her senior year of high school, I took her on a ten-college tour. The following year, I helped her move onto the campus she had chosen, and set up and decorate her dormitory room. I did everything that I knew to do for Lorna at that time, and I did it all out of love. Still, I **very** much wish that I could have been much more present in her life during her adolescent years.

CHAPTER SIX

GRADUATE SCHOOL AND MY EARLY PROFESSIONAL CAREER: THE COMMON THEME

I began my Master's Degree program in Philosophy at The University of Connecticut in September 1974. My very first response to being in Connecticut was that with all of its natural, wooded areas and streams, it was an absolutely beautiful place! I fell in love with the rural Connecticut landscape, and took many long rides in the country whenever I wasn't studying. Then came the Fall, and WOW! Having never seen Fall colors (when the seasons change in New Orleans, the leaves on the trees simply turn brown), I was astonished! I was delighted!

As a result of my childhood experiences with racism, followed by my civil rights activism at UNO, I left home for graduate school determined to do whatever I was able to do to help young African Americans reach their greatest human potential. That determination led me to found and charter the UCONN Black Graduate Student Organization (BGSO), the purpose of which was to provide a forum within which black graduate students could academically tutor, counsel and support black undergraduate students. Mine was only a one-year Master's program, after which I left UCONN, so I don't know whether the BGSO continued after my graduation from the university, but I do hope that it did and that if so, the life of at least one African American student, undergraduate or graduate, was positively influenced through it; that at least one student was encouraged; that through the organization, at least one student was profoundly inspired. I hope that the Black Graduate Student Organization made **some** difference. I shall never know.

I enjoyed my year of grad school at UCONN, and graduated from the university with my Master's Degree in Philosophy in May, 1975. I was 21.

Lorna (12) and me (21) at my Master's Degree Graduation
May 1975

I very much wanted to go straight from my Master's Degree program in Philosophy to a Ph.D. program in Eastern Philosophy, but I decided to work for two years in order to earn some money in preparation for my doctoral studies. Two months after graduating from UCONN, I was extremely fortunate to be hired as Assistant Dean of Admissions at Wesleyan University in Middletown, Connecticut. I started at Wesleyan on August 1, 1975, two weeks before my twenty-second birthday. It wasn't until after I had been at Wesleyan for a few weeks that I began to understand the affluence of the world I had entered – old New England wealth.

Wesleyan, Williams College in Williamstown, Massachuettes, and Amherst College, in Amherst, Massachusetts, are known as "The Little Three" (Little Ivies - Wikipedia), i.e. the little three ivy leagues, in an allusion to "The Big Three" Ivys, Harvard, Yale and Princeton. Many of Wesleyan's students came from families that had that kind of wealth. It was unlike anything that I had ever experienced in my life to that point. The campus itself, with its ivy covered buildings, mahogany furniture, and plush carpeting in the administrative buildings, was certainly nothing I had ever seen at either UNO or UCONN. The lavish catering of university events was utterly new to me. The experiences of the prospective students whom I interviewed as part of my responsibility as an Admissions Officer, were positively amazing to me - summers abroad, family ski vacations in Aspen, expensive sports camps, and weekend trips to Manhattan to see Broadway plays, to name just a few.

In the midst of that affluence, I was fully aware of the irony that as a twenty-two-year-old Assistant Dean of Admissions at one of the country's most prestigious universities, just eleven years earlier, I could by law neither drink from the same water fountains nor use the same restrooms as European American children. How things had changed in just over a decade!

LAUREN LYN JOICHIN
Assistant Dean of Admissions
Wesleyan University
Middletown, CT 06457
Tel. (203) 347-9411

During my first year at Wesleyan, along with two colleagues (Donna Ireland, an Admissions Officer at Trinity College in Hartford, Connecticut, and Ron Ancrum, an Admissions Officer at Connecticut College in New London, Connecticut), I was invited to a meeting at Harvard of ABAFAOILSSS (pronounced "Abafoils"), the Association of Black Admissions and Financial Aid Officers of the Ivy League and Seven Sister Schools. Ron, Donna and I were highly impressed by the meeting and, as a result, formally requested admission to the organization. Our three universities, while among the nation's most highly prestigious and competitive liberal arts institutions of higher education, were not part of the Ivy League and its Seven Sister Schools. We were a tier below. As a result, our request to join was rejected, leaving the three of us wondering why we were even invited to the meeting in the first place. Donna, Ron and I were determined, however, to provide to the student applicants of color to our, and similarly ranked universities, the same benefits that the ABAFAOILSS universities provided their student applicants of color. Within months, on June 4, 1976, Ron, Donna and I founded NECBAC, the New England Consortium of Black Admissions Counselors.

I was one of six admissions officers at Wesleyan. We each had two student populations for which we were responsible in the admissions process. Not surprisingly, one of mine was applicants of color. Over the course of my two years at Wesleyan, I recruited dozens of primarily African American and Latin American high school seniors in Westchester County, New York, Brooklyn, Philadelphia, Atlanta, Miami, Chicago, New Orleans, San Juan, Puerto Rico, and a host of other cities.

The student whom I recruited from the farthest location was Kofi. Kofi was a kid from Accra, Ghana, whose path I quite accidentally crossed while traveling in Ghana during a Summer 1976 sightseeing tour of the country. We met by chance on his neighbor's patio during a ping pong game on a rainy July afternoon.

Actually, I no longer believe that anything happens by chance. We are all, I believe, in each other's lives for a reason. I was obviously destined to be there on that patio, in that ping pong game, on that rainy July afternoon, at the exact time Kofi arrived.

Some of the Latin and African American students I recruited to Wesleyan were from privileged, upper-class backgrounds, often the children of attorneys and physicians. Some were from middle class families. Most, however, were from pretty tough circumstances, the projects of Brooklyn, the Bronx, Chicago, Atlanta and Miami. I feel privileged to have been fortunate enough to have played just a small part in the process of affording those kids the opportunity to attend an institution of Wesleyan's caliber that surely changed the trajectory of their lives.

NECBAC is still in existence, with the same acronym, but under a new name, "The New England Consortium Bridging Access to College". For more than forty years now, the organization has helped thousands of kids of color to attend college. I am humbly grateful for having played a small role in its inception.[74]

When I began working at Wesleyan, I planned to work for two years and then return to graduate school. Eastern Philosophy and Religion (Hinduism, and Buddhism, primarily) were my passions, and I desperately wanted to pursue an academic teaching career specializing in them. Thus, in the Fall of 1977, I left Wesleyan and entered a Ph.D. program in Comparative Philosophy and Religion at the University of Pennsylvania, or Penn, as it is often called. I was eager to begin serious preparation for my career in academia. I was twenty-four.

One of my most significant growth experiences in understanding, for the first time, a form of oppression that was not racism happened during my time at Penn. The oppression was sexism. Within my first month on campus, one of the professors in the Women's Study Department spoke to me about being the

74 Interestingly, for a time after it was the New England Consortium of Black Admissions Counselors, and before adopting its present name, the organization's NECBAC acronym stood for The New England Consortium of Counselors of Color Bridging Access to College.

student representative on the department's Board of Directors. I agreed to serve. Several weeks later, the Board asked me to attend the first International Women's Year convention that was taking place that year (1977) in Houston, Texas. Attending that event, at which thousands of women from across the world were present, opened my eyes to the issues of sexism, patriarchy and misogyny. At that time in my life, I was aware of sexism as only an oppression that deprived women of professional opportunities. Learning about the history of sexism around the world was transformative for me, but unfortunately, in a sad way. I remember experiencing a profound sadness when I learned about the history of bride burning in India, clitorectomy in Africa, foot binding in China, the denial of education to girls in parts of the Middle East, and rape as a weapon of war around the world. I also learned about American statistics that illustrated how far American women and particularly American women of color lagged behind White men in every way imaginable. Interestingly, in response to that information, it wasn't sadness that I felt, but outrage. After the conference, I began reading the works of feminist scholars. I learned that a feminist, whether female or male, was a person who believed in equal rights for women and men. Period. Full stop. It was a very straightforward definition, and as simple as that. Before my twenty-fifth birthday, I became a feminist, a lifelong feminist, and decided that in addition to speaking out about and working against racism, I was also going to use my voice to speak out and work against sexism.[75] Later in my young adult life, after coming out as gay, I learned about heterosexism and homophobia, and naturally, decided to speak out against those as well. Still later as a young adult, I learned about other forms of oppression, antisemitism, ableism, and ageism, among others. Needless to say, upon learning

75 Even more than my subsequent volunteer work with women's organizations (the Tompkins County, NY Task Force on Battered Women and the Washington, D.C. Rape Crisis Center), and my work as Staff Attorney for the Women's Equity Action League, I am most thankful for my work as an Organizational Development trainer during which over thirty years, I trained hundreds of women in effectively addressing sexual harassment in the workplace. I am thankful for the opportunity to have played a part in empowering many women to confront, with strength and confidence, men who were sexually harassing them on their job.

about them, I made an internal, personal commitment to be an ally to people most directly affected by **those** oppressions and to educate and speak out against **them** as well.

For reasons explained in my spiritual memoir, I spent only a year in my Ph.D. program, after which I decided to pursue a very different profession. I decided that since I wasn't going to earn my Ph.D., I would go to law school. My dream was to be a university Professor of Philosophy, Eastern Philosophy specifically, and my thought was that since I wasn't going to follow **that** path (the path that was the response to the first of my two compelling heartstrings - my deep spiritual orientation), I would follow the **second** of my two heartstrings – social justice. I thought that as a lawyer, I would have the skills to make what I hoped would be a significant contribution toward that goal. I decided, once again, however, to work for a couple of years before returning to school, so following my year of doctoral studies, I worked as an Equal Opportunity Specialist in the Office for Civil Rights' (OCR) Higher Education Division of what was then the U.S. Department of Health, Education, and Welfare, HEW. I began in its Region III, Philadelphia office, then transferred to the Region II, New York City office.[76]

LAUREN L. JOICHIN
EQUAL OPPORTUNITY SPECIALIST

U. S. Dept. of Health, Education & Welfare
OFFICE FOR CIVIL RIGHTS, REG. II

26 FEDERAL PLAZA
NEW YORK, N.Y. 10007
(212) 264-3829

My job at OCR was, as a member of a team, to investigate complaints of discrimination and harassment filed by employees of colleges and universities, and subsequently write a Report of

76 Years later, HEW was split into two separate Federal departments, the Department of Education, and the Department of Health and Human Services.

Findings in which the university was found either guilty or not guilty of having engaged in alleged discriminatory employment practices. The Report of Findings was then submitted to the agency's Regional Attorney's Office where, if the university had been found to have engaged in discrimination, a decision was made concerning the method to be used to bring the institution into compliance with Title VI of the Civil Rights Act of 1964. In such cases, complainants were awarded some combination of back pay, damages and reinstatement of their job. For me, the work was both intellectually exciting, and an emotional high. During my time at the Office for Civil Rights, I saw OCR help people who were innocent targets of discrimination, and/or harassment receive fairness. I saw them receive justice. I saw up close, the tremendous difference that the work of the attorneys in the Regional Attorney's Office made in the lives of people who had been hurt by discrimination and harassment.

Many years later, looking back on my time at UCONN, Wesleyan, Penn and OCR, I realized that a common and very familiar thread ran through them - social justice. Two years later, I entered Cornell Law School in Ithaca, New York to pursue a career in social justice. The year was 1981. I was twenty-eight.[77]

---

77 In my life during the years 1970 to 1981, my college, graduate school and early professional years, I did not experience any institutional racism. I did experience racism during those years, however, through the countless daily racial indignities that occur in society-at-large. One such indignity during that time stands out in my memory. It occurred while I was a Federal employee in the Office for Civil Rights and involved being followed around a small, open-front New York City produce store. As I walked from one aisle to another, the store owner walked to and stood at the front of whichever aisle I was on, looking at me. When I noticed the owner's behavior, I was so outraged that I slammed down on the table in front of me the package of raspberries that was in my hand, and as I stormed out of the store, yelled at him, "I'm not a thief!" I was particularly infuriated because two European American customers who had come in after me, were shopping without being monitored in any way. As it turns out, I needed that "break" from institutional racism at school and work in preparation for my very challenging three-year experience with racism that I was about to have at Cornell Law School.

CHAPTER SEVEN

LAW SCHOOL AND MY BRIEF PRACTICE OF LAW

CORNELL AND RACISM: A REPEAT PERFORMANCE

Cornell Law School, located in Ithaca, in the Finger Lakes Region of upstate New York, was overwhelmingly white, with only eight-to-ten African American students in my class, a handful in the two classes above me, and an even smaller number of Latin, Asian and Indigenous students. It is one of the country's five Ivy League law schools, and its student body reflected that status in that many of its students were from very wealthy families. The campus was stunningly beautiful. It was quite large, and on a hill that overlooked Lake Cayuga. Like Wesleyan, Cornell had many Ivy-covered buildings. It also had a lovely creek on one end, and a deep, breathtaking gorge on the other. While the physical campus was quite beautiful, however, a number of my experiences there were painfully ugly.

Entering Cornell law school in September of 1981 took me right back to my entrance to Holy Angels High School fifteen years earlier. Just as was the case at Holy Angels, the majority of European American students at the law school, while not visibly hostile, were visibly uncomfortable with people who did not look like them. And, not unlike the majority of my white high school classmates, many exhibited the resulting chilly, aloof behavior toward us. It felt very much like a repeat performance of the racism that I experienced fifteen years earlier upon entering Holy Angels high school.

First year law students shared their locker with one other student. The classmate with whom I was assigned to share **my** locker was European American. For the **entire** year that we shared our locker, my locker mate did not speak to me. The experience was always the same. If I happened to get to the locker first either at the beginning or end of the day or between classes, she stood behind me, saying nothing, and waited until I left. If she reached the locker first, she hurriedly got her things and then quickly scurried off. If I said "hi," she would respond, but with only a serious-faced, low, muted, "hi." That was the full extent of my locker mate's interaction with me the entire year. I was deeply saddened that my feelings of frustration and level of fatigue with the racist behavior that I was receiving felt so hauntingly familiar even after more than a decade had passed since I'd last felt them in that context. I just felt emotionally exhausted by the situation. My feeling was, "Enough! I've had enough! I'm a human being just like you! Why can't you **see** that?!"

The most serious consequence that racism has ever had to my life was that of potentially getting kicked out of law school on a trumped-up honor code violation filed against me by one of my professors. My mistake was that of very honestly sharing during a meeting of the Women's Law Caucus (WLC) during my first semester how I was experiencing the law school, or more precisely, how my European American classmates were responding to me as "other." Two months later, I found myself in a class taught by the WLC's Faculty Advisor who was present at the meeting. She both gave me an "F" in the class and alleged that I had intentionally plagiarized the paper that I wrote for it. Several weeks later, during my hearing before the law school's Honor Board, with the help of my student attorneys, my friends Gretchen and Ellen, not only was I able to prove that the **allegation** was false, I was **also** able to prove that at the time that my professor **filed** the charge against me, she had to have **known** that it was false. I was exonerated. The administration directed her to change my grade. She gave me a "C." Had I been found guilty of the charge, I would have been expelled from law school, which would have had an enormous impact on my life. I am not aware that the professor faced any consequence for her actions.

THE LOSS OF MY FATHER - FEELING ORPHANED

LATE IN MY FIRST SEMESTER, IN DECEMBER 1981, I CALLED MY FATHER early on a Sunday morning, as was my practice every Sunday morning, to touch base with and check up on him. He had retired by then and was living alone.[78] There was no answer. I found it strange that he didn't answer the phone because Daddy was always at home on Sunday mornings, cooking his breakfast and dinner before heading out for the golf course in the afternoon. It was his Sunday ritual which he carried out every Sunday. Having received no answer, I called Lambert, who lived ten minutes away in New Orleans East, to ask if he'd heard from him. His response to my question, "Have you talked to Daddy recently?," which he uttered with a deep sadness in his voice, was "Uh, well, Daddy's in the hospital but he didn't want me to tell you, Lemar Jr. and

78 After thirty-three years of service in the U.S. Post Office, and two years of service during World War II, my father retired with thirty-five years of Federal service.

Lorna. He didn't want to worry you." Four months later, in April of 1982, my father died, one month before the end of my first year of law school. Thirty years of smoking had taken their final toll on his lungs. He was turning fifty-eight that year, and I was twenty-eight. My father **knew** me, so he knew that I was innocent of the honor code violation allegation. The hearing hadn't yet occurred at the time of his death, so tragically, my father died worrying that I might be expelled from law school for something that I hadn't done, and specifically for cheating, which he knew I would **never** do.

It wasn't until after Daddy died that I got fully in touch with how much he loved us. He took good care of Lorna and me after Mama died. He cooked (which he did very well) almost every day, and when he didn't, he'd give me a twenty-dollar bill and the car keys and sent me to "the highway" (nearby Chef Menteur highway on which there were shopping centers and fast-food restaurants) to get burgers, fries and malts for us. He washed and folded the laundry every week, leaving our clean, folded mound of clothes on the foot of my and Lorna's beds. He paid our high school tuitions and my college tuition. From his regular question to me, "Have you heard from your brothers?" during Lemar Jr. 's thirteen months in Vietnam, and Lambert's year in the Philippines, it was obvious to me that he was very much concerned about and loved them too.

In retrospect, I realize that during the first seven years after I left home, the years before my father died, I lived with the unconscious awareness that if, for whatever reason, I ever needed to return home, my bedroom at the end of the hall of 5019 New York Circle would be there. It was my security blanket. I never thought about it after I finished college and moved away, but Daddy's death suddenly made me hyper-aware of the level of safety and security I had felt in the world during those years because on an unconscious level, I knew I had that security blanket—my father and my childhood home. We still owned the house, but with Mama and Daddy both gone now, the house alone, despite my love for it as the repository of all of my childhood memories, wasn't enough to maintain my emotional safety blanket. With my father's death, it was gone.[79]

My grief over losing my father, coupled with my feeling of being a true orphan at that time, quite abruptly made **whatever** racial insanity I was experiencing at school (including my locker mate's inability to treat me like a human being) no more than a minor annoyance. I was both grieving Daddy's loss and crushed by my deep regret that he would never see me graduate from law school. Those two very personal hurts consumed **all** the space in my heart and wedged out, for a time, the cruel sting of racism at school.

MY LAW SCHOOL REFUGE AND PARTING LETTER

THE BEAUTY OF ITHACA'S LANDSCAPE WAS TREMENDOUSLY HELPFUL to me after my father's death. I have always absolutely loved nature. Stunning landscapes and beautiful soft, ambient, meditation music are among the things in life that more than all others provide me with an **unparalleled** inner peace. The two together (with one exception that I describe in my spiritual memoir) give me a feeling that is as close to heaven on Earth as I believe I can ever have. I took more drives out to Ithaca's waterfalls and rural areas than usual after Daddy died.

I was extremely fortunate that the racism that I withstood throughout my time in law school was often abated by those drives. Ithaca has a kind of natural beauty that is no less than magnificent. Its Spring season is filled with young, light green leaves, and azaleas of utterly saturated pink, red, yellow, fuchsia, purple and white. Its Fall colors of amber, orange, red and brown are no less radiant than those of Vermont's Green and New Hampshire's

79 I used that security blanket in March of 1979 when, while living in New York City, I very quickly made a plane reservation and went home for a week because of my fear of the partial nuclear meltdown that occurred at Pennsylvania's Three Mile Island nuclear facility. I wanted to feel safe, so I went home.

White Mountains. It has winters of brilliantly white first snows; and summers of deep blue skies filled with mesmerizing white, puffy, cumulous clouds. Ithaca is surrounded by rolling green hills speckled with farms, red barns and old rusty wagons that date from at least the 1930's, and has, from many vantage points, absolutely stunning views of Lake Cayuga. Most of all, though, Ithaca has waterfalls! The then popular local bumper sticker, "Ithaca is Gorges," is literally true. Ithaca's gorges were my life savers throughout law school. Within a few minutes' ride from campus were three **stunning** falls, Taughannock, Buttermilk, and my unqualified favorite, Treman. All three were for me a safe harbor. Being able to get into my car, no matter how cold it was (indeed, the snow-white winter landscape had its own unique beauty), play one of my Gregorian Chant cassette tapes,[80] and take a peaceful ride out to either the country or to one of the falls was my personal retreat. It was my way of regaining my center and then returning home in peace and serenity, no matter what degree of frustration I was feeling after the latest racial incident at school. Being in Ithaca softened, significantly, the emotional blow of my experiences with racism at Cornell. It's incredible natural beauty was my refuge.

Two years after my father's death, in 1984, just before graduation, I wrote an article that was published in the May 20th edition of the *Dicta*, the law school's student newspaper, describing my experiences and those of some of the other black law students at Cornell. In it, I described what it felt like to be racially objectified by the majority of our peers throughout our entire law school experience. I was thirty when I wrote it in May of 1984. The article follows below in its entirety:

I wish that for a day, for just one day, I could make half of America's white population experience American society as black Americans experience it. Twenty-four short hours would suffice. What would they experience during those twenty-four hours? They would experience the American culture from a

80 Ambient music, my absolute favorite musical genre, didn't yet exist, making Gregorian chant, at the time, my soft, relaxing music default.

perspective which, for most, would be shattering, shattering myths, stereotypes, preconceived ideas, lies. Within those brief twenty-four hours they would gain an awareness of the subtleties of racism of which they otherwise may have remained totally ignorant. They would experience being the fourth person in a supermarket checkout line, seeing all three people ahead of them receive a friendly, "hello," from the cashier and they not a word; they would experience white people's assumption that they are interested in only "black things", which manifests itself, for example, in white peoples' questions to them regarding what they think about Jesse Jackson's campaign or Martin King's birthday becoming a national holiday, or some other such "black concern." They would experience what it feels like to have white people tell them all about the black people whom they have known in the past. They would experience what it feels like to be in a society in which the vast majority of its members harbor an entire set of often unconscious but nonetheless firmly entrenched beliefs and attitudes about them, all of which are based almost exclusively upon the color of their skin, i.e., that they are less intelligent than white people, that they lack the full range of human emotion, sensitivity and sensibilities that white people, by their very birthright, naturally possess—the ability to appreciate nature's beauty, to be touched by a poem, to look up at the stars with awe. In essence, they would experience what it is like to be thought of and responded to as inferior, to lose their individuality, to be responded to as "a black person," to lose their personhood, to be dehumanized. They would no doubt see quite clearly that many white people are totally and utterly unconscious of their preconceived notions about black people. They would see the specific ways in which many white people relate to black people differently from the way in which they relate to white people, and they would understand, no doubt with far more depth than "real" black Americans, that the ways in which white people relate to them is the result solely of their social conditioning. They would see clearly that most white people are not deliberately or maliciously racist, but they would truly and experientially understand that that lack of deliberateness and malice does not alleviate the pain of losing their individuality, their personhood, a big piece of their humanity. They would see clearly that it does not alleviate the pain of being objectified, the pain of dehumanization.

On still another level, in addition to experiencing the feelings of being a member of a group that is consciously and unconsciously thought of and treated as inferior by the majority of society, they would also experience the reality of being a member of a group that is a ***numerical*** *minority in this society—to walk into a movie theater, restaurant, bookstore, classroom, one's work environment—and be one of only a handful of brown faces, and possibly the only one....*

I am convinced that it can be fairly safely assumed that most white people, after only half of that day, would probably be driven to cry out, "I am white! I am white! This is going to wear off in only twelve hours! I am white!" Most could simply not take being classified, being responded to by automatic impulse on the basis of the color of their skin, walking through city streets and just being in society in general with the knowledge that when white people look at them, they (white people) see a black person first, their sex second, and not much else. With their exclamations, they would in essence be proclaiming and reclaiming their full personhood, their humanity. They would be shouting to the world that they really are a "regular person."

After those twenty-four hours had elapsed and the "black/white" people had returned to their ordinary state, I would like to sit in on a discussion in which the "black/white" people try to explain to the inexperienced half of the white persons present, what it was like to be black for a day. I would love to listen to them attempt to explain how differently they, the inexperienced half, responded to them (when they responded to them at all), as black people, what it felt like to be denied the common courtesy of a "hello" from a supermarket cashier, to have white people talk to them about "black things," obviously with the assumption not only that they are interested in nothing else, but also that they probably do not know much about anything else. I'd like to listen to them try to explain what it felt like to walk into a movie theater, bookstore, restaurant, classroom, one's work environment...and be one of a very few or the only black face present. I would like to hear them describe what it was like to experience the American media and advertising industries as a black person. I would ***love*** *to listen to that conversation.*

My thirty years of experience as a black American unequivocally inform me that the inexperienced white people would respond to their comments and perceptions with total skepticism and even disbelief. They would be utterly unable to hear, to really hear, to listen to the descriptions of the patronizing, rote manner in which the inexperienced white people related to the "black/whites". Without actually having lived as a black person for a period of time, albeit a very short one, there is simply no way for the inexperienced whites to understand the experience of being black in America. Finally, they would, for the very first time, truly understand that most white people simply do not see the racism in their interactions with black people.

My three years at Cornell Law School have, not surprisingly, proven that the law school reflects the racism in society-at-large, the kind of racism described above. I wish that for just one day, I could make the entire white Cornell Law School student body truly understand what it is like to walk through Myron Taylor Hall as a black law student—to sit in those classrooms knowing that the majority of your white colleagues view you as...less intelligent and less articulate than they, solely because of your race, that you are incapable of thinking very well in the logical, coherent, comprehensive manner which is required of attorneys.... They would learn much from experiencing what it feels like to have your intelligence, your ability to think critically and analytically, your articulateness, your ability to be an excellent attorney, discounted, ignored, indeed, not even seen.

Obviously, one cannot magically transform white people into black people. One cannot through mental telepathy make them suddenly aware of their unconscious racism. How then does one make them understand the invidiousness of unconscious racism? How can they be made aware of the all-pervasive extent and effects of that unconsciousness on those of whom they are unconscious? How can they be made aware that their unconscious racism also adversely affects their own lives? How does one expose myths for what they are? How does one open eyes? Minds? How does one force white people to grow, to identify, and subsequently eradicate their world view in which to be a white person is to be a person and to be a black person is to be a black person? How does one give them the simple ability to see and respond to people who are racially different from themselves as intelligent, sensitive human beings? How is that awesome feat accomplished? Do I go around the law school proclaiming that my favorite composers are Sibelius and Rachmaninoff, that I write poetry, that I keep a journal, that I love orange sunsets and rocky beaches? Do I go around explaining that I don't spend every waking moment of my day wallowing in my oppression, that I enjoy skating, exercising, and writing letters to friends? Do I yell out that my mother loved poetry and opera, that my father, a postman of thirty-five years was a science enthusiast and part-time mystic and Egyptologist?

I do not have the answers to those questions. Freeing minds and changing solidly established behavior patterns is extremely difficult work. That task requires generations. I am greatly encouraged, however, by the good, serious anti-racism work which so many black and white feminists have recently done and are presently doing. After six long years of working arduously in feminist organizations in Philadelphia and New York City with Indigenous American women, Black women, Asian American women, WASP women and Jewish women on issues of racism, anti-Semitism, sexism, classism, homophobia, ageism and able-bodied people's discrimination against the physically challenged, the past three years at Cornell Law School have been excruciatingly painful for me. The following are but a few of the numerous racist incidents which have occurred during my three-year tenure at Cornell Law School: A Law Practice Dynamics lecturer very clearly implied that all Black people are thieves and hustlers; a guest speaker judge addressing a group of students in the West lounge referred to his Nigerian law clerk's countrymen and women as running around in the woods throwing spears (for which he later apologized); a professor informed two Black students whom he planned to call on the next day what their question was going to be; placement office personnel continually informed a Black student about opportunities in a District Attorney's office despite her constant and adamant indications that she was not interested in prosecutorial work….

Consciousness raising can indeed be done, but not without both a sincere desire and serious commitment on the part of white people to work on their racism. It requires reading, consciousness-raising groups, an awareness in the moment of one's reaction to a person of color, as well as the reasons that underlie them. It requires a vision, a vision of what their life could be like if they were emotionally free to respond to every single person as an individual and a desire to have that life to the extent that it is possible. It requires a vision of what the world should and can be.

I have a list of several very good sources of information (primarily books and pamphlets) on how to "unlearn" racism and will be more than happy to provide it to anyone who drops a note in my Pendaflex.

Among the stories that I didn't share in the article was a conversation that I had with one of my African American classmates at the beginning of our third year. During the conversation, she described her sheer shock and horror in response to an incident that she had experienced while working as a summer associate at a major New York City law firm. At one point during the summer, she attended a social function of some kind at which several of the firm's partners, associates and law student summer associates were present, along with a few New York City judges. Two of the judges, one of whom was African American and the other European American, had an apparently well-known history with each other as what might be described as professional competitors and perhaps even rivals. At some point during the evening, my friend saw the European American judge, after he'd had "a few too many" walk over to the African American judge and overheard him say to his rival, "You know, if slavery ever came back, I'd love to own you."

Upon hearing of my friend's experience, I shared her horror. I then felt immediate and absolute empathy for the African American judge. And **then** I thought, "**Nothing**, not being an intelligent person, not being a good person, not a college degree, not an Ivy League law degree, **not even being a judge** can insulate you from that insanity."

The day the article was published, I ran into my first-year locker mate as she was entering and I was leaving the women's room at school. After neither speaking to nor even acknowledging me for three years, she looked at me and said with what sounded and appeared on her face to be utter shame and guilt, "I really like that article you wrote." In that moment, I could do no more than respond with a very cool, austere, "Thank you," and walk off. After sharing a locker with me for an entire year, after sitting in a number of classrooms with me for three full years, after seeing me five out of seven days a week over the course of those three years, I believe that, as a result of reading my article, that young woman (whose name I don't even remember because we never interacted) **finally** saw my humanity. Perhaps my stoicism in that moment gave her quite a lot to think about. I wish, however, that I had been able, in that moment, to have both felt more compassion for and shown more compassion to her. I wish I had possessed the maturity in that brief exchange, to have actually smiled at her and said warmly, "Thank you. I appreciate your saying that." It is what my mother would have done.[81] A few days later, I graduated from Cornell Law School with a Juris Doctor degree.

MY PRACTICE OF LAW: A BRIEF BUT MEANINGFUL COMMITMENT

Upon graduating from law school the following month, May of 1984, I moved to Washington D.C. and worked there for several years as a public sector attorney. I wanted to do whatever I could to contribute to making the world, and especially American society, more ethical, more just, more fair, and I wanted to use my law degree in that endeavor. My initial plan, upon graduating from law school, was to work on Capitol Hill, eventually as a Legislative Assistant to a Congressional member, preferably in the Senate. I thought that my work would have had the largest societal impact if it was at one of the highest levels of government. I spent the Fall of

81 I can become "cool" toward those whom I feel have treated me or others insensitively. Simultaneously, however, I remain both professional and personally respectful toward them. But in addition to being professional and respectful, continuing to be warm toward the person after we have have discussed the matter at hand and an apology has been given, is an individual personal growth objective on which I continue to work. I'm making progress.

1985 volunteering in the office of Senator Howard Metzenbaum of Ohio, researching and writing a comprehensive analysis of Affirmative Action. Although the Senator's legislative assistant informed me that the plan was to hire me at the beginning of the new year, cuts in the next fiscal year's budget prevented the office from hiring additional staff. I was **sorely** disappointed. It was the 99th Congress.

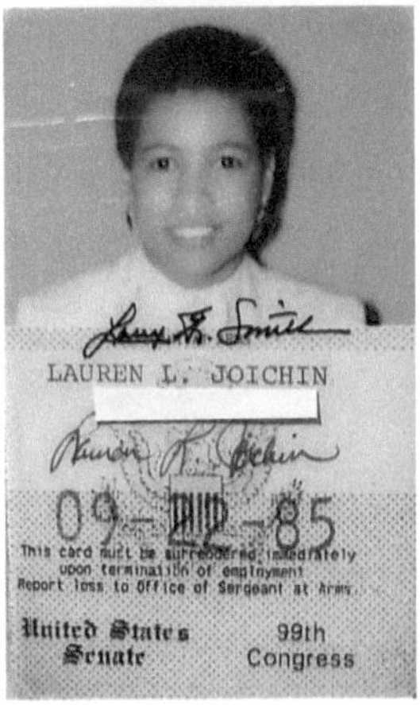

United States Senate ID Badge

My dream of working on Capitol Hill having not materialized, I went to work as a public interest lawyer in Washington. I began as a law graduate with the Maryland Legal Aid Bureau, then as Staff Attorney for the Women's Equity Action League, and finally as one of a number of Staff Attorneys, union lawyers, for the National Treasury Employees Union. At both Legal Aid and as a union lawyer, I represented clients who were not financially able to afford private legal representation. I felt very good about the work that I did during those years because whether my clients received Social Security Disability benefits or not, received Unemployment Insurance benefits or not, and indeed in many cases, whether they were **employed** or not, depended upon the quality of my representation of them. In an important sense, I had my clients' very lives in my hands, and I knew it. For that reason, I took my job as a lawyer very seriously. It required me to use my mind, however, in a way that was for me, far from either fulfilling or even comfortable. I had to focus on minor factual details upon which my clients' entire case might depend, details such as: "Did you re-apply for benefits within thirty days of your receipt of your denial letter?" "Why didn't you attend your appeal hearing for reinstatement of your benefits?" "Was there a reason you didn't apply for at least three jobs last week as required for your unemployment insurance benefits to continue?" "What specific reason was given to you for your demotion?" "What was the date of your letter of dismissal? When did you receive it?" "In informing you of your demotion, what were your manager's exact words to the best of your recollection?" "Were there any witnesses to your supervisor's behavior?" After years of studying both Western and Eastern Philosophy in which I was engaged in the intellectual pursuit of some of the most fundamental and fascinating questions about the very nature of reality, using my brain in that way felt to me like a mental prison. Nonetheless, during my six years of practice, I was absolutely dedicated to my clients, most of whom very much needed the representation, and did my very best for them with a level of success about which I felt very good. Because of the difference that my work and that of my colleagues made in the lives of our clients, I found my legal work very meaningful. It was, for me, however, just not a good intellectual fit. I was most intellectually comfortable with the work that I did during the two years that I served as Staff Attorney for the Women's Equity Action League, WEAL. In that job, I worked on discrimination against women in the military and the insurance industry. I also greatly enjoyed working during that time, in coalition with attorneys from other national women's and civil rights organizations.

After six years of legal practice, however, I grew restless. I wanted to write, to teach, to do public speaking and to facilitate adult learning about oppression/liberation issues. I was absolutely **driven** by a desire to open minds and soften hearts.

CHAPTER EIGHT

MY CAREER AS A TRAINER: A TRANSITION IN FOCUS FROM BIAS AND OPPRESSION TO THE ONENESS OF HUMANITY

THE UNEXPECTED BUT WELCOME BEGINNING

In 1990, six years after graduating from law school, I stopped practicing law. I was fortunate enough to be able to begin a career in the field of organizational development (OD) consulting and training, the decision that proved to be **the** best of my professional life. I **loved** being a trainer.

It was actually my passion for the issues of diversity, equity, and inclusion (DEI) that afforded me the opportunity to transition from the legal to the OD training field. I was a labor lawyer at the time, a staff attorney at NTEU, the National Treasury Employees Union (NTEU). I don't know exactly how, but somehow someone brought to the attention of NTEU's management that while there was a considerable amount of racial diversity among the union's staff attorneys, there was none among either its Chief Attorneys or its officers. Indeed, there was only one woman among the ranks of the union's officers. All of the other members of the union's top administration were European American men. The conversation about NTEU's lack of racial diversity on its leadership team led to diversity, equity and inclusion training for staff members. Whether the session was voluntary or mandatory, I do not remember. What was significant is that it became the springboard that launched my career as an organizational development trainer.

The workshop was my first experience participating in facilitated dialogue and interactive exercises about race, the objective of which was for all of us to leave with a heightened awareness of the ways in which we can all be more culturally competent. It was the very first time that I had participated in a learning endeavor designed to raise awareness of issues of racial privilege and disadvantage, racial sensitivity and insensitivity, racial justice and injustice. **I was utterly enthralled**.

At the end of the two-day session, I immediately walked up to Lucia, the African American trainer, and said to her with resolute determination, "Lucia, I want to do what you do." Lucia looked at me and, with sheer astonishment, uttered, "But Lauren, you're a lawyer." "Yeah, and a very unhappy one, too," I responded without missing a beat. The conversation ended with an invitation to attend a party at Lucia's home three weeks later, allowing me to meet other trainers and thus begin making connections with professionals in the field.

As one who has never been very comfortable at informal social gatherings, when the day of Lucia's party arrived, I hesitated. Deciding, as I ultimately did, to go to the party, changed my life, for it was at that party that I met Bill, the Director of a group of internal trainers at a Maryland-based consulting firm. Upon meeting Bill, we spoke for about twenty minutes. We talked about Lucia's gorgeous, ultra-modern home for the first two or three, then, for the remainder of the time, discussed his work, about which I had **many** questions. After that part of the conversation, Bill and I had the following exchange:

Bill: So what do **you** do?

Lauren: Well, I'm a lawyer, but I don't like it.

Bill: So.…What do you **want** to do?

Lauren: What **you** do.

Bill: After a few seconds of obvious contemplation and while looking at me with a noticeable degree of surprise, "Well...I'm looking to hire someone."

Lauren: After a few seconds thought, "Well, I'm looking to be hired."

From that moment, my days as a lawyer were numbered. Bill hired me, I joined his training team and began a new, thirty-year career. The field was organizational development (OD) training and my entry into it was unexpected, but certainly welcome!

DIVERSITY, EQUITY AND INCLUSION: MY PROFESSIONAL PASSION

Over the course of my career as a trainer in organizational development, both as Director of Training for the National Multicultural Institute in Washington and as an independent trainer for fifteen years, I trained in a myriad of organizations from small nonprofits to large corporations, in educational institutions, and at all levels of government. I trained in venues from a small, Virginia furniture store to the White House. My workshops have been in the areas, among others, of leadership, team building, communication, workplace etiquette, ethics in the workplace, working effectively with temperament differences, time management, conflict resolution, and training of trainers. I also facilitated hundreds of sessions in the areas of working effectively with cultural diversity and minimizing and effectively responding to sexual and other forms of harassment in the workplace. **I loved my work!** Over the course of my career as a trainer, I felt no less than called to do training. My true **passion**, however, was facilitating diversity, equity, and inclusion (DEI) workshops—helping us to see and to experience our shared humanity across all of our differences.

In my diversity, equity, and inclusion workshops, we focused on issues of racism, sexism, antisemitism, ageism, heterosexism, homophobia, ableism, other human prejudices, and unconscious workplace bias. Although as an OD trainer, I wasn't focused on my first passion, The Mysteries, I was often focused on my second—social justice. In much of my work, I hoped that I was helping people become aware of latent prejudicial thoughts, feelings, and behaviors about those whom they perceive as different from themselves. The goal of that work was to assist them in becoming both more self-aware and more compassionate toward their colleagues. I loved it.

In my DEI workshops, I developed agendas that I hoped would raise both the participants' awareness and their **empathy** in relating to their colleagues who they perceived to be different from themselves. I wanted them to understand both the universality of our humanity, and the serious consequences of our being blind to it.[82]

As serious, however, as such sessions by their very nature can, and in some segments must be, in most, there were also periods of lightness and laughter, which greatly helped to "crack the ice", to defrost the chill in workshops in which matters of racism and other forms of oppression were discussed. Then, when it was safe

82 Employers also often wanted me to discuss the legal prohibitions against workplace discrimination, harassment and retaliation, and of course, I did that as well. Both my experience in HEW's Office for Civil Rights, and my legal background were a tremendous help in that regard.

enough, i.e., when the participants felt that they were in an environment in which there was no shame, blame, guilt or judgment, they began to share their personal stories. I found over the three decades during which I facilitated DEI workshops that it is when we can listen to each other's experiences with neither judgment nor blame (similar to the way in which members of twelve-step programs share and listen to each other's stories), minds can change and hearts can open. For that reason, among my most important jobs as a trainer was that of making the room safe enough for people to both share and deeply listen to each other with an open heart. I discovered that workshops often truly start when the story-telling begins. There is **tremendous** power in our stories, each and every one of us.

I have listened to the stories of second and third generation Asian Americans sharing the frustration of not having their specific and very distinct Vietnamese, Japanese, Laotian, Cambodian, Thai and other Asian cultures acknowledged. It is the pain and frustration of being seen as a member of one large Asian monolith, Chinese specifically, and living with the consequences of the "All Asians are alike" stereotype.[83] I have listened as some Asian Americans have described the pain and anger of having people speak to them v-e-r-y s-l-o-w-l-y a-n-d l-o-u-d-l-y and with exaggerated expression. I've heard Asian Americans, born and raised in the United States, describe their experiences of being asked in that same tone, "Where—are—you—from?" I've heard about many of the different ways in which some Asian Americans respond to the "model minority" label. I've listened to what have often been compelling personal stories of Asian Americans who grew up poor, in contrast to the stereotype that the vast majority of Asian Americans are upper middle class. I've heard the accounts of other Asian Americans of how it felt throughout twelve

83 In that instance, two important points are missed—that there is much rich diversity among both Asian and Asian American populations of many nationalities, and that that same abundance of diversity exists **within** Chinese, Chinese American and the many other populations of Asian and Asian-American people.

years of elementary, middle and high school, to be considered "weird" because they loved literature, or art, for example, and had neither any aptitude nor interest in math, engineering or computer science.

I have listened to Latin Americans in many DEI workshops also talk about how frustrating and distressing it is to have others assume that **they** are not American. I have heard Latin Americans from Nicaragua, Ecuador, El Salvador, Costa Rica and other Latin American countries describe their many instances of being assumed to be Mexican, i.e., of having the uniqueness of **their** cultures also erased by others' mental tapes that all **Latin** people are **Mexican** and that all **Mexican** People are alike.[84] I have listened as young Latin American men describe their experiences of being stopped by police for no apparent reason. I've heard numerous Latin Americans describe the pain and embarrassment of having many of their elementary school teachers assume that because they had not yet learned English they were of low intelligence. I've listened to the accounts of Latin Americans who were born and raised in the United States, describing how it feels when they are assumed to be not only "foreign", but also "illegal."

Over the thirty years of my training career, there were, unfortunately, very few people in my workshops of Indigenous ancestry as far as I was aware.[85] As a result, both I and the thousands of workshop participants whom I trained over that time are much less aware of the reality of the lives of Indigenous People than we otherwise would have been had we been privileged to hear some of **their** stories as well. I did learn a lot, however, from being on a training team with two Native American colleagues some years ago, both Blackfeet, one female, the other male, one of whom grew up on a reservation and the other of whom did not. I learned

84 The same two points are missed in this instance, as in the categorizing of all Asian Americans as Chinese, i.e., the richness of both the diversity of the many nationalities of Latin Americans, as well as the diversity **within** Mexican, Mexican American and the many other Latin American populations.

85 There may have been many instances in which an Indigenous or Native American person was present in the session, but I was unable to physically identify them as such, and nothing they said informed me that they were indeed Indigenous.

a great deal from hearing their extremely different growing up stories, which resulted in part from the differences between their two families, but also from the completely different cultures in which they were raised.

In the absence of the voices of Indigenous People in the room, I tried, to the best of my ability, to include the historical and present-day experiences of Indigenous People in all discussions of our different experiences with diversity in the United States. In so doing, I was never confident that I had done an adequate job, and indeed, in most instances, despite both my sincere desire and valiant attempt to do so, probably did not. Indeed, the very fact that I lack the lived experience of an Indigenous Person made it impossible for me to have done so. I did my best, however, and genuinely hope that as a result the participants left the workshop with at least a slightly deeper understanding of the history and experiences of our Indigenous sisters and brothers.

I have listened empathically to African American men in many, many workshops, over three decades, try to help others in the workshop understand the feeling of being stopped by the police numerous times, a phenomenon that for many, began in their early adolescent years. I have listened, in many workshops, to an African American man share what it feels like when the simple physical manifestation of the combination of his race and his gender, i.e., the very fact that he **is** both black and male, instills obvious fear in strangers on the street; that the same thing often happens with a person with whom he is interacting and that depending upon the situation, he might attempt to put the person at ease. I have deeply listened as African American men share how psychologically and emotionally exhausting it is to continuously both **experience** people being afraid of them, **and** to go through the "It's ok, I'm really a good guy. Really. I'm not dangerous or anything. I'm a good guy" exercise on the numerous occasions on which they have done so in their lives. I have watched as **every**

other African American man in the room nodded his head in understanding each time the experience of people being afraid of them was shared.

I have listened with much empathy to the painful stories of African American women who worked very hard in their jobs in corporate America, in academia and in a myriad of other employment settings, earned a promotion on the basis of that work, and were then subsequently told by a colleague, often "in jest," that the only reason they received the promotion is that they were a "twofer," black and female. I have listened to African American women share their outrage, sorrow and disappointment when an African American man harasses them in the workplace. The sentiment that I've heard them express most often in this regard is, "How **dare** he! How dare **he**! **He** should know better, given his experiences with racism! He should **know** better!" I have listened to African American women's stories of not being sure whether the discrimination or harassment they are receiving in a particular instance is the result of racism, sexism, neither, or both, and as a result, not knowing how to respond.

I have listened as African American women **and** men have described their frustration and anger when they experience the phenomenon sometimes referred to as "shopping while black," i.e., of being watched carefully and often followed by sales people in retail establishments. In many sessions, African American parents tearfully shared on more than one occasion painful stories of their child having been put into the "slow" reading group in school without ever having been tested. I have listened to the heartbreak of African American parents as they described both the pain and the resentment of having to have "the talk" with their young sons, the talk in which they tell their boys that they must be deferential to the police if they are stopped, specifically **how** to be so, and that their life could very well depend upon just how **successfully** deferential they are.

THE POWER OF OUR STORIES

TWO STORIES, BOTH OF WHICH WERE SHARED IN DIVERSITY, EQUITY, and inclusion sessions that I facilitated more than ten years ago, are particularly powerful for me. One was told by a young African American man; the other, by a young European American woman.[86] The young man worked in management for a large Florida-based supermarket chain. During the afternoon of the first day of the workshop, he described a personal experience that had occurred at a gas station convenience store earlier that morning:

> On my way to the training this morning, I stopped at a gas station convenience store to get a cup of coffee. After pouring my coffee, I got in line to pay for it. The guy in front of me was also black. All of a sudden, for no reason that I could see, this guy started going off on the cashier, who was white. I mean he was screaming at her, calling her names, everything. I think maybe the guy was mentally ill. He left, then **I** was next in line. When I walked up to the counter, that lady looked at me like she saw a ghost. I know what she was probably thinking. She was probably thinking, "Oh God. Here comes another one!" I didn't even **know** that guy. I didn't know him from Adam. Now, if I had been a **white** guy in line behind **another** white guy who had just gone off on her like that, she probably would've looked at me and said something like, "What was **his** problem?!" But as a **black** man, I was in her mind, automatically linked to the crazy black man. I have no individuality. That hurts like hell.

86 Although I tell the two narratives in first person, they are not strict verbatim accounts. They do, however, accurately represent the speaker's message.

In my brief interaction with that young man, I experienced him as polite and soft spoken. Absolutely nothing about him was threatening.[87]

The following was the story of the young woman, an employee of a large Federal agency in Denton, Texas:

> When I was growing up, people used the "N" word all the time. They talked about Black People really negatively and had all the stereotypes. Then, once when I was in elementary school, we moved and for a little while right after the move, I had to go to a school that was mostly Black. I'll never forget the classrooms in the school. They had no world globes. They didn't have the clocks on the wall that teachers use to teach kids how to tell time. The alphabets that were hung above the blackboard were hand made by the teachers. There wasn't an abacus in my classroom. We had no record players, no science table, no maps. We had no reading corner. Other than the old textbooks, there weren't even any **books** in the classroom. I remember, even as a kid, thinking that there was no way

---

87 That young man's story reminded me of an experience that my cousin Joe had many years ago, and that he shared with me (with what I perceived was both anger and pain), immediately after it occurred. Joe's story was essentially the following, "Laurie, I just came back from Walmart, buying oil for my car. As I walked down the main, center aisle of the store, a white woman was walking in the other direction, toward me. Now, mind you, it was the middle of the day, with hundreds of people around in a big store, and the second that lady looked at me, she clutched her purse and moved way over. Laurie, I'm so tired of people responding to me like that! This is how God made me. I can't look any better than this. I'm a good person, Laurie." Even though Joe shared that story with me years ago, I remember very clearly that he was dressed, as he frequently did, in meticulously ironed pants with a crisp crease, a polo shirt and loafers. Joe is dark brown-skinned so it's possible that the woman's fear of him was exacerbated for that reason. All I could say to Joe, a young man of deep religious faith who lives his life consistent with his faith, was, "I know, Joe. I know, man." In that moment, I hurt for him. My heart ached for my young cousin.

The irrationality of the fear that many European Americans have of African American men and other Americans of Color becomes crystal clear when seen through the lens of American crime statistics. Those statistics demonstrate conclusively that in the history of the United States, many tens of thousands more Americans of Color have been beaten, tortured, lynched and in other ways murdered by European Americans than the other way around. Additionally, American history demonstrates irrefutably that many more synagogues, more Muslim temples, and more African American churches have been defaced and bombed by European Americans, and far more homes and businesses of Americans of Color have been burned by European Americans than the other way around.

> these kids could compete against white kids because they had nothing. How **could** they compete?
>
> While I was at that school, I made friends with a little Black girl. One day after school, I walked her home. When we got to her house, I went in. I noticed the floors. They were beautiful, shiny hardwood. There was a very nice piano in one corner of the living room. The furniture, the curtains, everything looked perfect. My little friend's mother came out, and she was dressed so nice and her hair looked so pretty. She introduced herself, made iced tea for us and then played the piano for us.
>
> After that, whenever I would hear one of my relatives, their friends or one of my friends use the "N" word and say racist things about Black People, I didn't say anything, but I would always think to myself, "Wow. They're saying those things and they believe those things because they've never seen what I saw. They don't know what I know. They just don't understand." I'm **so** glad that I had that experience. Going to that school for a few months and especially that **one** afternoon at my friend's house saved me. They saved me from a closed mind that would have really limited my thinking, my understanding, and my whole life. I'm so thankful for that.

Those are the kinds of stories that can **deeply** touch our hearts and in so doing help all of us to understand each other on a level much deeper than we almost ever do. If we could learn how to both share our own stories and with neither judgment nor defensiveness, listen to those of others, we would grow in wisdom at a rate that I don't think many of us even believe is possible. In listening, for example, to an Irish American friend recount the story of his immigrant great grandparents and the discrimination and harassment they faced upon their arrival in Boston in the late 1800's, I want to be able to experience curiosity about their experience, ask questions and learn about their experiences, about which I formerly knew virtually nothing. I want to be able to hear my friend without feeling resentment, without thinking, "Well at least they weren't slaves." I want to be able to give my friend the great human gift of my full presence as he tells me his story, and to listen to him compassionately, with a clear mind and an open heart.

Similarly, I would hope that my friend would be able to listen with an open mind and heart to the stories of my grandmother, Gramzie's formative years, to my parents' experiences and to my own experiences of racism growing up in New Orleans. I would hope that he would be able to hear me without thinking, "Why do they always have to play the race card? They weren't the only ones who had it hard. My great grandparents had it hard when they came over here too." I hope that my friend would also be able to be curious, and to ask questions about our experiences, hear my stories with empathy and compassion and as a result, have opened to him a world of understanding of an experience that before our conversation might have been virtually unknown to him in any significant way.

The power of our stories, all of our stories, is enormous. When we can listen to one another's stories without defensiveness, without guilt, without shame, without blame, and without judgment, when we can listen to our stories with deep curiosity, a desire to learn, and with an open mind and an open heart, our stories can be transformative.

MY WORK ON RACISM: THE GOAL

In the few workshops that I facilitated outside of the employment context that were focused specifically on the issue of race as opposed to the other forms of human diversity, I wanted the European Americans in the session to understand:

- The pain and suffering of racism, including the unconscious and thus insidious racism of low expectations that has historically been the cause of significant discrimination against Americans of Color in all aspects of life, including in employment, education, and housing. I also wanted them to understand both the source of **structural** racism, and the myriad ways in which it has historically manifested in our country.
- How unconscious racism so often results in the hurtful daily indignities with which Americans of Color live—shopping, driving, walking, sleeping in a car, indeed **living** while Black, Hispanic, Native, or Asian American.
- How racism has emotionally and psychologically impacted Americans of Color.
- How racism has mentally and emotionally disabled many millions of European Americans as well and that, as a result, **their** lives have been limited in ways that they simply cannot imagine.[88]
- I wanted the European American participants to see what is possible for their lives were they to begin the long, difficult, but also exceedingly rewarding journey of unlearning racism, of being able to see themselves as equal, not superior members of the human family. I wanted them to want that personal growth for themselves and their children.

88 I am not a trained psychologist. Based upon my three-decades long experience of conducting workshops that were focused on race and racism, however, I very strongly believe that when racism, not unlike all other isms, is rooted in one's psyche at a deep enough level, it is indeed a mental disability.

- I wanted them to be aware of the good, solid anti-racism training being done by many European Americans—training that is focused on helping European Americans to become more aware of racism both within themselves and in society-at-large. I wanted them to enroll in some of those courses, at the completion of which I wanted them to understand:
  - ◊ The history and dynamics of structural racism, and how it has impacted and continues to impact the lives of Americans of Color.
  - ◊ The importance of being anti-racist themselves.
  - ◊ How they might become effective anti-racist allies to Americans of Color. I wanted them to feel deeply motivated to become an ally to People of Color both at work and in their personal lives.

In order for that depth of learning and understanding to occur, however, I was aware that before receiving **any** of that information, whatever possible shame and guilt the European American participants might have been feeling **had** to be addressed. Were it not, those feelings would likely have been like a twenty-foot high, ten-foot-deep cement wall impeding their ability to hear any of the material being offered in the session. They **had** to be told that they are to blame for neither racism nor for its many horrible, inhumane manifestations. They had to know that they were **born** into the insanity of racism in which we all live, and that if they come from a family that participated in the ghastly institution of slavery, they are not responsible for what their ancestors did. They had to hear that **no one** can be held responsible for ills committed before they even existed on Earth. Rather than feel **guilty** about our nation's racist past (a past that they had nothing to do with), I wanted their sentiment to be something like, "Wow! What happened to Americans of Color during that time was horrendous! I'm so glad that as human beings, as a country, while there's still

much to be done to achieve racial equality, we've come a long way from **that**! I hope that if **I** had been alive at that time, I would have been active in the anti-slavery movement; or if I had worked on the railroad out West, I hope that I would've shown humanity to the Asian Americans who worked on it and been an advocate on their behalf; or if my work or my life-in-general caused me to have contact with Native Americans or Hispanic Americans, I hope that I would've been an ally to them." For learning to occur, guilt must be eradicated. One trainer whose DEI workshop I attended many years ago, Sherry Brown, said that, "Guilt is the glue that holds prejudice in place." I believe that she is correct. I do not want European Americans to feel guilty about racism. I want them to be allies in the struggle to **eradicate** racism—to eliminate all of its pain and ugliness from the face of the Earth.[89]

In addition to the message that they are not responsible for historical racism, the crucial, essential, critical message that I believe European Americans must receive **simultaneously,** however, is that **while they bear absolutely no guilt for the past, as a beneficiary of that past** (regardless of a sincere wish to **not** be a beneficiary of it), **they bear a tremendous responsibility for the present, a responsibility to be anti-racist in all aspects of their lives.**

89 That view may lead some readers to think that I am buying into what has been referred to as "white fragility," the discomfort, denial, defensiveness that many White People feel and express in discussions of racism and white privilege. It may sound to some that I am engaging in a very distasteful, familiar pattern of a Black American person making a tremendous effort, and expending a lot of energy to make White Americans comfortable in conversations about racism. My effort, however, is not to make White Americans comfortable. It is simply to get them to be able to **listen**, to actually **hear** both the presentation and the comments of the People of Color in the room. Just as I cannot be held responsible for anything that happened in the world before August 15, 1953 because I was quite literally not on the planet at that time, in the exact same way, no other human being can be held responsible for anything that happened before **they** existed. Any other position is simply utterly illogical. The simple truth is that none of us can be held responsible for events that took place at a time during which we weren't even alive. If telling that truth helps White Americans to both learn how historical racism has impacted the lives of Americans of Color, and understand their responsibility to help dismantle it, I will continue to tell that truth unapologetically.

In those sessions, I wanted the Americans of Color to:

- Fully grasp the concept of internalized oppression, to honestly consider whether it impacts them personally and, if so, how they may recover from it and go on to live their lives emotionally and psychologically free from its debilitating effects. Among ways that internalized oppression has impacted us, I wanted them to think specifically about how colorism has affected us in both our communities and our families.
- Be aware of, to understand, to claim, and to have pride in the greatness of their ancestors' ancient civilizations.
- Know about the many contributions to the western world made by members of their race.
- Boldly cast off the psychological cloak of inferiority from around their shoulders, and valiantly emerge from beneath it, proud to be Native American, proud to be African American, proud to be Asian American, proud to be Hispanic American.
- Acknowledge that we, as People of Color, **also** have both conscious and unconscious biases (sexism, homophobia, anti-Semitism, classism, colorism, and others) that can be enormously hurtful to **others**; and that some of those "isms" that we may not **personally** experience may greatly impact the lives of others; that we have a compelling moral responsibility to eradicate those biases from our minds and hearts, and that we must be effective allies to people who experience forms of oppression that as members of our racial groups, we may not experience. I want the People of Color in the workshop to understand their responsibility to interrupt and dismantle non-race-based oppressions.
- About European Americans, I wanted the Americans of Color to know:

◊ That while the skin color privilege that they possess is unquestionably a tremendous advantage in the United States, generally making life much easier for European Americans than it is for Americans of Color, it does not necessarily make life a "cake walk" because those who enjoy the privilege can still experience tremendous pain in their lives in other ways—as the result, for example, of having suffered physical, sexual, or psychological abuse, or having a disability.

◊ That while contemporary European Americans on a practical level **are** and historically **have** been the **beneficiaries** of racism, they are **also** its victims, albeit in a radically different way from the way in which Americans of Color have been. That both conscious and (especially) unconscious racism have mentally and emotionally imprisoned European Americans for centuries, and how **living** within that mental and emotional imprisonment has severely limited their emotional and intellectual growth, and indeed their entire lives.[90]

◊ That the average European American who grew up in the United States had virtually no chance of escaping that imprisonment.

◊ kThat had they themselves, the People of Color in the workshop, been raised in the same way, **they** would very likely harbor the exact same prejudices, and the exact same unconscious feelings of superiority to People of Color.

◊ That there are thousands of European Americans who are **sincerely** committed racial allies.

90 To suggest that the ways in which racism has historically impacted European Americans compared to the ways in which it has historically impacted Americans of Color as anything **but** "radically different" would be a dangerously false equivalency. Historical racism has unquestionably impacted the lives of Americans of Color in far more devastating ways than it has impacted European Americans.

◊ That true allyship between themselves and European Americans who are sincerely doing anti-racism work of all kinds is actually possible.

I wanted **all** participants in the workshop to understand the actual history of racism both in the United States and internationally, for it is only by holding up to the light the mistakes of our **past**, that we can avoid the **shadows** of those mistakes in our **present**. Most importantly, however, I wanted the participants in my workshops to understand the profound reality that all seven-plus billion human beings on Earth, **all** of us, irrespective of what we call "race" are members of one large extended family. I wanted them to understand on a very **deep** level, the oneness of humanity.[91]

OTHER "ISMS": WALKING IN EACH OTHER'S MOCCASINS[92]

I WANTED THE HETEROSEXUAL PEOPLE IN THE ROOM TO UNDERSTAND in a profound way, how both heterosexism and homophobia impact the lives of lesbian, gay, bisexual, transgender, gender non-conforming, and inter-sex people. I wanted the heterosexual people in the room to understand what it would feel like if they lived in a predominantly LGBTQ world and had to pretend to be an LGBTQ person at every turn, with family, with friends and all day, five out of seven days a week at work. My desire was for them to understand the discomfort of being in an office conversation about everyone's weekend and not feeling free to talk about the get-together of several of their heterosexual friends that they attended Saturday night. I wanted them to know what it would feel like to be a heterosexual person of deep faith and hear at their worship service on a regular basis how morally bankrupt they are for being heterosexual. I wanted them to understand what it would feel like

91 Much more detail is provided about my diversity, equity and inclusion work in my book, *On Race and Racism: Humanity's Bottom Line*

92 "Oh Great Spirit, keep me from ever judging a man until I have walked a day in his moccasins."
Sioux Indigenous Prayer

to have to prepare for family visits by having their partner assist them in totally "sanitizing" their home by removing all pictures and every other trace of their relationship, by having their partner then leave their home and not return until after they entertained their family for several hours, and upon their family's departure, calling their partner to return home, after which they went through the exhausting exercise of once again putting back in place all of the pictures and other evidence of their shared lives. I wanted them to understand the threat of physical violence with which many LGBTQ people live every day, sometimes for just being who we are, i.e., for just "showing up" as our authentic selves, and at other times for engaging in an act as simple, as innocent, as loving and as natural as holding the hand of our partner or spouse in public. I wanted them to understand the discrimination that we often face on a regular basis in every life context—education, housing and employment. I wanted them to see, understand and acknowledge the magnificent, rich diversity that exists within the community of people who are LGBTQ. I wanted them to understand what it feels like to experience what may be the most common discomfort for many LGBTQ people—simply others' personal discomfort with us as human beings, discomfort based on stereotypes about LGBTQ human beings.

I wanted the people in the room who are Christian to gain an intense awareness of the ways in which religious exclusion, even the most subtle and unconscious, affects their workplace colleagues who are not Christian. I wanted them to understand what it would be like to live in a culture that is predominantly Jewish, for example, and to experience being a religious minority in that society, a society in which the majority both knows very little about their Christian faith, and in a number of contexts, has historically been either unwelcoming or downright hostile toward people of their faith. I wanted them to understand how it would feel to live in a society in which hate groups that target Christians for unspeakable violence exist, a society in which Christian churches are defaced and bombed, simply because they **are** Christian. I wanted them to truly comprehend the feelings associated with living in a society in which Christians have been historically excluded from social clubs, from neighborhoods, from jobs and even from entire professions. I wanted them to deeply understand the experiences of their children at school during the Chanukah season.

I wanted **all** of us, those of us who have religious/spiritual faith of all kinds, as well as those of us who are atheist and agnostic, to see, understand and acknowledge the magnificent, rich diversity that exists within both religious and spiritual communities, as well as those which gather in observance of non-religious, non-spiritual, ethical, humanistic principles. I wanted people of faith to understand that there are millions of people who do not believe in a Divine Creator, who are highly ethical and compassionate and deeply caring about the lives of their fellow human beings; and I wanted people who are secular to not "write off" their brothers and sisters of faith as either unintelligent, or bamboozled.

I wanted the able-bodied people in the room and those with no emotional and learning disability to deeply understand the stories told by people with physical, mental, emotional and learning disabilities. I wanted them to understand, to the extent possible, their experiences of being patronized, the experience, for example, of having others assume that because they have a **physical** disability, they are also **intellectually** challenged; of having the restaurant wait-person ignore them and ask their able-bodied dinner partner, "And what would s/he like?"; of having others assume that because they have a learning disability, they are not intelligent. I wanted the sighted people in the workshop to understand the experience of a blind person who reports that because they are blind people often speak to them as if they are also hard of-hearing, i.e., very loudly. I wanted them to know what it feels like to have well-meaning people give them unsolicited help in performing the simplest of tasks, which they are fully capable of doing for themselves. I wanted the able-bodied people in the room to understand to every extent possible the ways in which both low expectations and patronizing attitudes and behaviors, **even the most unintentional**, impact the quality of life, including the career opportunities, of people living with physical, mental, emotional and learning impairments. I wanted them to see, understand and acknowledge the magnificent, rich diversity that exists within communities of people with disabilities.

I wanted the people in the room who did not grow up poor to deeply understand that people who are living in poverty are **not** genetically "lazy, shiftless and trifling," that as children they have the **same** dreams as all other people. I wanted them to see, to understand and to acknowledge the magnificent, rich diversity that exists within communities of people who are poor. I wanted them to understand what living in poverty and the hopelessness that often accompanies it can do to the human spirit. I wanted them to know that as a group, people who are born into poverty have the same intellectual ability and human potential as all other people.[93]

I wanted any harassers in the room to deeply understand how sexual, physical, and psychological harassment impacts the person who is the target of the harassment. I wanted them to "get," on a deep level, how emotionally debilitating workplace harassment can be on the targeted person and how it can severely impact the targeted person's physical, mental and emotional health, as well as their life **outside** of work.

93 Dr. Maya Angelou once told Melissa Harris Perry, host of a past political cable TV show, the story of her encounter some years prior with a young high school student who was in an urban school for kids who had been involved in the criminal justice system. In introducing herself to Dr. Angelou, the young woman could do no more than mumble in a thick urban dialect. Years later, that same young woman met Dr. Angelou again, this time by happenstance. During that later encounter, the young woman was extremely articulate, had earned B.A. and M.A. degrees and was a student in a Ph.D. program. About her, Dr. Angelou said the following: "That young woman was just waiting to become herself." I wanted the people in my workshops who did not grow up in poverty to know that, **with opportunity**, children of **all** races, Native American, Hispanic American, African American, European American, and Asian American, who are born into poverty and whose lives reflect the negative consequences of poverty, can "become themselves."

I wanted the people in the room who do not experience the daily indignities of "the isms" and "the phobias" (racism, sexism, anti-Semitism, heterosexism, ageism, ableism, Islamophobia, homophobia, etc.) to understand on a deep level what it feels like to experience the double blow of first **living** through the indignity, then upon **talking** about it to be met with one of the "common responses": "You're being too sensitive;" "You're looking for it;" "That's happened to me too, so it couldn't have happened to you because of your race;" "Maybe the cashier was just having a bad day;" "Why are you always playing the race (or gender, etc.) card;" "Yeah, but that happens to everybody;" "Well, if I went to the Black (or Latino, or Native American, or Asian, etc.) part of town and went shopping, the same thing would happen to me;" "The police see all those teenagers the same. Race has nothing to do with it." I wanted the people in the workshop who respond in that way to understand that one of the results of those common responses is that they erect cement walls of deep emotional distrust among people, distrust founded in the knowledge that the other person in the conversation isn't open to even **learning** about the indignities and about the emotional and practical consequences of the indignities in the lives of those who experience them.

In essence, in the workshops that I facilitated, I wanted the participants, for at least a few hours, to walk in each other's moccasins to whatever extent it may have been possible. The objective of doing so was for those who are members of majorities, racial, physical ability, sexual, identity, gender expression, sexual orientation, religious, and other majorities, to leave the session with a deeper understanding of and as a result, **compassion for** those who are members of minorities; and, for those who are members of minorities to leave with a deeper understanding of and as a result, **compassion for** those who are members of majorities.

My goal in **all** of my diversity, equity and inclusion training was to have participants leave the session with a heightened awareness of whatever unconscious biases they may have. I wanted them to leave with a genuine commitment to work on those biases, and to make a sincere, concerted effort to relate to **all** of their colleagues as equals, and in a kind, respectful manner.

Finally, and perhaps most importantly, I wanted the participants in my workshops to get a least a glimpse of what it means to live life consciously, conscious of human oppression in all its myriad forms, and with the intent to courageously oppose the oppression of their fellow human beings when and wherever it rears its ugly head in their life.

At the end of my training career, primarily when facilitating workshops outside of the employment arena, I shifted my focus from diversity, equity and inclusion to the oneness of humanity. I wanted people to **truly** understand the scientific basis of the truth that all human beings on the Earth, all homo sapiens, are equally human, possessing in equal measure, all of the characteristics that make us human. I still do that work, and shall continue to do until I am no longer capable. It is **deeply** gratifying.[94]

94 I wrote extensively on the daily indignities, the common verbal responses given in conversations about them, and the scientific basis of the oneness of humanity in *On Race and Racism: Humanity's Bottom Line*.

Lauren Training

MY LIFE TODAY AND FINAL THOUGHT

MY CHILDHOOD EXPERIENCES OF GROWING UP UNDER SEGREGATION IS a history that I share with Oprah Winfrey, with Condoleezza Rice, with Morgan Freeman and with many, many other well-known African Americans. All of us who grew up Black, in the South and at that time, under segregation. We lived through it ourselves and saw our parents and grandparents endure it as well. I will end my racial journey, however, fully acknowledging that as painful as my life experiences with racism have been, I have in comparison to millions of others, experienced very little of the potential pain of racism. In New Orleans, I experienced the hardships of both segregation and newly-imposed integration, but millions of African American kids who grew up at that time in Birmingham, Montgomery, and Selma, Alabama, in Jackson and Philadelphia, Mississippi and other southern cities experienced actual domestic terrorism—the bombing of their churches, meeting places and for some, their homes. Millions of African American children who were growing up in rural areas of the American South at that time lived through terrifying night rides through their communities by the Ku Klux Klan. In one of my workshops, an African-American woman, my age, who grew up in a small rural Alabama community, privately shared with me at the end of the session that during her childhood, her best friend's father had been lynched, for a reason I do not remember, by an angry white mob. Unlike the millions of Black kids who lived in either the rural south, or in one of the southern cities in which the Civil Rights Movement was being led by Dr. King and others, I was filled with all of the hope but none of the terror of the Civil Rights Movement, the terror of its child demonstrators who faced the full wrath of racist Mississippi and Alabama police forces. Even in my hometown, dark brown-skinned kids, and the thousands of Black kids who grew up in the projects of New Orleans suffered far more than I did. Millions of African American children who grew up at that time in the northern ghettos of Newark, Detroit, St. Louis and Chicago and in ghettos all over the country, in L.A., and Baltimore, in Washington, D. C., and Atlanta, and in so many other American "hoods," suffered the results of the long history of racial oppression in the U.S. far more than I.

All over these United States, millions of Latin American children who grew up in barrios, Asian American children who grew up in poverty—in Chinatowns, Koreatowns, Japantowns and pockets of Asian American poverty all across the country, and Indigenous children who grew up in incapacitating poverty at that time, both on and off reservations, suffered the social consequences of racism much more than I. For that reason, I am very well aware that the pain of my experiences pales in comparison to many who had either the same or much more God-given intelligence and creativity than I, but who, due only to the circumstances of their birth, tragically became statistics. My heart bleeds for those millions of innocents. I honor their stories. I honor their lives.

Over the course of my thirty-year career as a trainer, I was fortunate to have trained with a number of very talented European American DEI trainers who not only train, but also live their lives with great insight about DEI issues, specifically, team members of the firms Strategic Interactions of Fairfax, Virginia, Tom Finn Associates of Reston, Virginia and Annapolis Professional Resources of Glen Burnie, Maryland, among others.[95] I feel particularly fortunate to have formed precious friendships with three European American trainers who are now among my very dearest friends—Theresa, Jack, and Tom. If asked, they would be the first to acknowledge that they still carry somewhere within themselves, the vestiges of many of the negative racial messages which, over the course of their lives, they have received from other European Americans, both in their families and from society-at-large. That fact notwithstanding, Tom, Jack and Theresa have a depth of understanding of race, our country's racial history, and the present-day experience of racism by Americans of Color that I have often wished all European Americans, and indeed all other human beings, could truly share. I fantasized about doing a mind meld with Jack, Tom and Theresa, making a copy of whatever it is in their minds that has allowed them, as European Americans, to overcome many of the negative messages they have received about People of Color. In that fantasy, I duplicate that mysterious substance, reproduce it hundreds of millions of times, and make it available to all who wish to live a more intentional, more conscious, more compassionate life.

After thirty years working as an OD trainer, I have retired from my career as a trainer. I now spend my time writing about the issues on which I have worked throughout my life. I do so in my very much still present hope that I may encourage and perhaps even inspire other young, would-be activists to continue the work done by so many in the generation before me, and indeed by many

95 Tom Finn's Book, *Are You Clueless*, provides many valuable stories of cultural diversity "cluelessness" within the employment context. Finn, Tom. *Are You Clueless*. Reston: Kells Castle, 2007. Print. www.areyouclueless.com

in my own, the work for justice, for peace, for compassion, and for the health of the Earth. My hope is that in my writings (as I hope I have done in my workshops), I will inspire at least one person to become, as I hope I have been, a compassionate activist. I hope that my words spark in them a keen desire to leave this Earth at least a little better than the one they entered, to make their lives matter, and to make a contribution to the evolution of our species.

I began my racial journey as a young civil rights activist. Beginning in my mid-teens in New Orleans, and continuing through my 20's in Philadelphia, in New York City, in Ithaca, New York, and in Washington D.C., I participated in marches and demonstrations for freedom and equality, and volunteered in non-profit organizations that worked on peace and justice issues. Over the years, I have participated in both local and national demonstrations for racial equality, women's equality, for women's safety, for LGBTQ equality, and in support of progressive environmental causes. In the third through sixth decades of my life, I devoted myself to continuing to help humanity to free itself from the mental and emotional shackles of prejudice through the vehicle of education. I am, at heart, an educator.

At nearly seventy years old now, realizing that I am in the Autumn of my life, I deeply hope that over the course of my life, in the many relationships that I have had with family, colleagues, workshop participants, and friends, and in the even more numerous interactions that I have had with many strangers, I have helped at least a few of my fellow human beings see the profoundly deep connection that exists among the nearly eight billion human beings on our planet. I hope that I have helped at least a few of us to both see ourselves in each other and the Divine in us all.

Here now, dear reader, is my final thought with which I end this, my racial memoir:

Every single person on Earth enters this world in the **exact** same manner—we **find** ourselves in these bodies of ours. We just find ourselves in them. **All** of us. **None** of us asked to be born into the racial group into which we were born. None of us chose to be born intersex, female, or male. We didn't choose our sexual orientation, gender expression or gender identity. No one chose to be born with a physical, mental, emotional or learning disability. None of us chose our national origin. We didn't choose our parents. We just found ourselves in our identities, whatever identities we happen to have.[96] Let us, as human beings, now become fully aware of that fact. Let us embrace each other as if, as a species, we had no eyes, "seeing" one another through only the lens of our experience with one another, judging ourselves solely on what is on our inside—our character. That, dear reader, dear friend, is our clarion call. It is the call to see our true unity, to see the oneness of humanity. It is among our species' most imperative challenges. We **can** indeed do it. We must simply be mature enough to want it.

Now that you have traveled with me along my **racial** journey, I invite you now, dear friend, to join me on another adventure – the adventure of my **spiritual** journey - my quest for The Divine.

96 It is appropriate to acknowledge here, however, the belief in pre-birth planning, i.e., the belief that prior to birth, we do indeed choose our parents, and thus, many of the circumstances of our lives. That concept will be more fully explored *in* my book, *On Religion and Spirituality: Humanity's Greatest Call - The Call to Spiritual Maturity*.

NOTES

NOTES

PART TWO

MY SPIRITUAL MEMOIR:

A LIFELONG ODYSSEY...A PILGRIM'S PATH

I dedicate my spiritual memoir to Gramzie, my maternal grandmother, Mrs. Victoria Edwards Gray. Gramzie's inexpressible love, charity, and sincere, profound compassion for others as well as the powerful example of her life, lived wholly consistently with her deeply-held religious convictions, have inspired me for my entire life. I am eternally grateful that I had Gramzie for the first twenty-two years of my life. I love you, Gramzie. This book is for you.

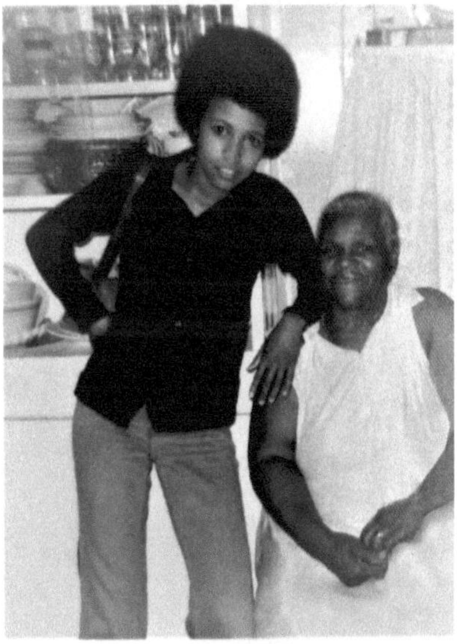

My Grandmother
Mrs. Victoria Edwards Gray (Gramzie) and Me
1974

ACKNOWLEDGMENTS

Reverend Edward A. Kennedy, Jr. was the minister of Bethany United Methodist Church, which I attended throughout my childhood and adolescence. Reverend Kennedy's numerous sermons about the ethical responsibility of Christians and indeed of all people of conscience to live both an examined life and a life of service, profoundly impacted my personal, social and spiritual development. His dual teachings of both the gospel of love and the gospel of social justice, and his exquisitely articulate explanations of the inextricable interconnectedness of love and social justice, were a source of major inspiration for me during my formative years.

Dr. Donald Hanks was a Philosophy Professor extraordinaire during my undergraduate years (1970-74) at The University of New Orleans. His brilliant lectures challenged and captivated my intellect and his unceasing humor personally endeared me to him. Dr. Hanks taught me to think like a philosopher. For that, I am eternally grateful, for the ability to do so proved to be a **critical** skill along my spiritual journey.

To my beloved friend of over 30 years, Physics Professor Dr. Jack Straton, I owe unending thanks for the many hours spent in what we refer to as our "cosmo raps." Jack's training in Physics and my training in Philosophy resulted in many "deep" shared dialogues between us, both wonderful and filled with wonder, in which we discussed, among many other things, the nature of time as a dimension, the relationship between chaos and order in the universe, the general theory of relativity, quantum mechanics, string theory and the possibility of intelligent extraterrestrial life. I cannot thank you enough for our cosmo raps, Jack. They profoundly deepened my curiosity about the mystery of existence. I am exceedingly happy that we recorded a number of them. Those old cassette tapes of our cosmo raps remain among my most cherished possessions.

With Mr. Junius Solomon, my dear friend of fifty years, I have had countless conversations, usually by telephone, about matters both spiritual and mystical in nature. Thank you, Junius, for those numerous discussions during which you reminded me, most compellingly, of the importance of maintaining a daily spiritual practice. I wish only that we could have had more of those extraordinary talks in person. Most importantly, thank you for being my cherished friend over the past fifty years. I deeply admire your commitment to spirituality and utterly respect your decades of work both as Director of the Virginia Tech Upward Bound Program and in the U.S. Department of Education's Office for Civil Rights. Junius, you are and always will be my friend.

I also acknowledge with gratitude my friend Lynn Worley for informing me of the CHIME signal discussed in Chapter 2, which was a valuable addition to that chapter.

INTRODUCTION

I am enormously thankful that despite having been born into an external public life of abject, state-sanctioned racism, both my external **private life and my internal** life were the total opposite of my external public life. My external **public** life was that which I lived as an African American child in the segregated American South. My external **private** life was that in which I lived with my family, my community, my church, and my school, in all of which I was deeply loved and supported. That life, my external **private** life, made my **internal** life possible.

Me at Four Years Old

As **for** my internal life, I was, for the most part, a free, happy little kid. My inner life was one of consistent awe, wonder and fantasy. That inner life was the result of the fierce curiosity with which I was born—my curiosity about the deepest mysteries of what we all experience as reality. Throughout my childhood, I was completely captivated by those mysteries—by questions that no adult was able to answer, questions to which there simply were no answers. Over the course of my life, I have come to refer to the mysteries about which I was so curious as a child as "**The** Mysteries."

My little child's mind was captivated by The Mysteries, by questions, among many others, about how the universe started, and since, as I was taught, it was created by God, about how God came into existence, about whether time travel was possible to the past, but especially to the future, about what heaven was like, and about whether there were intelligent civilizations elsewhere in the universe.

I think that it was the combination of my curiosity and my very vivid imagination that resulted in my having such a rich inner life as a child. Using all the powers of my imagination, I read nearly all of the stories in the ten-volume set of Collier's Junior Classics that came with the set of Collier's Encyclopedia that we had throughout my childhood.[97] As I did, vibrant colorful pictures of what I was reading appeared in my mind. While reading the stories, I was actually there in my imagination, in the plot, as the story's protagonist. In my imagination, it was I, not Jack, who was climbing the beanstalk and then wandering around what I fancied to be a magical kingdom in the clouds at the top of the beanstalk. It was me who was running away from the witch's gingerbread house in the forest, not Hansel and Gretel. I, not Gulliver, was standing on the island of Lilliput, looking down at a throng of miniature Lilliputians at my feet.[98]

97 Later, as a young teenager, beginning with the letter "A", I started reading the adult encyclopedia set with the goal in mind of reading the entire encyclopedia. Having never gotten out of the "A's," I fell far short of that goal! In school, I enjoyed learning about the Dewey Decimal System (Dewey Decimal Classification - Wikipedia) because it gave me access to entire libraries of information.

98 I was a young adult in my mid-twenties when I began reading feminist analyses of social realities and societal issues. It was then that I began to analyze, through a feminist lens, those same children's fantasies. Incredibly, it wasn't until then that I began thinking about the fact that all of the primary characters whose adventures I had so vividly seen in my imagination were boys. The female characters in those stories were primarily wicked witches, evil stepmothers and either weak little girls or weak women in need of being rescued by a man. I could not identify in the least with any of those characters. I could identify with neither their helplessness nor with their evil. Of course I knew on a conscious level that the leading characters and heroes in all of the stories were boys, but as a child, I never thought about it. I never thought, at least not consciously, about the fact that all of the main characters who were strong and heroic were male, and that all of the weak, helpless, or evil characters were female. At the time, it was just the way it was. Equally as interesting is that while I can't believe that I wasn't aware of it on some level, it was also not until that time in my early adulthood that I became consciously aware that kids of my race were also totally absent from all of the stories I read as a child. The fact that all of the characters in those children's stories were white was just the way it was. It was normal. There were no exceptions. Indeed, it was so normal that the question, "Why aren't some of the kids in these stories black?" never even occurred to me nor, I venture to guess, did that question occur to most black children at that time. It wasn't a matter of having to get used to not seeing yourself depicted. You never were depicted. You never had been. You were born into that kind of invisibility. Your invisibility was the only reality you knew. It was the only one your parents had ever known, and their parents before them. All of the people who were portrayed as important and heroic in children's stories, as

Collier's Junior Classics

My imagination (greatly influenced by those and other books I read along with the movies and television shows I watched) often transported me into scenarios in which I traveled either deep into space, or far into the future. Among the things I most enjoyed thinking about and imagining as a kid was how human beings might live in the future, and how much smarter and wiser we'd be by then.[99]

well as in the real world, were both white and male. In the 1960s and before, it was just the way it was. For the most part, the only exceptions, i.e., generally the only times we were not invisible, were when we were being portrayed negatively and specifically as either dumb, lazy, or criminal. Such was true, among many other examples, of the popular 1930s and '40s Buckwheat character, the African American children in the Shirley Temple movies of the same time period, and of most of the characters on the Amos and Andy radio and television shows of the 1920s through the 60s. I wonder how the United States, the country of my birth in which I have lived my entire life, might today be different if a critical mass of contemporary white American men had, as children, read amusing, whimsical adventures in which the protagonists were all and only smart, strong, brave, little black girls, and if they never saw in those stories children who looked like themselves—children who were neither male nor white. I wonder how it would have affected them if by and large the only representations that they saw of themselves in society were racist stereotypes of White People as unintelligent, lazy, or criminal. It would be extremely interesting to know how such a childhood would have affected their self-esteem, their self-confidence and their overall self-image. It is, however, and thankfully for them, something we shall never know.

99 As an older child and young teen, I thought that as a society we were learning a great deal from both the Civil Rights Movement (especially from Dr. King's speeches and sermons which even though I was young were **very** powerful for me) and from the peace and anti-war movement, specifically the anti-Vietnam war movement. I remember vividly that my childhood thought was that by the time I was an adult, and certainly by the time I was thirty (which seemed like an eon away) humanity would most assuredly have matured beyond both racism and war. I love and am extremely thankful for the innocence and the optimism with which I was fortunate enough to live as a child.

On the wings of my imagination, I soared the skies. My experience of that profound inner freedom comprised a full half of my emotional template as a child. The deep love I received from both my mother and my grandmother comprised the vast majority of the other half.

Throughout my youth, science was my vehicle for attempting to understand the universe...and **I loved it**. I was a little science nut from the time I first learned what science was! I may well have inherited my science orientation and my obsession with The Mysteries because my two older brothers, Lemar Jr. and Lambert, had the very same science bug I had. In his adolescence, Lemar Jr.'s dream was to be an archeologist. For Lambert, it was life as a neurosurgeon. Years later, when we were all adults, I asked Lemar Jr. and Lambert about the source of those dreams. I asked them how as children, they even became aware of archeology and neurosurgery as disciplines. Lemar Jr. said that he saw a television documentary about an archeological dig in Egypt when he was young and was hooked on it from then on. Lambert said he actually didn't know why at a time when most of his little friends wanted to be police officers and firefighters he wanted to operate on people's brains. Always the consummate teaser, however, he told me many times as we were growing up, that he wanted to be a brain surgeon so that he could operate on my brain to see what made me so stupid![100] Whenever the two of us, as adults, discuss some

100 In retrospect, I now wonder if as teens, after the innocence of childhood had faded, Lemar Jr. and Lambert ever thought about the discrimination they would surely have faced as young black men trying to pursue careers in archeology and neurosurgery in the 1960s and early '70s. Courtney Milloy, a well-known African American columnist for the *Washington Post*, said in a May 20, 2001 column, "Adults in my neighborhood could wage war on racism, even risking their lives, while enabling their children to feel safe and secure—even special—in the midst of it all." That was also abundantly true of my mother, and of so many of the other adults of Pontchartrain Park. They made us feel safe, secure, valued and loved, and told us that there was nothing that we couldn't grow up to do if we applied ourselves. That was certainly my mother's consistent message to my brothers and me. Thus, despite the fact that, to my knowledge, there were no African American women research scientists at the time during which I was dreaming of becoming one, amazingly it never ever occurred to me that I couldn't be one when I grew up. My mother's message bestowed on me the dual gift of my wonderful childhood confidence and my childhood dreams. While neither of my brothers followed the path of their childhood aspirations, they both did just fine. Lemar Jr. was a successful business owner for thirty years and Lambert retired from a management position of a large, urban transportation system in which he worked for over twenty years. Both maintain their interest in science to this day.

subject or another about the brain, Lambert will undoubtedly say at some point during the conversation, "The mind is baaaad. The mind is **so** bad." He seems to be quite fascinated by one particular fact that he learned about the human brain in his youth, i.e., that **everything** that we experience in life, literally every single thing, is permanently recorded somewhere in our memory banks and never forgotten, never, no matter how long ago it occurred. He comments on that from time to time with total awe, saying, "I wish we knew how to access all those memories, cause they're all there. I just wish we knew how to access them." Inevitably, he'd then follow up with his familiar closing, "The mind is bad. The human mind is so bad." Lambert has truly been fascinated with the human mind nearly his entire life.

If my brothers and I **are** genetically inclined to have a science orientation, we inherited our "science gene" from our father. Our father, who worked as a United States postman and retired after thirty-five years of federal service (two years in Normandy, France during WWII, and thirty-three years in the U.S. Post Office), loved science.

My Father, Lemar Louis Joichin, Sr.

In one of the talks we had when I was a young adult, I asked my father what, as a little boy, he had dreamed of being as an adult. He told me he had always wanted to be a doctor. My father was an extremely intelligent man, and I'm sure that had the circumstances of his life been different (i.e., had he either been born to an African American family of some means, or had he not had the serious barrier of racism to overcome in the 1940s and early '50s) he would most certainly have pursued a medical career. I realized at that moment that my father's interest in medicine was why, for as long as I can remember, he had two giant green medical books under his bed that he pulled out and read from time to time.

Interestingly, my father never talked to Lemar Jr., Lambert and me about either science or his childhood ambition to be a doctor, so, we definitely didn't get our science orientation through conversations with our father. I do believe it was much more his nature, i.e., his genes than his nurturing that impacted the three of us so profoundly.

My younger sister Lorna was my parents' wonderful mid-life surprise. When she was born, Lemar Jr. was nineteen, Lambert was fifteen, and I was almost nine. Lorna didn't seem to have in her childhood the interest in science that Lemar Jr., Lambert and I had in ours. She may not have gotten my father's "science gene." Perhaps she inherited more of our mother's orientation, who to my knowledge, didn't have any particular interest in science. That may well be why she has more of our mother's spiritual orientation than either of my brothers or me.[101]

101 Genetic research indicates that our tendency toward religion and spirituality, in addition to being very strongly influenced by environment, is also influenced by genetics. Perhaps the most well-known treatise on the subject is molecular geneticist Dr. Dean Hamer's work, *The God Gene: How Faith is Hardwired into Our Genes.* https://www.nature.com/articles/ng1204-1241#:~:text=It%20might%20be%20that%20some,able%20to%20tease%20them%20out.

Lorna, my best friend
Gay and me - 1964

Lorna's High School
Graduation - 1980

Being the serious little science geek that I was, I started every Saturday morning, without fail, with Mr. Wizard, https://www.youtube.com/watch?v=j_RJtkKGw4c a popular kids' science show of the 1950s and 60s.

I enjoyed the science-based television shows of my childhood—National Geographic Society specials, The Undersea World of Jacques Cousteau, and Mutual of Omaha's Wild Kingdom—and often watched them with my father who unfailingly had the day and time on which they aired circled in the current week's *TV Guide*. Documentaries about space and space travel and movies and television shows about space and time travel, however, were my absolute favorites.

Not surprisingly, I was a total science fiction fan as well. Although they sometimes scared me to death, I rarely missed an episode of Rod Serling's "The Twilight Zone" and the American Broadcasting Corporation's "The Outer Limits." When it aired in 1966, however, "Star Trek: The Original Series" immediately became my all-time science fiction crown jewel of television. I was 13 and a freshman in high school.

The 1950's and 60's science fiction films including, "The Day the Earth Stood Still", (https://www.youtube.com/watch?v=IN-wC0Pfe5G4), "Journey to the Center of the Earth" (https://www.youtube.com/watch?v=_7WHpfhc_2o), "The Invisible Man" (https://www.youtube.com/watch?v=5o-UUIrdIcY), "Fantastic Voyage" https://en.wikipedia.org/wiki/Fantastic_Voyage, and "The Nutty Professor" http://www.dailymotion.com/video/x32gl0r. totally seized my imagination. "The Day the Earth Stood Still" left me wondering whether there really were intelligent peaceful civilizations on other planets that were aware of what I thought of as our infantile human violence. "Journey to the Center of the Earth" left me enthralled by the thought that there could be an entire prehistoric world complete with an ocean and giant plants deep within the Earth. Total fascination with the concept, indeed with the possibility of invisibility, was my obsession after seeing "The Invisible Man." "Fantastic Voyage" had my young mind spinning with thoughts of the possibility of changing the size of people and objects, and indeed making them small enough to be injected into a human body.[102] I saw all of those movies on television. My mother took me to the movie theater, however, to see "The Nutty Professor" when I was ten. We saw it at the Circle, one of New Orleans' segregated movie theaters, in which we sat up in the Colored balcony. Jerry Lewis' amazing adventures as absent-minded professor Dr. Julius Kelp began my fascination with what might be possible to do in a chemistry lab filled with various sizes and shapes of test tubes all bubbling to the brim with both scalding hot and freezing cold bright orange, purple, green yellow, red, blue, gold and clear liquids. I thought about the cures to diseases that might be possible in such a lab and about what chemical concoction might be able to make human beings smarter. I even thought about myself, one day finding the fountain of youth in a chemistry lab!

102 While the movie's plot focused on only the miniaturization of humans and objects, it left me also curious about the possibility of maximizing the size of people and things as well. I imagined a world of giants!

After seeing the movie, one of my favorite games was playing "Chemistry Lab." I'd stand in front of the bathroom mirror wearing my white sweater, pretending that it was a lab coat. Then using water glasses for test tubes, I'd mix lotion, toothpaste, mouthwash, my mother's Noxzema, and whatever else was available in the bathroom, making believe I was a chemist in search of the fountain of youth. I don't have a clue why the fountain of youth was my holy grail, but for whatever reason, that was my fantasy. For Christmas that year, I asked for a chemistry set, and when I woke up on Christmas morning, I ran to the Christmas tree and found my brand-new Gilbert chemistry set. I was ecstatic! I expected that it would be in a cardboard box like other toys, so when I saw its shiny tin case, complete with a handle, I was over the moon with excitement!

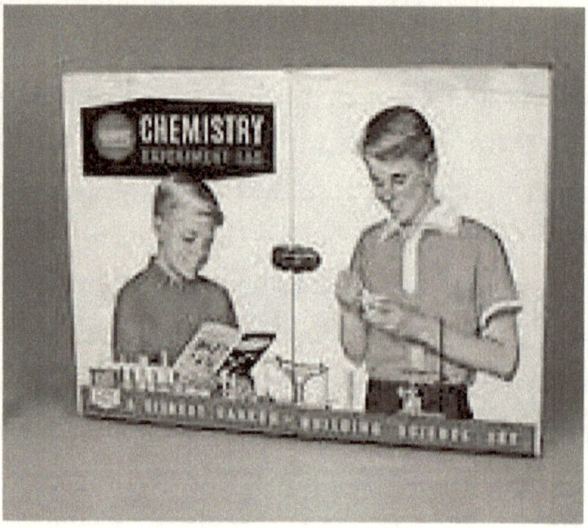

My 1964 Gilbert Chemistry Set[103]

After opening the set, I couldn't wait to start playing with its test tubes with their metal stands, magnifying glass, small cardboard boxes of red and blue litmus paper, steel wire, and clear,

103 As was the case with my chemistry set, all of the kids whose pictures appeared on all of my childhood toys were white, and because I was attracted to toys that could be played by both girls and boys (among others, my marionette puppet show, my Crazy Clock and other board games, Slinky, Etch-A-Sketch, Silly Putty, Give-A-Show Projector, viewfinder, bicycle, pogo stick, and skates) and had no interest in "girls' toys" (dolls, doll houses, tea sets, miniature vacuum cleaners, toy make-up, manicure, and hair kits, etc.) they were also often not only white kids, but boys as well. I am deeply thankful that despite that fact, I always thought, as a child, that when I grew up, I could be anything that I wanted to be. My mother and grandmother's love and the example of my mother's strength were wholly responsible for the healthy, balanced self-confidence I developed early in my life.

square glass jars of chemicals. As I played with my chemistry set for hours at a time, I imagined that I was a chemist, working in a lab on some immensely important experiment that was going to help all of humanity in some profound, history-making way. The following summer, my brother Lambert and I had an accident with the set in the kitchen. I remember very little about it, only that it involved test tubes, a few chemicals, the kitchen stove, a loud "Pow" sound, and then lots of black smoke that stuck to a large section of the kitchen ceiling. My father was furious. The day of the accident was the last day I ever saw my chemistry set. I suspect that my father had something to do with its disappearance.

As a child, I lived everyday with the mysteries that mesmerized me and consumed my inner life. They were at the very core of my interior. It feels to me on a very deep level that I was simply born with my questions about the nature of reality. I simply don't remember a time before my curiosity. I was only about seven years old when in response to my Sunday School lessons about living forever without end in heaven, I began wondering about the nature of eternity as my first mystery. I thought, "How is it possible to live forever, and ever, and ever?! Ok, so you have a day, then you go to sleep, then you have another day, then you go to sleep, then you have another day…then another one, then another one, then another one, and that **never** ends?! **Ever**?!" I remember, as a child, finding the thought of it actually disturbing. I now wonder why.

My childhood and teenage curiosity about The Mysteries was so profound that it was at times both intellectually and emotionally uncomfortable. Among my most persistent thoughts were, "We don't know how we started or even where we are in space because we don't know whether the universe ends at some point, or goes on and on forever." I'd then always respond with the same series of thoughts: "I **really** want to know this. Doesn't everybody?! I have to know this. How can we human beings live in the midst of such incredible mystery and not be haunted by it? Why isn't everybody talking about this?!" "How" I wondered, "can we not be spending the majority of our time and intelligence searching for the answers to the complete mysteries in which we all live every single day of our lives—Where did this universe come from, where did **we** come from, and where are we? How can those questions not be our total human focus?"

It was because I thought that I'd find the answers to The Mysteries through science that I absolutely loved it and wanted to be a scientist when I grew up. As I matured, however, there came a point at which I realized that ultimately science was incapable of giving me the answers to The Mysteries for which I searched insatiably. Specifically, once I learned in college, the Big Bang Theory of how the universe began—incredibly, that the entire universe started from a simple singularity, a single very tiny speck that exploded approximately 13.7 billion years ago and spewed out all of the pulsars, quasars, galaxies, solar systems, dark matter, and every other single thing that exists in the known universe—I knew beyond question, that science would never be able to answer the following very simple question I wondered about constantly, "Ok, the universe started from a single speck of something, but where did that little speck come from? Where...did...it...come...from?" That, more than any other, was my question. It haunted me. I wondered, "How did that speck get there? How did it come from nothing?" But two more questions about our Big Bang origin also bothered me tremendously...First, "What **was** that spec? What was it made of?" and secondly, "How could the entire universe have possibly begun from a tiny speck?" I knew that science would **never** be able to answer those questions. As a young teen, I felt helpless, both not knowing the answers to my questions, i.e., not knowing how the universe began, and also not knowing how any human being could possibly find the answers. Intuitively, I felt that

I had to go deeper, deeper than anyplace science could take me. I had no idea, however, what that deeper place could possibly be.

Fortunately, several years later, I found that very place: the study of Philosophy. I eagerly dove right into it as an undergraduate, and to my father's initial utter disappointment, majored in it with the intention of ultimately becoming a university Professor of Philosophy.[104]

Philosophy, to my mind, was both the broadest and the deepest of all intellectual disciplines, and thus the only one that was potentially capable of providing the answers to The Mysteries. It was, therefore, the only one I could even consider pursuing. It raised and theorized about precisely the kinds of questions that I so acutely felt it was my life's mission to have answered, many of which, to my surprise, even my insatiable curiosity had never formulated, e.g., "What is the nature of consciousness?," and "What is beauty?," among many others. I remember thinking in a number of my classes, "Of course that's a question. Why didn't it ever occur to me? Why haven't I ever wondered about that?"

In addition to both the breadth and the depth of its inquiry, I was thrilled that my study of Philosophy was also training my mind by, among other things, requiring me to study Logic. As a Philosophy major, I was being trained to think critically and analytically. In my logic course, I learned about the 13 logical fallacies in thinking and speaking. I learned how to do critical analysis; I learned, in essence, how to think. Studying Philosophy, I thought, was making me smarter. I loved it, and eagerly looked forward to my adult life as a Professor of Philosophy.[105]

104 My father was a very intelligent man, but was not a college graduate. He was a freshman at Southern University in Baton Rouge Louisiana when he was drafted to serve in the Army during World War II. He wanted me to major in either elementary or secondary education and become a teacher. In my father's world, raising a daughter to grow up and become a teacher was a parent's ultimate pride. I explained to my father that I intended to get my Ph.D. in Philosophy, and was going to be a teacher, but that instead of teaching elementary, junior or senior high school, I was going to teach at the university level and be a college professor. I went on to remind him of something he knew well from his college days, i.e., that at that level, rather than being called "Ms. Joichin," my students would refer to me as "Dr. Joichin." Needless to say, my dad was thrilled by that possibility, surpassing as it did, his wildest imaginings for me. From that time on, my father was very supportive of my Philosophy studies.

105 Much later on, I learned about other ways of thinking and learning, other ways of

About three quarters of the way through my undergraduate studies, however, I realized that while Philosophy exposed me to many deep questions about the nature of reality and fascinating analyses of them, it was utterly incapable of answering those questions. I came to the realization that while Philosophy, unlike any other discipline, raised many "ultimate" questions, it, like science, actually had no answers to those questions. None. It was totally unable to **solve** The Mysteries. Thus, before graduating, I arrived at the realization that as with science, Philosophy would also in due course, leave me with no answers to my questions, no insight into The Mysteries. I understood once again, that I had to go deeper still, deeper than the deepest depths of my first voyage into science, and deeper than those of my second voyage into Philosophy.

Fortunately, the very last Philosophy course I took before graduating became the portal to my next and last voyage. That course was "World Religions." It was in essence, a survey of all of the world's great religious traditions. It was during that course that I was introduced to Eastern Religions with their emphasis on a concept of which up to that point, I had been utterly unaware, the concept of not **knowing** Ultimate Truth but indeed **experiencing** it. It was then that in search of answers to The Mysteries, I began my third and final voyage—my journey down the dual path of Religion and Spirituality.

Lebanese-American writer and poet Kahlil Gibran's incisive observation concerning science, philosophy, and spirituality perfectly describes my spiritual journey. Gibran said:

> There is a desire deep within the soul which drives man from the seen to the unseen, to philosophy and to the divine.

"knowing" that are quite distinct from the Western logical, analytical method. I learned about intuitive knowledge and about seeing systems wholistically, which are more common African and Eastern ways of thinking, learning and knowing. Over time, I grew into a deep appreciation of those methods, for they can result in not only understanding. They can, indeed, lead to wisdom.

I think of "going from the seen to the unseen" as the scientific method since using that method in our attempt to understand the "seen" universe (i.e., the material universe that we perceive and experience in our everyday lives) physicists discovered that the very foundation of the "seen" universe is an entirely unseen universe – a microscopic universe of atoms protons, neutrons, electrons, and even smaller entities. Thus, Gibran's thought is a perfect description of my journey from science to philosophy to the Divine.

"My Spiritual Journey: A Lifelong Odyssey...A Pilgrim's Path," is the story of how I responded to that deep desire within me, that desire that was so compelling that it was impossible for me to ignore. As you will see as you travel with me along my spiritual journey, it is the story of the little girl whose early love of science turned out to be the precursor of a life-long spiritual quest. It is the story of my spiritual journey, the source of which, using Gibran's words, was a desire deep within my soul that drove me from the seen to the unseen, i.e., from science to Philosophy, and from Philosophy to The Divine. The story of that, my ultimate quest, begins now.

CHAPTER ONE

MY EARLY CHILDHOOD AND MY LOVE OF SCIENCE

THE THREE MAJOR MYSTERIES

During the earliest years of my childhood, I was plagued by what I refer to as my three Major Mysteries.

By the time I was seven, the concept of eternity had become the first. I went to Sunday School every Sunday at Bethany and learned in my third grade Sunday School class that after we die, we go to heaven and live forever. Not long after I heard that concept, it began to haunt me. I remember playing alone on the front lawn of my house, and as I did so, thinking, "So after you die, you wake up in heaven, and at the end of the day you go to sleep, and then the next day, you wake up and then go to sleep and then the next day, and then the next day, then the next day…and that never ends? Never? I tried to imagine it, but was, of course, utterly unable to do so.

While I was entirely captured by the idea of living forever, interestingly enough, I remember also feeling actually troubled by it. Indeed, for a reason I am unable to articulate, I found it frightening. I am today fascinated by my childhood fear of the thought of living literally forever and even now cannot explain it. But much more than my fear of the notion of eternity, I remember my curiosity about it. I asked my mother, my Sunday School teacher and, when I was alone, I asked myself, "How can we live forever and ever? How can time never end?" I was totally consumed by the question. The answers I received, that some things are a mystery we can understand only when we're in heaven or that it is God's will and therefore a mystery we can't understand, were just not satisfying. They were not good enough explanations for me.

Infinity was the next Major Mystery. I'm not sure just how old I was when I was introduced to the idea of infinity, the concept that the universe might go on and on in space forever and ever without end, but it was probably in my fourth, fifth or sixth grade science class when I was eight, nine or ten. I also don't remember whether I was immediately fascinated by the concept, or whether my fascination developed over time. The one thing I do know for certain is that as with eternity, the concept of eternal, i.e., never ending time, I was also absolutely intrigued by infinity, the concept of eternal, never-ending space. I wondered about whether the universe ends at some point far, far away, leaving only empty space beyond its borders. Later, as an adolescent, I thought that there might not even **be** space beyond the borders of the universe. I thought that if that were the case, we, the universe, was surrounded by pure nothingness...but then, my young mind wondered, "Pure nothingness? Not even space? What is that? What would pure nothingness **be**?" At first, I imagined it as total blackness. Then I thought, "Well wait. Maybe it's total and utter whiteness."

But then my next thought was, "But black and white are both colors. They're things, they're colors, so even total blackness or total whiteness are impossible because they exist on the light spectrum (I thought). So what could absolute nothingness be?" Then, utterly unable to fathom it, and thinking that pure nothingness is an utter impossibility, I thought, "Well, maybe the universe does go on forever and ever and ever and doesn't have boundaries... maybe it doesn't ever end!" But of course my thought in the very next second was, "But how can **that** be? How can **anything** go on and on and on forever without end? The universe either **has** an end or it doesn't," I thought. Both possibilities, i.e., that the universe is finite and surrounded by mysterious nothingness and that it is infinite, going on without end, were sources of equal torment for me.

As a kid I often looked up at the sky as I thought about this mystery. I found the daytime sky stunningly beautiful. I'd lie on my back in my backyard, knees up, with both hands behind my head, staring at the beautiful, white clouds against the deep blue sky, seeing all manner of both animals and objects in them. It was one of my all-time favorite ways to spend time alone. More than a half-century later, I'm still an enthralled watcher of daytime skies, of the magnificent swoops and swirls of cirrus clouds, of the remarkable puffiness, infinite shapes, and utter grandeur of cumulus clouds, of rainbows, of amazing lightning, of orange sunrises and purple sunsets.

But it was the night sky that completely captivated me. I wasn't allowed to be outside of the house by myself at night, but whenever I was out at night, usually with my mother returning home from either shopping or my grandmother's or returning home from one of my aunt's or my uncle's house, between getting out of the car and going into the house, if I was awake enough, I often looked up at the sky. Because we lived in a residential area that was quite a distance from downtown, and just blocks away from Lake Pontchartrain, on which, of course, there were no lights, light pollution was minimal, rendering a view of a very dark night sky in which hundreds of billions of stars looked like tiny shimmering diamonds. I wondered constantly whether there were any intelligent beings up there looking up at **their** night sky wondering if **we** were here. I thought surely that in the vastness of our grand universe, we simply could not be the only life. I was sure that we could be and indeed were not alone. I thought, "I'll bet the people on other planets are a lot smarter than we are. They're probably so much more advanced than us that they have all kinds of inventions we don't have. Maybe they even have powers that we can't even imagine. Maybe they can do time travel. And I'll bet they don't discriminate against each other either. I'll bet they don't have segregation. Everybody's equal on their planet. And I'll bet they don't have poverty or war either. I'll bet they live in peace. If they came here and saw us living with segregation and believing that people are better or not as good as other people just because of their color, if they saw all the poor people on our planet, if they saw us fighting with each other, having wars, they'd think we were barbarians." I thought that surely, if they were advanced enough, they had matured beyond racism, poverty, and war, the three social ills of which I was aware as a child. The thought of life, intelligent, advanced life on other planets, fascinated me. I wanted life on our planet to be advanced in all of those ways.

Not surprisingly, after wanting to be "a scientist" when I was very young, after two to three years of fantasizing about that generic career in science, being an astronomer became my first specific childhood science career ambition. I wanted to know everything about the entire universe.

I wished that I could see at least as far into the universe as our technology would allow. I remember wondering, "If the universe **is** finite, where in the universe are **we**?" I wondered if we were in its northwest quadrant, or maybe at the tip of its southeastern corner. Maybe we were in its northeastern or southwestern section, or maybe we were right in the very middle of it. I wanted to know. I thought that I'd learn about this in school when I got older, and I'd therefore know much more about this in just a few years. I couldn't wait!

I wanted to see beyond the confines of Earth. I wanted to see what was "out there." I thought that if I had a telescope, I'd be able to see at least Mars and Venus up close, and while I was excited about that, what I really wanted was to see beyond our solar system. I wanted to see other solar systems and other galaxies. I wanted to see as far and as much as was humanly possible. I was absolutely captivated by the thought that the universe might be filled with billions and billions of other planets on which advanced civilizations lived, civilizations that might have been centuries and perhaps even thousands of years ahead of the human race not only in technology, but much more importantly, and of much more interest to me, in wisdom. As a kid, I thought that if I had a telescope, maybe, just maybe, I might see one of their spacecrafts flying around out there!

Then, on a warm, sunny, late summer Sunday afternoon in 1965 on my twelfth birthday, I walked into the house to find a long, elegantly wrapped, long, rectangular box on the dining room table with a beautiful bow and birthday card attached. As I suspected, it was from my mother, another one of her many surprises that she loved giving me. As I eagerly tore off the gift wrapping, I wondered from the size and shape of the box whether it was the telescope that I'd desperately wanted for some time. It was...I was ecstatic! My mother loved surprising me with gifts and, for me, this was a big one!

As it turns out, my 1965 Jason telescope was powerful enough to see the craters on the moon. I stared at those craters through the lens of that telescope for several years, over and over and over again. It lives on in my office to this day.

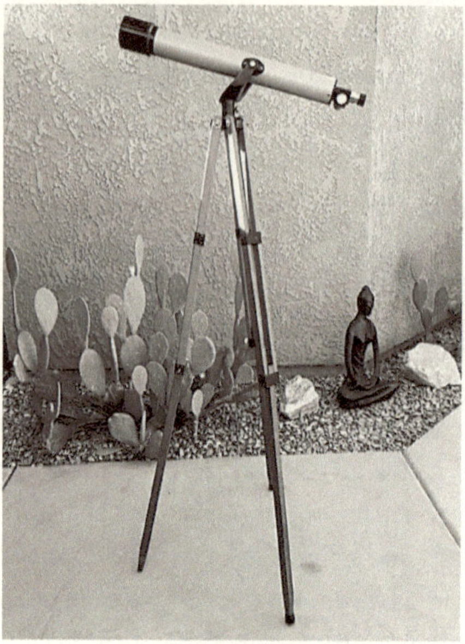

My 1965 Jason Telescope

I read the Astronomy Section of the Colliers and World Book encyclopedias that we had at home, and even though I understood very little of what I read, I was fascinated by what I did understand. I asked my mother to buy me an Astronomy book. She did, of course, buy several Astronomy books for kids. My first was the Whitman World Library's 1965 edition of the book, *Astronomy.* I was twelve when I got it and I devoured its chapters, "The Study of Space," "The Beginning of Matter," "The Sky," "Our Galaxy," "The Milky Way," "The Solar System," "The Asteroids, Meteors and Comets," "The Frontiers of Astronomy" and "The Coming Conquest." As I read, I got lost in the book's many colorful illustrations. *Astronomy* still today remains a treasured part of my library.[106]

106 On page 46 of the book, in a section that explained the calendars of ancient peoples, the Egyptians are depicted with dark brown skin. It was the first time I had ever seen people with brown skin represented as figures of historical significance. I was twelve. I was astounded by that picture. After seeing it, I remember thinking, "Wow. I wonder what else we've done in history." I was also terribly confused because I'd previously and consistently seen pictures of the ancient Egyptians in which they had been portrayed only as white. Additionally, until well into adulthood, every other pictorial portrayal of the ancient Egyptians that I saw, also depicted them as white. It was through my adult research of the ancient Nile Valley Civilization

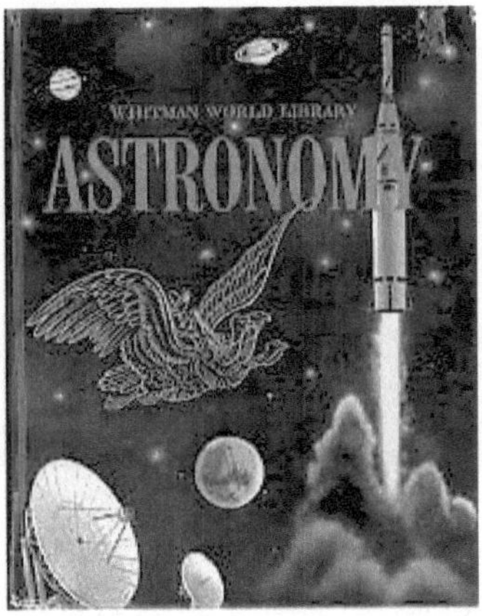

My First Astronomy Book

The childhood Astronomy book I remember most clearly, however, is the Scholastic Book Services' 1967 *Environments Out There*, by Isaac Asimov. I was thirteen when I read it, and its chapters, "The Inside Planets," "Mars After Mariner," "Mysterious Asteroids," "The Giant Planets," "Moons of the Giants," "The Search for Other Planets," and "At Home in Space," utterly enthralled me. To this day, some fifty-six years later, I also still have *Environments Out There* in my personal library. I absolutely lost myself in it and in all of my Astronomy books.

(reading the work of Dr. John Henry Clark and Dr. Martin Bernal, among others) that I learned that the ancient Egyptians were neither white nor olive-skinned people, but were indeed (as they represented themselves on their pyramids) dark-skinned African people. In *On Race and Racism: Humanity's Bottom Line*, I discuss the psychological effect on American children of color, of being taught both World History and American History that includes almost no mention of the contributions made by people of their race to either the world or to the United States. It often results in feelings of inferiority and the resulting low self-esteem and self-hatred that usually accompany them. "Internalized oppression" is the term that is frequently used to describe that psychological state.

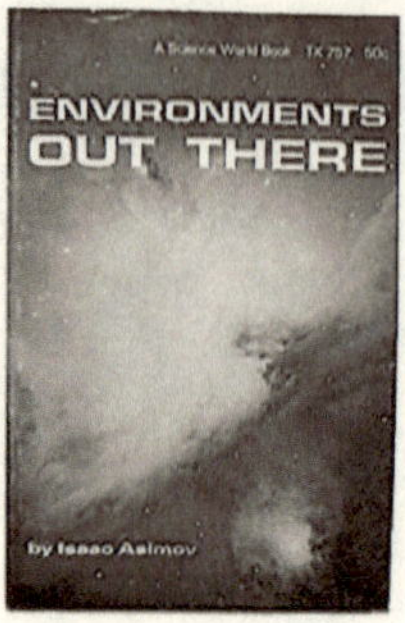

The origin of the universe, and ultimately the origin of God, became my third Major Mystery. I don't know how old I was when I began to ponder it, but certainly since I was in junior high school, I would have been either eleven or twelve.

Regarding how the universe began, as with the question of whether the universe was finite or infinite, there were only two possibilities. My thinking was, "The universe either **was** created or it was **not** created. That's it. Those are the only two possibilities."

I had been taught in Sunday School that the universe indeed **was** created, and that it had been created by God. Initially, I accepted that as true, and never questioned it. There came a time, however, at which I thought, "Ok, the universe came from God. But then where did **God** come from? Who created **God**? Another creator? Then who created **God's** creator? And then who created **that** creator's creator, and so on." As I reached adolescence, the answer to the question that I had been given of how the universe began, that it had been created by God, and that as God, He is supreme and eternal, and therefore does not **need** a creator, just didn't work for me anymore. Since, as I was taught, the **universe** had to have had a creator, then why didn't **God** have to have a creator too? If it didn't make sense for the **universe** to exist without ever having **come** into existence, how does it make sense that **God** exists without ever having **come** into existence?

I found the only **other** possibility, i.e., that the universe was not created, but simply always has been, just as troubling. "How could **that** be?" I wondered. "How can something that exists now, never, at any point, have **come** into existence? How could **anything** just always have been without ever having come into being? Ridiculous!", I thought. Neither of the only two possible explanations of the universe's existence, i.e., that it was or that it was not created, was rational. Neither made any sense to me. So, the origin of the universe, the very fact that there **is** a universe, was for me, the source of great mystery during my early years. My young mind spun in a quandary, and in time, that question, "What is the origin of the universe?, more than any other, became **the** question that plagued me, far surpassing my captivation with both eternity and infinity. For me, my **third** Major Mystery was the **ultimate** mystery.

On a deep intuitive level, despite the fact that God's origin was a total enigma to me that gave me no rest, I nonetheless sincerely believed in God, and that God was the creator of the universe. I had been taught to believe in God, it's true. My mother was a person of deep faith and her faith formed the foundation of her life, so I can never know how much I was influenced by my mother's faith, but what I do know is that in addition to being taught to believe in God, I also had what was an extremely strong intuitive feeling that God existed. My complete childhood scientific orientation notwithstanding, I have felt a very deep and abiding connection to The Divine since I was a very young child, so I never doubted that God did indeed create the universe. I just yearned to understand God, to understand how it was that God could have no beginning. I was burning to know.

THE THREE MINOR MYSTERIES

The Three Major Mysteries of eternity, infinity, and the origin of the universe were far from the only ones that captivated me as a child. Three of what I think of as minor and, for that reason, less important mysteries, but mysteries nonetheless, also plagued me. They were the concepts of the fourth dimension, a parallel universe, and time travel.

First was the idea of a fourth dimension. As a kid, I knew that we lived in three dimensions, the dimensions of length, width, and depth, all of which I understood. I don't remember how I was introduced to the concept of a fourth dimension, and I definitely didn't know what the fourth dimension was. I do remember, however, that that introduction included a hypothetical about a train in the fourth dimension passing through a room in our three-dimensional reality without our even being aware of it. The possibility that a train in another dimension could be passing right through my room, and maybe even right through me, while I was sitting in my room at my desk doing my homework or lying on my bed reading captivated me. I knew that the people on the train in that dimension had absolutely no idea they were passing through my room, but thought that if I tried hard enough—if I used extrasensory perception, or "ESP," as it was called at the time, and said with a lot of concentration (in the typical eerie, slow, monotonic hypnotist's voice that was popular in movies and television shows of that era), "You are passing through another dimension. You are in another space. You are now passing through Lauren's room"—maybe, just maybe, somebody on that train might feel something and maybe I might in that very same moment, feel something too. I tried my experiment to telepathically connect with my fourth-dimension train-riding friends more times than I can remember, but to my utter disappointment, I never felt a thing.

Even though my telepathic experiment with my imaginary fourth-dimension friends never worked, I was nevertheless intrigued by the concept of mental telepathy, the possibility of both mind over matter and ESP. The board game, "Kreskin's ESP" that

I asked for and got for Christmas when I was fourteen was one of my all-time favorite toys.

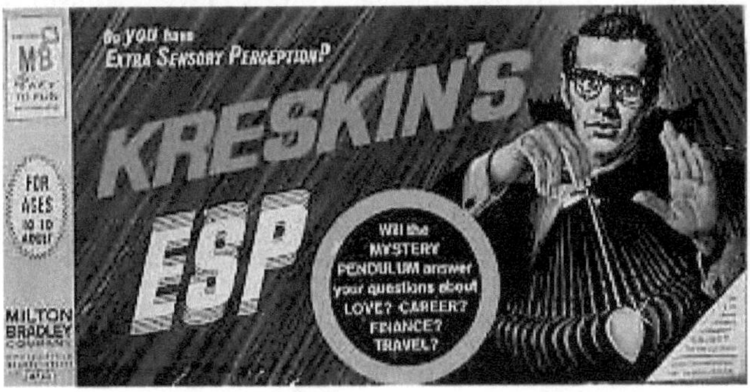

I deeply wondered about what the world of the fourth dimension was like. I wondered how we might experience the people of the fourth dimension who somehow managed to break through into our world.[107] I wondered if the world of the fourth dimension was more technologically advanced than ours. I wondered whether it was more socially advanced than we were. I truly wanted the ability to telepathically transport myself into another dimension. I wanted that kind of freedom—the freedom to roam the universe! [108]

The possibility of a parallel universe, one in which everything was for the most part, exactly the same as in our universe

107 Some years later, as a young adult, I read Edwin Abbott's book *Flatland*, Flatland - Wikipedia which describes how it would feel to people who lived in two dimensions, for one of us to break through into their world. It is my absolute favorite illustration of what it would be like for people who do not live in our three-dimensional world to experience us. Flatland is the story of an entirely flat world filled with inhabitants who are entirely two-dimensional, i.e., entirely flat. In the story, the two-dimensional Flatlanders experience only length and width. They are utterly unable to experience depth. The message of *Flatland* is demonstrated by the scenario in which someone from our three-dimensional world suddenly steps into Flatland. To the shock and amazement of the Flatlanders, it appears that the shoe of the three-dimensional person (of which they can see only the length and width of the sole) has appeared literally out of thin air. The message is that we may, in the future, discover the answers to phenomena that we currently experience as utterly impossible and mysterious. The original *Flatland* was an 1884 social satire of Victorian culture. What I read was a short, simplified rendition of it with no social satire. It was, of course, a purely fictionalized and utterly delightful consideration of the concept of dimensions.

108 We now know that in reality, we actually do live in four dimensions, and that the fourth dimension is time. To this day, however, I do not understand this concept at all, the concept that time is a dimension. Contemporary physicists have now informed us of the possibility of the existence of infinite dimensions. I don't even know how to begin thinking about such a thing.

except for a few minor details that were the exact opposite in our world, was my second minor mystery. The 1960 Twilight Zone episode, "Mirror Image" (https://www.youtube.com/watch?v=QSegeI5Qn6A&t=13s) was the first dramatization of a parallel universe that I remember. The episode of Star Trek's original series, "Mirror Mirror" (https://www.youtube.com/watch?v=8_rTTXCOpL8&t=8s) was the second.[109] The movie, "Journey to the Far Side of the Sun," https://www.youtube.com/watch?v=Zyv6n2TLWco which premiered a few years later in 1969, raised the possibility of a parallel planet on the other side of the Sun. I was intrigued by that thought, but knew that the astronomy upon which the movie was based—that there was a planet that was the mirror opposite of the Earth, which was invisible to us because it was on the other side of the Sun—was absolutely scientifically flawed.[110] Several years before that, however, when I was perhaps eight or nine, I remember thinking that what we see when we look into a mirror is really another universe. I have absolutely no idea why such a thing even occurred to me (maybe it was a storyline in one of the hundreds of comic books that I read), but I have a clear memory of standing many times in front of the bathroom mirror, making a really fast move trying to "fool" it. I thought that if that **is** another universe in the mirror, I could prove it by seeing a split-second lag between my movement and the movement of the kid in the mirror. I must've tried that move a hundred times, and was sorely disappointed when my experiment never succeeded.

In my young mind, I mistakenly entangled the concept of a parallel universe, which theoretically exists in other dimensions, with the concept of space, and thought that just maybe, the parallel universe I imagined was in space, out there somewhere far, far away. I regularly spent extended periods in my backyard lying on my back, looking up at the sky, absolutely lost in thought about the

109 Several other Star Trek series also featured episodes in which a parallel universe was present.

110 https://www.youtube.com/watch?v=8_rTTXCOpL8

possibility of a universe that was in some ways exactly like and, in other ways, exactly the opposite of ours. I wondered what things would be exactly the same in that universe and ours, and in what ways the two universes might be exact opposites. I wondered about the young Lauren in that universe, lying in **her** backyard, looking at **her** sky, wondering about **me**. Sometimes, I'd fall asleep in the grass, and my wonders became my dreams.

My third Minor Mystery was time travel. The idea that nothing can exceed the 186,000-mile-per-second speed of light, and that clocks begin to slow down as they approach that speed, sent my little brain spinning into orbit. My first thought, of course, was, "Well, why **can't** anything travel faster than light? I mean suppose, just suppose we were able to travel at 186,00**1** miles per second. What would happen then?" I don't remember how (perhaps it was from Mr. Wizard, the weekly kids' science show that I watched every Saturday morning without fail), but somehow, I learned that what would happen is that we'd begin to go backwards in time. "Go backwards in time?!" I thought. And if we **were** able to travel back to the past, I wondered, "Would we be able to change anything, any tiny little thing about it, and if so, would that change alter the future, i.e., our present?" Without knowing it, I'd stumbled upon two of Physics' most profound questions: Can time be traversed and, if so, can the timeline as we know it be altered? I had countless daydreams about time travel.

Interestingly, I was always going to the future in my daydreams about time travel, never to the past. In them, I was an adult, and was always making speeches to throngs of crowds, trying to help humankind understand that rather than spending our energy on things such as segregation, war and inventing better television sets and other machines, we should be spending our energy on trying to solve our human problems, problems such as racial prejudice and discrimination, problems such as how to end hunger, how to end war, how to cure disease, and how to educate the children of the world. In those daydreams, I was teaching the world that humankind **had** to grow up, that we had to resolve those problems, and that we had to do so for two reasons. First, it was the right thing to do. I learned that lesson from my mother, in my Sunday School classes, and from the sermons that our minister, Reverend Kennedy, delivered in church about the social justice responsibilities that resulted from our Christian faith. I felt strongly that discrimination was both immoral and immature, that war was both immoral and immature, and that it was absolutely wrong and indeed intolerable for any human being on this Earth to be hungry, thirsty and without a home, medical care and education. I believed that working non-stop to have every one of those needs met for every person with whom we share the planet, was above all else, humanity's first and overwhelming moral responsibility.

Second, I thought that since before doing anything else, we had a moral responsibility to stop human suffering, our continuing to not do so kept us from being able to focus on solving The Great Mysteries in which we all live, and that thought was simply intolerable to me.

I was a true geeky little kid, wondering about my three major mysteries, my three minor mysteries and what I refer to as the host of Miscellaneous Mysteries—among them, the possibility of intelligent, advanced life on other planets, whether mental telepathy really existed, and whether we will ever be able to achieve invisibility.[111] Although I had the social awkwardness that often accompanies geekiness, I simply cannot imagine being a kid without my curiosity. I wouldn't trade it for the world. I didn't know it at the time, but it was my connection, very early in life, to The Divine.

> I have a deep-rooted, intense feeling that there is a profound connection between science and spirituality, and that if one delves deeply enough into science, one will, by necessity, begin to touch the fringe of spirituality. I be-

111 The 1933 movie adaptation of H.G. Wells' novel, "The Invisible Man" The Invisible Man (1933) - YouTube that I saw as a child was what no doubt spurred my interest in the concept of invisibility.

lieve, indeed, that the two are flip sides of the same coin. In 1935, Albert Einstein wrote about the relationship between science and religion:

> "Everyone who is seriously involved in the pursuit of science becomes convinced that some spirit is manifested in the laws of the universe. One that is vastly superior to that of man. In this way the pursuit of science leads to a religious feeling of a special sort which is surely quite different from the religiosity of someone more naïve."

Further on in the letter, Einstein went on to make clear that the religious feeling to which he referred was not related to any traditional or mainstream religion. Specifically, he commented that,

> "The word of God is for me, nothing more than the expression and product of human weaknesses. The Bible is a collection of honorable, but still primitive legends, which are nevertheless pretty childish. No interpretation no matter how subtle, can for me, change this."

I do not condone the characterization of the stories in the Bible as childish. With the mind that Einstein had, however, I understand why he might have done so.

SUNDAY SCHOOL – MY INTRODUCTION TO RELIGION

Throughout my childhood, I attended Sunday School and later church service every Sunday without fail. My mother required it of my two older brothers and me. In many African American communities, that is exactly what is meant when you say you "grew up in church." I grew up in church.

What is often thought of as a black church is one filled with black people, all dressed up in their Sunday best, women in huge "church hats," with all the people enthusiastically responding to a vibrant, spirited gospel choir, female ushers in dresses that resembled nurse uniforms, male ushers wearing white gloves, and a minister delivering a fiery sermon all the while bouncing, singing and wiping his face with a "sweat rag." I have absolutely no doubt that growing up in that kind of church provided a spiritual foundation to millions of African American children that was both incredibly life sustaining and culturally affirming.

I grew up in a black church, Bethany Methodist Church.[112] Louisiana UMC | BETHANY New Orleans Louisiana (la-umc.org) Bethany, however, was a different kind of black church. Because Bethany was a Methodist church, we had no deacons, no female ushers in dresses that resembled nurse uniforms, no male ushers in white gloves, no testifying, no raising of arms, no waiving of handkerchiefs, no gospel music.[113] Bethany's congregation, while indeed dressed in its Sunday best, was quite reserved.

Bethany, one of two churches in Pontchartrain Park, was chartered in 1957 when I was four, two years after Pontchartrain Park opened. My mother was one of Bethany's twenty-three founding members, the lead soprano of its Sanctuary Choir, Chair of its Pastor-Parish Relations Committee, a member of its Building Committee and its Bi-Racial Dialogue Group. To say that my mother truly loved Bethany would be an understatement of mammoth proportions. My mother was totally committed to Bethany. It was **exceptionally** close to her heart. She had a profound and abiding religious faith. Indeed, my mother's deep-seated faith in

112 After the 1968 merger of the Methodist Church with the Evangelical United Brethren Church, the name of the Methodist Church was changed to the United Methodist Church, after which Bethany, of course, became Bethany United Methodist Church. In researching the history of the Methodist Church as an adult, I was surprised by that merger because I had always thought of the Methodist Church (especially in comparison to Catholicism, New Orleans' predominant religion) as enlightened, modern and liberal, anything but evangelical, which in my mind was synonymous with fundamentalist, or orthodox.

113 Even though I wasn't exposed to gospel music as a child, I've developed a keen appreciation of it as an adult. There's something no less than spiritually stirring about the unique harmony of twenty, thirty, forty, fifty or more strong female and male African American voices singing gospel music. I find the music of the Winans, Andre Crouch, and Kirk Franklin, among others, very moving. Gospel music, complete with the choir robes, the synchronized swaying, the dramatic stops and starts and more recently the drums and wind instruments that often characterize gospel choirs, now has an appeal to me that actually feels visceral. In listening to Negro Spirituals, I have also developed a deep emotional connection to them as well.

God was one of the pivotal foundations of her life. I'm sure that Gramzie, also a woman of deep faith, was her role model.

Bethany was filled with adults who were active in the community, and who were warm and loving toward us kids. It was also filled with lots of children who were my friends. I was happy and felt safe as a child growing up in Bethany Church. It provided me, as a child, with three of my childhood treasures – Saturday night kids' movies, summer day camp, and Sunday School.

Bethany's Saturday night kids movies was my mother's project. Throughout most of the time that I attended Bethany, the church was involved in a building fund campaign for the construction of a new sanctuary. My mother, a member of the Building Committee, in order to help raise money for the campaign, and also to give the neighborhood kids something to do on Saturday nights, showed kids' movies at the church. I went with her up to the movie rental store just off of Canal Street every Saturday morning to choose and rent the movie to be shown that night. Next, we'd go to the bank to get lots of change for the admission box. Finally, on Saturday afternoon, we'd go to Bethany to set up for the movie show—bring in the popcorn, popcorn bags, napkins, and sodas, set up the popcorn popper, set up the movie projector, load the movie and set up the chairs. My mom coordinated those kids' movie shows for no more than a year or two, but I **loved** those Saturday night kids' movies at Bethany.

As for summer day camp, when the school year ended, I looked forward every year with great anticipation to starting day camp at Bethany. It was the Pontchartrain Park Community Summer Day Camp that Bethany ran on the church grounds. Mrs. Jeanne Green, wife of the Choir Director, Mr. Eugene Green, was the Camp Director. I remember Mrs. Green as a really nice, soft-spoken woman. I liked Mrs. Green.

At camp, we played shuffleboard, Ping-Pong, softball and volleyball. We had daily exercise routines and relay races. We did a whole host of different kinds of arts and crafts, and whenever the torrential rain fell in the afternoon, which it often did during the hot New Orleans summers, we played password, dominoes, and a variety of board games. Checkers, Chinese checkers, and chess were my favorites. We also played charades, read stories, had stories read to us, and sang kids' songs. I loved it!

Every Monday morning, Reverend Kennedy's father, Mr. Edward Kennedy, Sr., drove the kids and camp counselors on an old school bus to Major Lanes, a bowling alley on Claiborne Avenue in the city's 7th ward, where as kids, we didn't actually bowl, but played at bowling. Since the earlier years of my attendance at Bethany's day camp were prior to the passage of the Civil Rights Act of 1964 that integrated all public accommodations, we had to go to one of the city's "colored" bowling alleys. The Mardi Gras Bowling Alley on Chef Menteur Highway in the Gentilly section of the city in which Pontchartrain Park was located was actually much closer. Major Lanes, however, was the closest "colored" bowling alley to us.

Every Tuesday morning, our field trip was to Lincoln Beach, the city's "colored" amusement park. Pontchartrain Beach was the city's other amusement park, and was much closer to us than Lincoln Beach, which was several miles away. Pontchartrain Beach, at that time, however, was "White Only." While Lincoln Beach had both swimming pools and rides (the Haunted House and Ferris Wheel were my favorites), we went to swim. I loved swimming in the Lincoln Beach pools!

I was both a highly curious and a highly sensitive kid. I felt things deeply. I was also fiercely competitive. Whatever the challenge—a spelling test at school, a relay race, a game of jacks, I wanted to win.[114] Whatever the nature of the competition, I felt as if I was competing against myself to do my best, and in my mind, winning verified that I had done my best. It made me feel

114 At the same time that I enjoyed my success, I also felt badly for the kid or kids who lost. I don't remember ever trying to console them, although I wish I had, but I do remember feeling badly for them.

successful. Even more than feeling successful, however, I wanted to make my mother proud of me—**always**, and I loved my mother so much that **nothing** was more rewarding to me than doing just that. I wanted to do my best at everything, whether it was in school, in Sunday School, at day camp,or in my piano lessons. I wanted to excel at whatever I did, at everything.[115] Needless to say, I brought that same spirit of competitiveness to my activities at Bethany's Day Camp.

One summer, I was named the camp's Outstanding Broad Jumper, for both girls and boys.

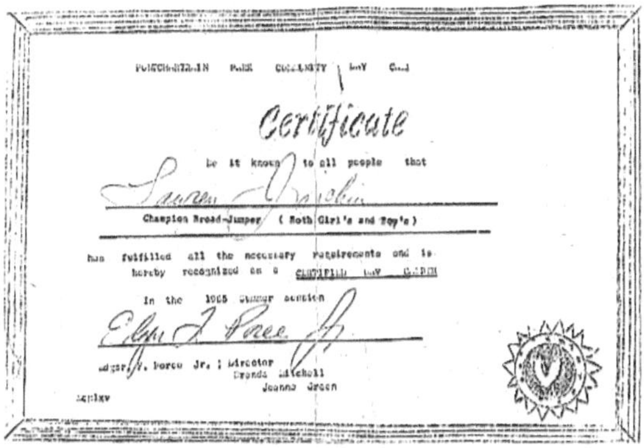
[illegible]

Certificate

be it known to all people that

Champion Broad-Jumper (Both Girl's and Boy's)

has fulfilled all the necessary requirements and is hereby recognized as a CERTIFIED DAY CAMPER

In the 1965 Summer session

Edgar F. Poree Jr., Director
Brenda Mitchell
Joanne Green

[illegible]

Pontchartrain Park Community Day Camp Certificate

During another summer, I was Captain of the Championship Shuffleboard Team.

115 There were many times, of course, during which I had done my best and not won, or not performed as well as I would have liked. I had to learn to manage my disappointment during those times, which was difficult for me. It helped, however, that my mother always told me that as long as I had done my best, she was extremely proud of me, whether or not I had won. Still, I felt disappointment in myself whenever I lost.

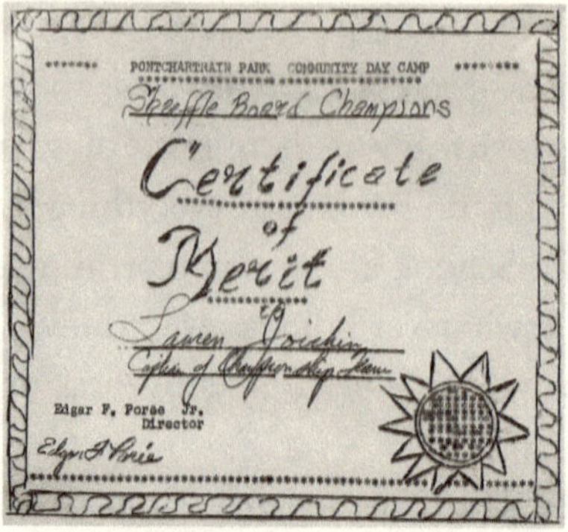
PONTCHARTRAIN PARK COMMUNITY DAY CAMP
Sheffle Board Champions
Certificate
of
Merit
Lauren Joichin
Captain of Championship Team
Edgar F. Poree Jr.
Director

Day Camp Certificate

At the end of my last summer at Day Camp when I was twelve, I was named "Most Outstanding Girl Day Camper."

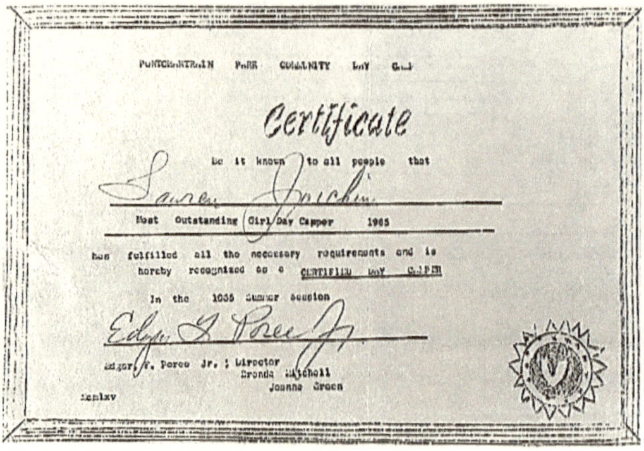
Certificate
be it known to all people that
Lauren Joichin
Most Outstanding Girl Day Camper 1965
has fulfilled all the necessary requirements and is hereby recognized as a
In the summer session
Edgar F. Poree Jr.
Edgar F. Poree Jr. ; Director
Joanne Green

Day Camp Certificate

As for my third "Bethany treasure," Sunday School, my first few years at Bethany were, of course, as a very young Sunday School student. Sunday School teachers read children's Bible stories to us, taught, and sang children's hymns with us, and engaged us in child-level discussions of religious themes. I was fascinated by both the Bible stories we learned and the lessons behind them, among them, Jonah and the Whale, Noah and the Arc, and, of course, David and Goliath. Those stories intrigued me every single bit as much as all of the non-Biblical children's stories that I read in the Collier's Junior Classics.[116]

I really loved Sunday School. It was fun, and the lessons were intriguing. I even remember the words to the dismissal hymn that we sang every Sunday when Sunday School ended, "Lord Dismiss Us with Thy Blessing". YouTube: "Lord Dismiss Us with Thy Blessing"

I enjoyed learning in Sunday School, but pretty early on, I also had questions about some of what I was learning. One of the first lessons we were taught in Sunday School was that God was a Trinity; God the Father, God the Son, and God the Holy Ghost. At Bethany, however (as is true of every other Christian church I have ever experienced) it was Jesus, His life and teachings that were the focus of what we were taught. I was about nine or ten when I began asking questions about that. I remember distinctly that my very first question was, "Why do we talk so much about Jesus? God the Father is the real God, the God that created the universe, all the stars, all the galaxies, all the planets, all the comets, and all the meteors. He created everything! He even created Jesus.[117] Jesus is just the Son of God. Why do we talk so much more about Him and hardly ever mention God the Father?[118]

116 The Bible stories that I was learning as a child all sounded fantastical to me, but we were taught that miracles happened during Biblical times, and that for that reason, the events of the stories could not be explained in scientific terms. I accepted that explanation.

117 I have not referred to The Creator in human, gendered terms in many years. I do so here in order to reflect the thoughts that I had been taught and learned about The Creator as a child.

118 While beginning in early childhood, I had many "mystery", i.e. **science** questions, my question about why Jesus received so much attention, and God the Father received so little, was my first **religious** question. Sometime later, I began wondering how God could be both three Gods but also, at the same time, only one. I'm curious about why that question didn't occur to me immediately upon learning about the concept of The Trinity. I just may have been too young at the time to formulate that particular question.

It's not fair that God the Father is kind of ignored." I remember very clearly that as a child, I liked Jesus, and sorely wished that the world would follow His fundamental teaching of love, but on some deep internal level, for a reason that I cannot explain, I felt closer to God, the Creator of the Universe. I felt a connection to God.[119]

Because I was uncomfortable with what felt to me to be an inordinate amount of attention given to Jesus over and above God the Father, as an adolescent, when I knelt next to my bed to say my bedtime prayers, I began saying one prayer to each. Also, not wanting to deprive the third personality of the Trinity, the Holy Ghost, I prayed a prayer to It as well. To God the Father I prayed the Lord's Prayer. In my adolescent mind, I knew that it was a

---

119 I don't know why my fervent childhood science orientation had absolutely no impact, even when I was a teen, on my strong faith in a loving, divine, personal Creator, but it did not. I now realize, in retrospect, that I was born a complete combination of my parents - of my mother, a devoutly religious and, as a matter of conscience, staunchly liberal Christian, and of my father, a totally science-oriented, avowed agnostic. Specifically, I suspect that I have my father's brain wired for curiosity and science, and my mother's heart, with its deep faith in The Creator, i.e., her "God Spot."

There is growing scientific evidence that brain circuitry, i.e., how our brains are wired, is indeed an inheritable trait. As brain circuitry is a biological characteristic, its inheritability is not surprising. Of course, determining the source of one's religious belief raises the issue of whether it is the result of nurture or nature. Specifically, it is very difficult to determine if a religious person who was raised in a religious household is religious because they were raised to be religious, or if regardless of upbringing, that person, due to the inherited wiring of their brain, would have been religious irrespective of their upbringing. It is a fascinating question.

The relationship between the anatomy of the human brain and a belief in God, and indeed whether such a relationship exists, is the fascinating focus of the field of Neurotheology, the neuroscience of religion. "It is the study of correlations of neural phenomena with subjective experiences of spirituality to explain these phenomena. This contrasts with the psychology of religion, which studies mental rather than neural states "of religion". Neurotheology: The relationship between brain and religion—PMC (nih.gov), and
The Believing Brain: Evolution, Neuroscience, and the Spiritual Instinct—YouTube

Additionally, scientific evidence exists that suggests that particular regions of the brain affect spiritual/religious faith. In *The Independent's* article, "*Belief and the Brain's God Spot,*" Belief and the brain's 'God spot' | The Independent | The Independen the following is reported:

A belief in God is deeply embedded in the human brain which is programmed for religious experiences;

There is not just one but several areas of the brain that form the biological foundations of religious belief (The term, "God Spot" has no literal corollary in that neurotheologists do not believe that any one scientific spot of the brain either determines or controls spiritual/religious networks); and,

Specific components of religious belief are mediated by well-known brain networks.

prayer to God the Father and not to Jesus because of its beginning words, "Our Father who art in heaven." To Jesus, I prayed the 23rd Psalm. Because of its beginning, "The Lord is My Shepherd," I was clear that it was a prayer to Jesus. Because Jesus was often referred to as our "Lord and Savior," I thought of God the Father as God and Jesus as the Lord. I don't remember the prayer that I prayed to the Holy Ghost.

I had very deep feelings about what I felt was the unfairness of Christians giving so much attention to Jesus as compared to God the Father, about God's ability to condemn us to hell forever, and about His requiring Jesus to suffer so much on Earth. Those feelings, I believe, were the result of my being, even at a young age, a highly sensitive person.[120]

I had several questions, however, about the things that I was being taught about God the Father: Why did God create a Son? Was He lonely? If so, why didn't He create a wife for Himself? When did He create His Son? In other words, how long was God by Himself before He created Jesus?

My paramount questions about what I had been taught about God the Father, however, were two that, unlike my other questions, the answers to which I was simply very curious about, actually deeply troubled me. Those questions were how God could be so angry at us that He would send us to hell forever, and how He could send His son to Earth to die such a horrible, excruciating death. Both felt extremely cruel to me.

120 Highly sensitive people What Is a Highly Sensitive Person (HSP)? (verywellmind.com) are born with a biological difference that results in the deep processing of information, and a heightened awareness of emotional subtleties. As a highly sensitive kid I wanted everything in the world to be fair. I wanted people to be kind to each other. When I was at Gramzie's for dinner and I didn't want to finish my meal, I was disturbed when she told me that I should eat all of my dinner because there were children all over the world who did not have enough to eat, and were starving. I was troubled by the prospect of war, and couldn't understand why the Russians hated us so much that they might start a nuclear war with us. I thought that the segregation in the society in which we lived was not only unfair, but also totally illogical and even silly, the result of thinking on a very low level. I cried easily during tender scenes in movies, and was moved by the lyrics of songs that spoke about the oneness of humanity, and the need for love in the world. More than anything else, I wanted to do something when I grew up to improve the human condition, and specifically to show us that it is possible for human beings to be loving toward each other and to live on the Earth in peace.

My thoughts about the never-endingness of eternity made the idea of being sent to and living in hell <u>forever</u> especially frightening. I asked my mother and grandmother that question: How could God be **so** angry with us that He would send us to hell forever? Their answer was always the same: "Laurie, we don't know the answer to that question. No one does. It's a matter of faith. You just have to have faith." Those answers were extremely unsatisfying, even to my child's mind. It was hard for me to believe that God could be so angry with us that He was **capable** of condemning us to suffer forever in hell. I just didn't believe it. Perhaps it was because at neither Sunday School nor later at church was there ever any talk about the devil, or hell, or our going to hell, or God's punishment. Certainly, when I looked at the beauty of the sky, and at the beauty in my calendar pictures that I collected of Yosemite, of Yellowstone, and of Glacier National Parks and other sites of natural beauty,[121] it just felt totally impossible to me that a God capable of creating such amazing beauty could also be capable of causing such extreme, everlasting pain. On a deep feeling level, it was totally incongruous to me. It just felt entirely wrong. God, I thought, was more loving than that. Indeed, He was infinitely loving, as I had been taught, and thus incapable of such cruelty.

Regarding the question of how God the Father could have not only allowed but indeed sent His son to suffer so much on Earth and ultimately be tortured to death, I thought about the teaching that I had received that God loves us more than anyone, including our Earthly parents. In that regard, I remember thinking that my Earthly parent, my mother, loved me so much that she could **never** have wanted me to suffer that much, and she certainly wouldn't ever have volunteered me for such pain and suffering. She would never have chosen that for me. So how could God do that to His

---

121 As a child, although I grew up both in a city, and in a family that didn't travel, I had an intense love of nature, the source of which I cannot explain. I collected many calendar pictures of the Grand Canyon, Montana's Big Sky, Virginia's Skyline Drive, and California's Pacific Coast Highway. I spent long periods in my room looking at all of my calendars, imagining that I was in the picture, hiking around the Grand Canyon, riding a motorcycle across Montana's Big Sky country, camping somewhere in Virginia's Blue Ridge mountains, or driving a convertible Corvette along the Pacific Coast Highway. I absolutely **loved** beautiful scenery.

son? Didn't God love His son as much as my mother loves me? I was taught that the fact that God did sacrifice His son for us was a clear indication of how very, very much He loves us, that that great sacrifice demonstrated His infinite love for us. My response, however, was, "Yes, but what about Jesus? Didn't God love Jesus, His son, just as much as He loves us? If He did, how could He have given up Jesus to suffer so horribly and die such an awful, painful death in order for us to be able to go to heaven? Why can't we just live a very, very good life to be able to get into Heaven? If, over the course of our life, we sincerely try to always treat all people with kindness and love; if we always earnestly try to show compassion for the less fortunate; if we always genuinely try to do our very best to make the world a better place, why isn't that enough?" If our hearts are good, couldn't God just forgive us for the times that we fail? Why did God have to sacrifice Jesus for Him to be able to let us into Heaven?" Why isn't He more forgiving than that? When I was older, as a college student, I also began to wonder why it was that a **sacrifice** was necessary to make it possible for us to get into heaven. I asked myself, "Didn't many religions prior to Christianity believe in and carry out the sacrifice ritual? Doesn't Christianity condemn such rituals? But isn't Jesus' death on the cross a sacrifice ritual? How can Christians believe in not only sacrifice as a ritual, but indeed a **human** sacrifice?! How can that be the centerpiece, the very foundation of Christian faith? Those questions deeply bothered me.

CHURCH AND REVEREND KENNEDY'S INSPIRATION

When I was ten, in June of 1964, I graduated from Elementary School, and later that summer, in August, two weeks after my 11th birthday, I was promoted from the elementary to the junior high class of Bethany's Sunday School.

Certificate

Lauren Joichin

has been PROMOTED to the

Junior High Class

of the Bethany Church School

New Orleans, La.

Place Signed

August 30, 1964

Date Signed

I was glad when they said unto me, Let us go into the house of the Lord.—Psalm 122:1

Sunday School Promotional Certificate

Three years later, after completing my Junior High School grades (7th, 8th, and 9th), I had my final graduation from Sunday School. I had attended Bethany's Sunday School for ten years, from kindergarten through 9th grade. I remember feeling sad about the fact that Sunday School was coming to an end for me.[122] I loved Sunday School.[123] Graduating from Sunday School felt like a real rite of passage for me that denoted that I was one step closer to adulthood. Following our graduation, I and all of my peers began attending church, either the 8 or the 11:00 A.M. service. I attended the 11:00 service. Our Sunday services followed a consistent ritual. It began with the choir, a meticulously directed group of about twelve to sixteen members who stood, sang, and then sat down in perfect precision on cue from the choir director,

122 I was in eighth grade at Rivers Frederick Junior High School in December 1965 when in Mrs. In Parker's Social Studies class, we watched on television parts of the Second Vatican Council, Vatican II, the historic Roman Catholic Ecumenical Council. I'm sure that Mrs. Parker must have explained the importance of the event to us, but I had no real appreciation of the importance of the event, and just how historic it was.

123 Unfortunately, I didn't send Lorna to Sunday School at Bethany after my mother died, and deeply regret that I did not. At the time, I had to get her ready for school every day, I was taking care of all of Gramzie's needs, and going to school myself. Having to get Lorna ready for Sunday School on Sunday mornings was more than at sixteen, in heavy mourning, I was able to do. I sincerely wish I had been up to the task. It would have been **very** good for Lorna to have attended Sunday School, and grown up in Bethany's church family as I had.

Mr. Green, a high school music teacher and band director. At the beginning of the service, the choir stood in the back of the church in their black robes and purple choir stoles singing the first stanza of the opening hymn. The congregation also stood. We had two acolytes for the service. When the choir began singing, the two boys (there were only boy acolytes then), walked in unison, followed by Reverend Kennedy, up the church's middle aisle, to the pulpit. All three wore black robes. Reverend Kennedy's robe was floor length and had a purple and gold clerical stole on the front. Once on the pulpit and at the altar, the acolytes, again in unison, lit the altar's candles. They, along with Reverend Kennedy and the congregation, stood while the choir finished the first stanza of the opening hymn. Upon beginning the second stanza, the choir began walking in unison, two-by-two, up the center aisle to the choir seats in front of the church. I always sat in an aisle seat next to and on the right side of the center aisle so that my mother, a member of the choir, could surreptitiously pass her purse to me as she passed me in the aisle. She was always one of the last members to march up the aisle because the choir took its seats from the back to the front row, and as a soprano, she always sat in the front row of the choir seats. Once at their seats, the choir, continuing to stand, finished singing the second and often third and fourth stanzas of the opening hymn. Then, upon Mr. Green's signal, they took their seats in perfect precision. The congregation and the acolytes then also sat, and Reverend Kennedy, continuing to stand, began the service. At the end of the service, the acolytes extinguished the altar candles and once again walking in unison, preceded Reverend Kennedy down the center aisle from the pulpit to the back of the church. The choir then followed, also walking in unison, two-by-two, down the center aisle, to the back of the church. The congregation would then begin to exit down the middle and side aisles as the organist continued to play the closing hymn. It was all quite formal, and I loved it.

I saw the adults during the service nodding their heads and sometimes smiling while listening to Reverend Kennedy's sermons. I saw them, both men and women, sometimes wiping away tears through the singing of hymns. In response to Reverend Kennedy's invitation to altar prayer, I saw them walk up Bethany's center aisle, kneel at the front altar, which spanned the length of the entire pulpit, and pray on bended knees with bowed heads, sometimes with their thumb pressed against a temple, and their index and middle fingers pressed to their foreheads.

Bethany's old sanctuary in the foreground

Bethany's New Sanctuary— Consecrated in December 1969

Not long after I began attending Sunday service, I began taking home, on my own, with no coaching from my mother, the program from the service and then on every night that week, before going to sleep, knelt by my bed and read the prayers from the program. I remember how surprised my mother was the first time she saw me do that, and heard her immediately call Gramzie to tell her, her voice overflowing with pride, about her little praying teenager. While on my knees, after I had finished reading the church service program, I prayed sincerely. I gave thanks for my mother and grandmother's love. I asked for blessings for my entire family, for Daddy, for my two older brothers and my younger sister, for Gramzie, and for my uncle, two aunts and their families. I asked for blessings for people who were poor, and for people and especially for children in other countries who were hungry. At a time during which as a child, through our "duck and cover" school drills, I was aware that "the Russians" (the USSR at the time) and the United States had thousands of nuclear bombs pointed at each other that could destroy human civilization, I also asked God for peace in the world.

I was, from the beginning, intensely moved by Bethany's service. I enjoyed the ritual, it's true. In addition to the ritual, however, there were two specific things about our service that touched me deeply.

First were the sermons of our minister, Reverend Edward A. Kennedy, Jr. Reverend Kennedy's sermons touched and inspired me. His sermons, while passionate, had an unmistakable cool, intellectual flair. They were always about our responsibility, both as Christians and as people of conscience, to have the courage of our convictions, to compassionately help those in need, and to be actively engaged in just social causes. He specifically called upon us, the residents of the city's most affluent African American community, to not rest in our comfortable homes and relative financial comfort while ignoring the plight of our less economically fortunate African American sisters and brothers. His consistent theme was that we are called to be Christians every day, in every way with our families, in our schools, on our jobs, with our friends, in our community, and indeed, in the world. Essentially, Reverend

Kennedy was calling us to live consciously, with intention, and consistently with our religious faith. Starting very early in my life, Reverend Kennedy's sermons inspired me beyond description.

I also felt close to Reverend Kennedy as a person. He looked a bit like my father, but was a very different kind of man. Indeed, except for the high degree of intelligence they shared, Reverend Kennedy seemed to me to be just the opposite of my father. I experienced him as very warm (Reverend Kennedy smiled a lot) and while strong, also very kind. Indeed, he was the sort of man that I wished my father could've been. I admired Reverend Kennedy immensely, both personally and as a minister.

Reverend Edward A. Kennedy, Jr.

Second was the music, those beautiful, old, liturgical Methodist hymns. I've always absolutely loved music, and the hymns that I heard in church every Sunday were among the musical genres for which I developed a very early appreciation. Both their music and their lyrics impacted me deeply. I'm sure, however, that the fact that my mother, who had a **beautiful**, Broadway/opera-strength soprano voice, sang lead in all of the hymns that required a lead was, in part, responsible for their effect on me.

Our organist, Brenda Mitchell, who was a young woman with a BS degree in music, was no less than gifted at her craft. I remember how Brenda's fingers and feet made Bethany's organ "sing." Mr. Green, our choir director, was also outstanding in his role. When I was younger, I'd sometimes attend the Thursday night choir rehearsal with my mother. I saw the choir, under Mr. Green's excellent leadership, rehearsing the hymns for the next Sunday's service until they had gotten each one just right.

Bethany's choir had a polished, professional sound. The sanctuary choir was so good, in fact, that I remember there was talk at some point when I was in highschool of the choir making a recording. Unfortunately, for reasons unbeknownst to me, the recording was never made. It was a real personal loss for me both because I would have loved to have had a recording of the wonderful church choir with which I grew up, but even more significantly, because I would have absolutely cherished a recording of my mother's beautiful, clear, strong soprano voice. In a number of arrangements, she and Mr. Arthur Robinson, who had a wonderful, deep baritone voice, would alternate the lead parts in such dramatic fashion that even Bethany's very traditional congregates, who rarely uttered a spontaneous reaction during the service, would respond with an emphatic, "Amen!" I truly wish that a recording of Bethany's brilliant choir had been made.[124]

About twenty-five years ago, having heard me say a number of times how very deeply I was moved by the hymns we sang in my childhood church, Mike, who was one of my close friends, gave me, as a birthday present, a Methodist hymnal.

---

124 I greatly enjoyed the choir's rendition of Christmas Carols during the Christmas season. It was beautiful. My memories of how exquisitely Bethany was decorated each Christmas with dozens of red, white and pink poinsettias, and at Easter with long palms and stunning lilies, tulips and chrysanthemums of yellow, pink and white, are among my favorite memories of Bethany.

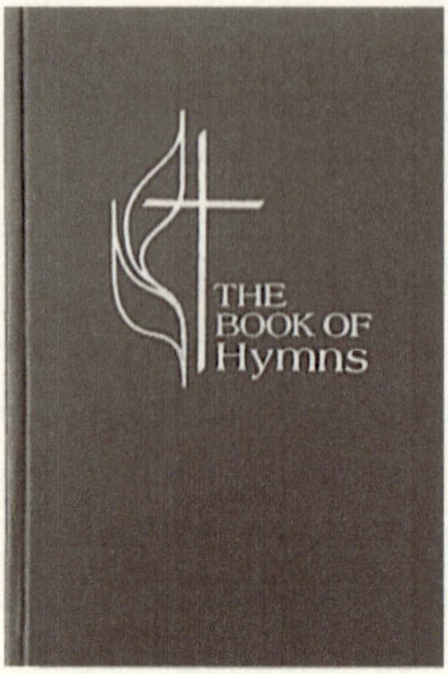

My Birthday Gift - The Methodist Hymnal

My mother, as did many adults in the church, had her own personal, leather-bound hymnal, which my brother Lambert now has.

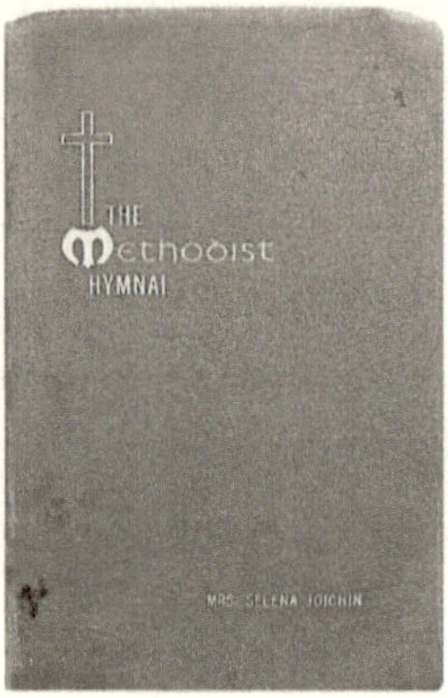

My Mother's Hymnal

To this day, I sometimes still open that little purple hymnal and sing one of the hymns we sang at Bethany during my childhood and adolescence. "Holy Holy Holy Lord God Almighty," "Be Not Dismayed What E'r Be Tide, God Will Take Care of You," "Open My Eyes That I May See," and "Come Ye Disconsolate," were among my favorites. There were two hymns, however, that I loved far and beyond **all** others. Although I was unaware of it at the time, in retrospect, I now realize that it was their descriptions of the beauty of the natural world that appealed to me on such a deep emotional level.

"This Is My Father's World" https://www.youtube.com/watch?v=bEE5MvoT3oI was one. I felt the sentiment behind the lyrics of that hymn as if I'd written them myself: "This is my Father's world and to my listening ears, all nature sings and round me rings the music of the spheres."

The hymn continues with rhyming references to birds, rocks and trees, to skies and seas, to morning light, to the lily white, and to the rustling grass in which we hear Him pass.

It concludes by declaring that no matter how strong evil may seem, this world is God's, and He is in control, a sentiment that had profound resonance with me as an adolescent. I loved that hymn.

But what was then and remains to this day my absolute favorite of all hymns is, "How Great Thou Art" https://www.youtube.com/watch?v=HudWItQDrJw on page seventeen of the Methodist hymnal. That hymn stirred my young heart like none other, especially the first two verses:

> O Lord my God, when I in awesome wonder consider all the worlds Thy hands have made; I see the stars, I hear the rolling thunder, Thy pow'r throughout the universe displayed.
>
> Then comes the refrain, an exclamation that upon experiencing nature's beauty, one's soul sings out about the greatness of God. Then the second verse...
>
> When through the woods and forest glades I wander, and hear the birds sing sweetly in the trees, when I look down from lofty mountains grandeur, and hear the brook and feel the gentle breeze.... Refrain.

I could not then nor can I even now get through that hymn with dry eyes. Although forty-seven years have passed since at 18 years old, I last stood in Bethany's sanctuary and sang those old liturgical hymns, and although my spirituality has for all of that time been fundamentally different from the religious doctrine that I was taught at Bethany, those old Methodist hymns touch me as deeply now as they did in my youth.[125]

Bethany United Methodist Church was my spiritual home from the time of my earliest memories as a young Sunday School student until I was eighteen, when for reasons explained later in "A Crisis of Faith," I stopped attending church. Growing up in Bethany was one of the true keystones of my childhood, and was indeed my introduction to spirituality.

125 Barbara, my wife, was also reared in the Methodist church, and grew up with many of the same hymns that we sang at Bethany. Whenever I spontaneously break out in song singing one of those old hymns (which I am known to do from time to time) she always joins me, and we both very much enjoy it.

CHAPTER TWO

HIGH SCHOOL AND MY INTRODUCTION TO ROMAN CATHOLICISM

A SPIRITUAL SHOCK

After attending Robert R. Moton Elementary School from kindergarten through sixth grade and spending seventh and eighth grades at Rivers Frederick Junior High, I was enrolled at The Academy of the Holy Angels High School (AHA, or Holy Angels, as it was often called), a small, Catholic girls high school. My mother believed that I'd get a better high school education in the parochial school system than at a New Orleans public high school. The student body at Holy Angels was overwhelmingly white. It was September of 1966, one month after my thirteenth birthday.

From the very start, I faced two significant challenges at Holy Angels. Two were emotional, and one intellectual.

Emotionally, I was challenged first by the racism that I experienced from many of my white classmates and a few of the nuns, all of whom were white. Although I had grown up seeing White New Orleanians, who at that time comprised the majority of the city's population, with only one exception, I had never really interacted with white people, not even in school, since both Moton and Frederick were segregated.[126] What I received from many of my white peers wasn't outright hostility. It wasn't overt racism. No one ever called me or, to my knowledge, any of my African American classmates any racial epithets. It was more subtle than that. It was more "coolness" than anything. Rather than antagonism, what I felt from my white schoolmates was a kind of emotional distancing, but I felt it strongly. Most of the AHA nuns, by contrast, were just fine with my African American classmates and me, treating us no differently than they treated the White students. A few of the older nuns, however, were noticeably uncomfortable with us, and that discomfort manifested itself in a kind of sternness that seemed to me to have been reserved for only us.[127]

My second emotional challenge at AHA was that I had begun to develop feelings, soon after my very first exposure to Catholicism, that it was a harsh, punitive religion. I had begun to develop those feelings, however, as a young child, years before I entered Holy Angels. I was in elementary school at Moton when my mother's brother, my Uncle Ikee, lost his wife, my Aunt Gerlie, leaving him with two young elementary school-age boys, my cousins Ge-

126 The exception was Gramzie's dear, dear friend of many years, Miss Maymie. Gramzie and Miss Maymie (whose last name I never knew) had been friends for many years before I was born. Unfortunately, I don't know how they met, but those two women were as close as sisters, sharing a true bond between them. Miss Maymie had two children, Don and Marion, who were young adults when I was a child. Don took my cousin Drexel and me for a ride around Gramzie's block on his motorcycle once, which for us, was a total thrill. Marion, I remember, was always very nice to my cousins and me. The relationship between Gramzie and Miss Maymie was my first exposure to an interracial friendship, and to anyone who knew Gramzie and Miss Maymie, it was exceedingly obvious that it was one of sincere love.

127 This was, after all, only two years after the passage of the Civil Rights Act of 1964 and all of the social turmoil that resulted from the integration of restrooms, water fountains, restaurants, public seating areas, the city buses, and all other public accommodations.

rard and Drexel. Following the loss of his wife, Uncle Ikee married his teenage sweetheart, my Aunt Deannie. Subsequently, they also had two boys, my cousins Kevin and Neville. What seemed really harsh to me was that because she divorced her first husband to marry my uncle, Aunt Deannie, a sincere, gentle, caring person and devout, practicing Catholic her entire life, was essentially shunned by the Church. A woman who was in an unhappy, childless marriage for years, who then changed her life by marrying her teenage love, raising his two older sons with as much love as if they were her own, bringing two more children into the world, and being a faithful, loving wife to my uncle, and an adoring mother to four children, was punished by her church for getting a divorce. I don't know whether Aunt Deannie had been formally excommunicated from the Catholic Church. I was too young at the time to be aware of such detail. I knew only that she was never allowed to return again to St. Gabriel, her parish church. As a child, I deeply felt that the way the Catholic Church treated Aunt Deannie was both horribly mean and unfair. The Catholic Church, and specifically St. Gabriel's loss of Aunt Deannie as a parishioner, however, was our gain, because shortly after her departure from St. Gabriel, Aunt Deannie became a loyal member of Bethany, which she attended until her death.[128]

Intellectually, I was challenged by what I experienced as a severe disconnect between some aspects of Catholicism that I both witnessed and was being taught, and the religious teachings that I had received all my life to that point, at Bethany.

The difference between the cross that we used at Bethany and the Catholic crucifix was my first disconnect, the first thing that made an impression on me. I was used to seeing the empty cross at Bethany. I remembered one of Reverend Kennedy's Easter Sunday sermons in which he explained that we use the symbol

128 In describing my introduction to Catholicism, I sincerely have absolutely no intent to be disrespectful to the billions of practicing Catholics whose faith is sacred to them. Indeed, I never wish to disrespect anyone's faith tradition. I have merely described here the musings and deep feelings of a Protestant adolescent, being exposed for the first time to 1960's Roman Catholicism.

of the open cross to signify Christ's resurrection, his victory over the grave, and our resulting salvation and everlasting life. While I was uncomfortable with the notion of God using Jesus as a sacrifice and the explanation of why he died, I wasn't uncomfortable (probably because I had seen it my entire life) with the sight of the Protestant cross, the empty cross. By contrast, I found disconcerting the sight of the Catholic crucifix with Jesus' limp body hanging from the cross, his head down, bleeding from the puncture wounds inflicted by a crown of thorns, his right-side bleeding after being pierced by the sword of a Roman soldier and his hands and feet bleeding from the large nails that penetrated them. I didn't like seeing it. It made me uncomfortable. After hearing Reverend Kennedy's sermon on why Protestant churches symbolize their faith with the open cross, I wondered why in using the crucifix, the Catholic Church emphasized Jesus' torturous death instead of what we had been taught was his victorious resurrection.[129]

In addition to being troubled by the crucifix, I was also unsettled by some of what I was learning in my religion classes. As was the case at all of the Catholic high schools, we were required to take a religion class every year in order to graduate from Holy Angels. The lessons that we were receiving in religion class were of great interest to me because they focused on the mystery of The Divine, on God and His nature, one of The Mysteries in which I had a deep and abiding interest. From the beginning, however,

129 The sight of the crucifix was indeed troubling for me as an adolescent, but as an adult, I find even the open cross used in the Protestant Christian tradition in which I was raised, disconcerting. I well understand the symbolism of the cross for Christians. It symbolizes the tremendous love that **God the Father** has for us, the enormous sacrifice that He made—that He loved us so dearly, that He gave his child, His only begotten son to suffer and die for us in order to save us from eternal damnation. It symbolizes the tremendous love that **Jesus** has for us—that he would, at the young age of 33, endure such an excruciating fate on our behalf. It symbolizes everlasting life, for it is through Jesus' crucifixion, through his sacrifice, that believers receive eternal life. As one raised in the church, I well understand that, the **theological** context of the cross. It is difficult for me, however, to not also see the cross in its **historical** context, specifically that it was an instrument of grievous human torture widely used by the Romans for hundreds of years. It is the instrument on which untold thousands of men and women breathed their last breath after dying an indescribably agonizing, insufferable death. It is for that reason that I find troubling the use of the cross, an instrument of torture, as a symbol of any religious faith.

from my earliest religion classes in my freshman year, I privately rebelled against much of what I was being taught.

One final thing that troubled me about being a Protestant kid in a Catholic school was that Protestants were referred to in my religion classes as "non-Catholics." I didn't like that label. The sentiment that I sensed behind it felt as if we were being called "non-Christian," and I was appalled by what I perceived as the complete arrogance of being assigned that designation. In view, however, of my feelings about several fundamental Catholic beliefs that seemed no less than outlandish to me, I wore my badge of "non-Catholic" with both a kind of secret pride and relief—relief that I wasn't Catholic. I thought that **my** religious training was both much more intelligent, and much more mature.[130] I'm not proud of it today, but thirteen-year-old Lauren, in my annoyance over being relegated to the inferior class of "non-Catholic," what was clearly thought of as an inferior kind of Christian, privately began referring to Catholics as non-Methodists!

I found three particular Catholic doctrines that we were taught utterly untenable.

First and foremost was the doctrine that the Catholic Church was the one true church, the one true Christian church. We were taught that Jesus started the church, that His apostle Peter was the first pope, and that every pope since Peter served in a direct line of succession from Jesus. The implication (although it was never overtly stated) was that since the Catholic Church was the one true Christian church, Protestant churches were not true Christian churches because they were started by men (Martin Luther and others), not by God. Well, all my thirteen-year-old mind heard from that claim was that Mama and Gramzie, women of deep, sincere faith whom I **fiercely** loved, were not true Christians. Needless to say, that notion went over with me like a lead balloon.

130 I realized years later in adulthood, that that thought, as well as my feeling of Protestant intellectual superiority that accompanied it, were quite arrogant, and not at all consistent with Jesus' message of humility.

Second was purgatory. Never, in either my ten years of Bethany's Sunday School classes or in my five years of listening to Reverend Kennedy's sermons, did I ever hear anything about purgatory. I knew only that if you were a good person, you went to Heaven, and if you were a bad person, you went to Hell. Period. Full stop. And while I knew that bad people went to Hell, Hell was never a subject of study or even discussion in either Sunday School or church. The idea of purgatory, of there being a third place where we go as a kind of way-station, a kind of holding place in which we stay until we've been cleansed enough to be able to get into Heaven, just seemed utterly untenable to me. I remember as if it were yesterday, sitting in religion class as a high school junior, thinking, "Where are they getting this from? In all my years of going to Sunday School and attending church, I was never taught anything about purgatory." I asked my mother about it. She told me that purgatory was a Catholic belief, that our faith didn't teach it and that Methodists didn't believe in it. Although I don't remember how, I do remember learning at some point that there is no reference to purgatory in the Bible. Not a single one. My thought was, "They made it up!"

Third was the belief, also taught in our religion classes, that during the communion portion of the mass, the priest's consecration of the Eucharist turns it into the actual body and the actual blood of Christ. It was called The Transmutation of the Eucharist. Upon learning about the belief, I rejected it out of hand. I thought, "Wow, now that's a belief in magic!" I didn't believe it and the thought that anybody believed it, that anybody believed that they were eating the actual body and drinking the actual blood of Jesus bothered me—a lot. I found it disturbing. In my Methodist Sunday School I was taught that the small thin white round communion wafers we ate, and the grape juice we drank from the little individual glass serving glasses were representations, symbols of Jesus' body and blood that we had to eat and drink in remembrance of him. As a little thirteen-year-old Methodist religion student of Catholic theology, I remember being amazed that people could truly believe that a human being was actually capable of creating Jesus' real physical body and blood. I was also extremely uncomfortable with the thought that people wanted to eat and drink Jesus' body and blood. I found it deeply disturbing.

In addition to what I think of as those three major theological teachings of the Catholic Church, which my adolescent mind simply could not accept, there was also a host of what I think of as minor Catholic beliefs (although practicing Catholics may indeed have considered them to be major Church tenets) that I thought were also simply untrue.

- Of all the sacraments, communion, i.e., eating the body and drinking the blood of Jesus, was the most sacred, and in order to get to heaven, one had to take communion. That, I thought, was probably why every mass included what Catholics refer to as the celebration of the Eucharist, and why according to Catholic theology, it is the apex of the mass. Of course I was accustomed to taking communion. At Bethany (and in many Protestant churches), we did so not at every service as Catholics did, but on the first Sunday of every month. I was never taught, however, that if you don't take communion, you couldn't go to Heaven. That was, according to Catholic theology, yet another of God's rules that again seemed so very punitive to me. "Suppose," I thought, "a person grew up in a family that didn't go to church. Would God send them to hell even though they didn't even know anything about taking communion?" Once again, I just did not believe that God was that cruel.
- Since taking communion was the most sacred of all the sacraments, one should never take it without first cleansing oneself by going to confession. I didn't be-

lieve it. I was pretty sure that I'd learned in either Sunday School or Vacation Bible School, or that perhaps I had heard in one of Reverend Kennedy's sermons, that somewhere in the Bible it said something about the need to confess our sins. I was confident, however, even as a high school freshman at the age of thirteen, that nowhere in the Bible was it stated that we had to confess our sins to another human being. My thought was that confessing our sins was probably meant to teach us to candidly acknowledge them to ourselves, to be truthful about them with others whom we have harmed, and to have an accompanying sincere commitment to do better in the future. Confessing one's sins felt to me to be the kind of thing that one would do privately with God. I was only thirteen, but as a result of the strong religious foundation I'd already received at Bethany, I was totally secure in rejecting out of hand, the idea that we were required to confess our sins to another person.

- Certain sins, called mortal sins, if committed even once, damned one to hell automatically. One such mortal sin, we were taught, was "French kissing" boys. During our initial discussion of it in my freshman year religion class, I didn't even know what French kissing was, and I remember neither how nor when I learned what it was, but when I did learn that it was using the tongue to kiss, while I was completely repulsed by the thought of it, I believed strongly that nobody would go to hell for doing it. I found utterly ridiculous the notion that God would damn a person to hell for all eternity for something like French kissing. I wondered whether some of my classmates may have engaged in such a gross act, but if they did, I was convinced that they wouldn't be going to hell for it. I knew that no one would!

- That on matters of faith, the Pope was infallible. "How," I thought, "can that be? The Pope is a human being," I mused, "so how can he be perfect about anything? Take the rule that women can't be priests. I'm sure he agrees with that, and yet he's certainly wrong about it. Sure, they say that men and women are equal in God's sight, and that they just have different, but not superior or inferior roles in the Church, but I don't buy it. The roles are different all right, but men have all the superior ones. I'm sure that nowhere in the Bible does it say that women can't be priests. This is yet another thing they just made up, and in going along with it, the pope is discriminating against women. He's absolutely wrong for doing so, and therefore cannot be and is not infallible."[131]
- The canonization of saints. The idea that a body of human beings could vote on and then declare that a person is a saint, I found totally implausible. Gramzie had always had an altar in her home, with statues of many saints on it—St. Peter, St. Paul, St. Francis, and others, so perhaps it was for that reason that I had never given any thought to the concept of the existence of beings that we called "saints." Regarding the Catholic practice of the canonization of saints, however, my thought was that, "Saints are saints and only God determines who they are. People can't decide something like that, and certainly not by majority vote!"

131 While at Bethany I had seen only male ministers, first Reverend Frank, when I was very little, and then Reverend Kennedy, I never heard it said that in the Methodist church women could not be members of the clergy. While at that time it may not have been common for a woman to be a minister in the Methodist church, had I been aware of either a church policy or a practice that prohibited women from becoming members of the clergy, I'm sure that I would have thought about it the exact same way I thought about the Catholic prohibition against women priests—that it was abominable. After beginning early in childhood, having received the consistent message that I could do anything that I truly applied myself to, the thought that I wouldn't be allowed to pursue a chosen career on the basis of my sex was simply detestable to me.

- Eating meat on Friday was a sin. I patently rejected it. New Orleans' French roots resulted in its being an overwhelmingly Catholic city when I was growing up. Perhaps it was for that reason that it was the tradition of even many families that were not Catholic to eat seafood instead of meat on Friday. My own was one such family. On those few occasions, however, on which we did eat chicken or steak or smothered pork chops or spaghetti with meatballs or hamburgers and hotdogs on Friday, we didn't think we were committing a sin for having done so. The belief that it was a sin, I considered to be pure rubbish. I thought, "God, the Creator of the entire magnificent, mysterious universe definitely does not care whether or not we eat meat on Friday. In fact, I don't believe that God cares what we eat on any day of the week. It's not in the Bible, and it just seems so petty. They made it up. Besides, with things like war, poverty and discrimination plaguing the world, God has more important things to be concerned with."

I remember thinking that my Catholic classmates were able to believe all of those things, that the Catholic Church is the one true church, in the existence of purgatory, in the transmutation of the Eucharist, in the "communion or hell" doctrine, in confessing one's sins to a priest, in venial vs. mortal sins, in the infallibility of the Pope, that women cannot be part of the Church's hierarchy, in the canonization of saints, and that it's a sin to eat meat on Friday, only because they had been taught from a very young age to believe all of those things, and that had they been taught something totally different, they'd probably believe those things just as strongly as they believe the Catholic doctrines that they had been taught. I remember feeling glad that **I** hadn't been taught any of those things in my religious education at Bethany.

My realization that Catholics believed whatever it is that they were taught to believe, led me to a realization that was for me, at that time, the most profound realization I had ever had – that most people around the world, including Protestant Christians, probably believe whatever it is **they** believe for the same reason, i.e., because they were **taught** to believe it. That realization was one of the most critical steps along my spiritual journey because it caused me to look critically and analytically at religious beliefs in general.

I still think that in terms of religion, most of us believe throughout our lives, and often with very strong conviction, whatever it was that we were taught as children to believe. If we were raised Muslim, and if we remained religious as an adult, we will probably remain Muslim for the remainder of our life. If we were raised Jewish, and remained religious as an adult, chances are quite good that we will remain Jewish for the remainder of our life. If we were raised Christian, and remained religious as an adult, we will in all likelihood remain Christian for the remainder of our life. Furthermore, it is probably likely that we will remain, throughout our lives, in the specific sect of the faith in which we were raised. Thus, for example, if we were raised as a Shia Muslim, it is unlikely that if we remained religious in adulthood, we would become a Sunni Muslim, or vice versa. If we were raised as a Reform Jew, it is unlikely that if we remained religious, we would, as an adult, become an Orthodox Jew, and vice versa. If we were raised an Episcopalian, it is unlikely that in adulthood, if we remained religious, we would become Southern Baptist, and vice versa. If we had been raised Hindu, Buddhist, as a Taoist or a Baha'i, and remained religious in adulthood, we would in all likelihood, remain faithful to whichever of **those** religions we had been exposed to as a child. It all seemed terribly random to me that one's fundamental beliefs about the most profound questions of life are determined not by a serious examination of what human beings have believed around the world and which of those belief systems resonates as truth to us, but simply by what we had been taught during our formative years.[132]

Despite my disagreement with those and other religious teachings I was receiving from them, I was intrigued in high school by the life of our teachers, the Marianite nuns. I was extremely curious about and interested in their daily lives. I knew that they attended mass every morning and then taught school until mid-afternoon, but I wondered what their evenings and weekends were like. I wondered if they had any time alone and, if so, how they spent it, or if they were in community until the time they went to bed every night. Being taught by nuns at Holy Angels was my introduction to monastic life.[133]

I was able to get a glimpse of that life in my last year at Holy Angels. On one otherwise uneventful morning of my senior year, my homeroom teacher, Sister Mary Rose Elizabeth, asked me to go to her room in the convent to get something that she'd forgotten earlier that morning.[134]

The convent was on campus and just a short walk away from the classroom building. I don't remember what it was the Sister wanted me to get for her, but I remember every other detail about my brief visit to the convent. Her room was on the second floor. Following her directions, I entered the convent at the back stairwell. I walked up the stairs and when I reached the second floor, looked at the long hall that stretched out in front of me. It was completely silent. The dark hardwood floors were unbelievably shiny and beautiful. The walls were hospital white with a very large crucifix hanging on one of them.

---

132 Of course, at the end of such an examination, two other possibilities exist for the examiner. They could decide that none of our human religious traditions resonate with them, and that ultimate truth is utterly unknowable, i.e., they could decide that they are agnostic. The other possibility is that the examiner could declare a disbelief in anything but the observable, material, physical universe, in essence becoming an atheist.

133 Unbeknownst to me then, that introduction began what has been for me a life-long intrigue with monasticism.

134 Not long after I was assigned to her class, I got the feeling that Sister Rose Elizabeth really liked me for some reason. If I am correct that Sister took a unique liking to me, it was completely mutual. Sister Mary Rose Elizabeth was one of my two favorite teachers. She was a middle-aged nun, and had a kind of compassion, sincerity, and gentleness of spirit that I both saw clearly and felt unequivocally.

As instructed, I walked halfway down the hall and arrived at Sister Rose Elizabeth's room on the right. What I saw when I opened the door was blissfully shocking and in stark contrast to the long, rather dark hall down which I'd just walked. Immediately after opening the door of Sister Mary Rose Elizabeth's room, I spontaneously broke into a big wide smile. What I saw upon entering was a bright, cheerful space with a vivid red theme—a red, busily patterned bedspread, a red doily on a bookcase, and a chair with a red pad on the seat. I'm not sure, but I think I remember a stuffed teddy bear sitting on the bed. I was intrigued. I found it both fascinating and refreshing that even in monastic life one was able to express one's personality and, even more importantly, one's individuality. I remember that the item that Sister asked me to get was in the precise spot she told me it would be. I picked it up, walked out of the room, quietly closing the door behind me, walking again on the beautiful, shiny hardwood floor to the staircase, down the stairs, out of the building and back to class, delivering Sister's item to her. The convent felt utterly peaceful. I distinctly remember feeling that I could very easily live in such a place, one that had such peace, such stillness and quiet. That short trip to Sister Mary Rose Elizabeth's room is one I'll never forget.

My trip to Sister Mary Rose Elizabeth's room was a bright, if very brief experience of one aspect of Catholicism. My introduction to Catholic religious beliefs at the age of thirteen, was for me, a spiritual shock. I was shocked by what I thought of as the Catholic belief in the cruelty of God, that God would damn us to hell forever for having committed certain sins, even once. I was shocked by the Catholic belief that priests are able to commute bread and wine into the actual body and blood of Jesus. I was shocked that Catholics believed that human beings are able to decide who is a saint. I was shocked by learning, as a young adolescent, about those and a number of other Catholic doctrines and beliefs to which I was introduced at Holy Angels. In truth, it made me very happy I was Methodist.

THE MYSTERIES DEEPEN

After spending my early years in total wonderment about "The Major and Minor Mysteries," among them how the universe came into being, eternity, infinity, and a fourth dimension, during my sophomore year at Holy Angels, I had my first specialized science course—Biology. Sister Mary Dominic Savio, the other of my two favorite high school teachers, taught biology. Sister Dominic Savio was young, kind, patient, warm, and very smart. It was a nice convergence of events that the person who up to that point was my favorite teacher was teaching what was my favorite subject.

Taking biology totally appealed directly to the young scientist in me. That said, I wasn't exactly enthralled with biology because it wasn't "deep" enough; it didn't focus on "the mysteries." Nonetheless, I so enjoyed, during lab, being able to see another universe, the microscopic universe, that I asked for a microscope for Christmas that year. It was 1967. In response, my mother told me that because microscopes were very expensive, it would be better for me to get it for my next birthday in August, as opposed to during the holiday season when there were so many other expenses. I understood and was just fine with that. When Christmas morning arrived, my mother woke me, telling me that she needed my help to open a box. I thought that was strange because my father was home. When I walked with my mother to the Christmas tree in the den, there, under the tree, open and displayed, was a Jason microscope! It was in a nice black case with a red felt interior, complete with slides and a few small dissection instruments. I immediately threw my arms around my mother and we both laughed and cried in each other's arms. My mother **loved** surprising me! [135]

135 On the morning of my seventh birthday, my mother woke me, said she wanted to show me something, took me by the hand to my brothers' room (the window of their room faced the backyard), and opened the curtain to show me, to my utter surprise, the swing/sliding

What I liked most about my microscope was that it allowed me to glimpse an entire whole other universe that existed within the larger, familiar one in which we lived and that was indeed the very foundation of the larger universe. Under the lens of my microscope, I looked at leaves, blades of grass, grains of dirt, drops of water, and anything else that caught my attention at any moment. Being able to see living cells through the lens of my microscope made me wonder, as I had at day camp on that hot summer day several years earlier, whether an entire universe like ours of galaxies and solar systems and even intelligent life existed on the microscopic level. That thought absolutely fascinated me. Over forty years later, I still have my microscope, and it too, is one of my most cherished childhood keepsakes.

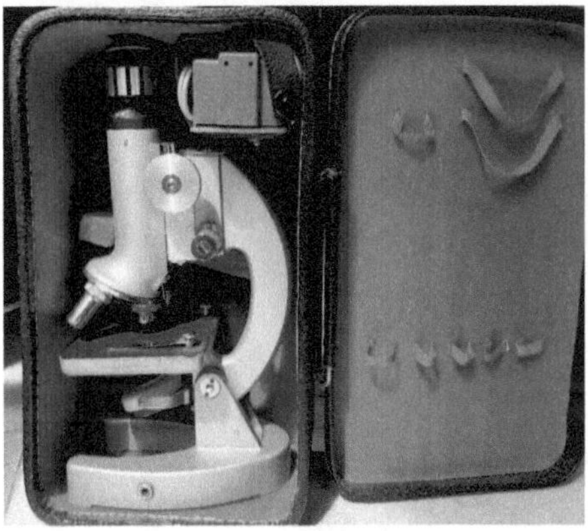

My 1967 Jason Microscope

board set I wanted so badly. On the morning of my fifteenth birthday, my mother was already at work, but I woke up to see on my desk a wonderful gift I hadn't even asked for—a portable, electric Smith Corona typewriter wrapped in a bright red ribbon with a big red bow on top. Next to it was a beautiful card on which my mother had, as always, written a very touching inscription. My swing set, telescope, microscope, typewriter, piano and bicycle are the surprises I remember. The many little surprises she often gave me when she came home from shopping are just too numerous for me to remember.

Me at Fourteen in My School Uniform with My Microscope

As it turns out, to my chagrin, my high school biology course was the last science course I ever took. The three-year science curriculum during my high school years at AHA was General Science in ninth grade, biology in tenth, and chemistry in eleventh grade. After having taken General Science as a freshman, and Biology as a sophomore, I would have loved to have taken chemistry in my junior year, but despite my love of science, I had been math-challenged since elementary school and was not good enough in math to take chemistry.

As a junior, however, even though I wasn't enrolled in a science course, I entered a project in AHA's Annual Science Fair. Surprisingly, all I remember about the project is that it had something to do with space and rockets.

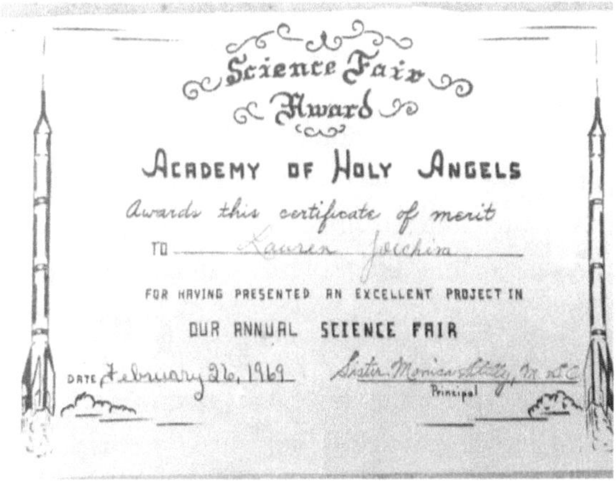

Certificate of Merit for Science Project Entered in
AHA's 1969 Annual Science Fair

Later that semester, my project was chosen to represent AHA at a regional high school science fair.

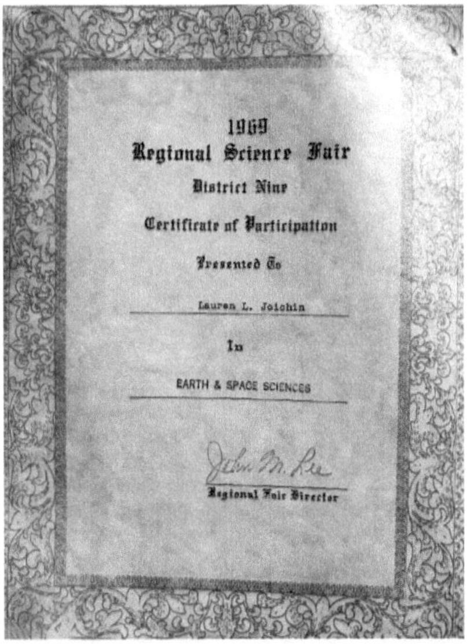

Certificate of Participation in 1969 High School
Regional Science Fair

Looking back on my high school biology class, the most significant fact I learned in the course was that chemical systems are the basis of all biological systems, i.e., that chemistry is the very foundation of biology. I distinctly remember being fascinated by that fact because it profoundly deepened my understanding of how the universe works. From my readings in Astronomy, I had gained a clear understanding of how the universe is organized, that there are stars, i.e., suns (and possibly planets circling them that comprise solar systems), that those suns exist in galaxies, and that those galaxies comprise the entire universe, but learning that chemistry is the foundation of biology was the first time I remember thinking, not "So this is how the universe is **organized**," but "Ah, so this is how the universe **works**! Biological systems are the basis of life, and chemistry is the foundation of biology. It's even deeper than biology." Not surprisingly, my next question was, "But what's the foundation of chemistry? What's deeper than chemistry?" I wanted to know. In terms of learning how the universe works, The Mystery had deepened.[136]

THE END OF MY CHILDHOOD AND THE BEGINNING OF A NEW HUMAN ERA

IT WAS THE SUMMER OF 1969. ON JULY 3RD, WITH MY MOTHER'S death, my childhood ended. Less than three weeks later, on July 20th, with its first lunar landing, a new era for humanity began. As utterly unbelievable as it was at the time, the human species achieved the most amazing accomplishment imaginable: we broke the bounds, the chains of Earth, and set foot on another celestial body. We landed on the moon! I was at my Uncle Ikee's house on

136 Had I taken chemistry in high school, I would most likely have learned at that time that physics is the foundation of chemistry. It was several years later that I learned that fact. As fascinating for me as was my learning that chemistry is the foundation of biology, my learning later on that physics is the foundation of chemistry was even more fascinating. It was so because when I was introduced to physics, I understood that I was being introduced to the "deepest" and, indeed, to the most profound of all sciences; the science that is the very foundation of all other sciences; the science that has as its focus, some of the most fundamental questions about the nature of reality. I knew this was it, that we can't go any deeper than physics. I knew that in physics, I had finally reached the "source science"—the science that, together with Cosmology, could lead me to the very Source of the universe itself. It still amazes me that Jack, one of my closest and dearest friends, is a physicist. How likely is it that I would ever even know a physicist, much less be good friends with one?! I am convinced that our friendship is no accident.

the Sunday afternoon that it happened. Even in my deep grief, I watched it. I watched all by myself on the television in my uncle's den while the rest of the family was in the backyard. If I had not lost Mama just a little more than two weeks prior, I would have been over the moon with excitement the moment the Eagle touched down, and then minutes later, the moment Neil Armstrong set foot on the surface of the moon. In my grief, however, I felt nothing. I was emotionless. I've thought several times over the course of my life about what that moment would have been like for me had I not just lost my mother. I know that it would have been one of the most impactful moments of my young life.[137]

Summer ended, and within a few days of the start of the school year, the nuns, in what was no doubt a sincere attempt to be charitable toward me, gave me a certificate showing that my mother had been enrolled into a purgatory society. Purgatory societies are groups of Catholics who pray and attend masses offered for the deceased in order to shorten their time in purgatory and accelerate their entrance into heaven. I was touched that the nuns had done that for my mother, a "non-Catholic," and I knew that they did so out of pure charity and compassion. Their kindness and sincere concern for me because I had lost my mother were absolutely not lost on me. At the same time, their having enrolled my mother in a purgatory society deeply upset me because I knew

137 In retrospect, I find it hard to believe that Uncle Ikee, his wife—my Aunt Deannie, and their two older sons, my cousins Gerard and Drexel, weren't interested in watching that historic event. I was quite young during the heyday of NASA's Mercury space program. Indeed, on May 5st, 1961, when Alan Shepard became the first American to go to and return from space, I hadn't quite turned eight, but I well remember the adults excitedly talking about it. I was excited by it too—a man in space! (I didn't know that the Russians had beaten us there by three weeks with the April 12, 1961 flight of cosmonaut Yuri Alekseyevich Gagarin.) I also remember, less than a year later, John Glenn's February 20, 1962 historic flight, the first flight (I thought) of a man to orbit the Earth. Again, I didn't know that the Russians had already accomplished that milestone as well. I was eight and a half. I don't actually remember watching the launch, but I do remember the adults talking about it. I was fascinated by, and had many questions about it. My father explained to me the difference between the Shepard and Glenn flights, that Shepard went straight up into space and then came back down, whereas Glenn went up and actually circled the Earth. I understood. My general interest in space, combined with my memories of Alan Shepard and John Glenn's early space flight were, I'm sure, why at fourteen and fifteen, I followed the preparations for the Apollo moon landing in total awe of the process and with great anticipation of the actual moon landing itself.

beyond any doubt that my mother was not in purgatory, a place I didn't even believe existed. I knew my mother was in heaven.

Certificate of My Mother's Enrollment in the Salesian Purgatorial Society

I couldn't understand why my mother had to die at such a young age when she had so many more years of life ahead of her. I couldn't understand why she had to leave us when Lorna was still so young. I couldn't understand why Gramzie had to experience the indescribable pain of losing her eldest daughter. I couldn't understand why my mother had to leave **me**. I didn't understand **any** of it.

I had questions at that time about the very foundation of the religious belief system in which I had been raised, questions about how God could sentence us to eternal suffering because during our short life we hadn't lived a good enough life; about how God, the Creator of the universe, could have a child; and about how God could require a human sacrifice, the crucifixion and death of His child, a sacrifice that He Himself required in order to save us from His own wrath. But even with those questions, for some reason, my mother's death did not shake my very deeply rooted faith in God. It was that faith, indeed, that carried me through that indescribably difficult time. My faith was that despite His having taken my mother away from us, God was loving. God was good and had some reason for taking Mama. I knew that my mother was in heaven with God.

In January of 1970, during my senior year of high school, six months after my mother died, I was elected President of the Senior Division of Bethany's MYF, the Methodist Youth Fellowship. I neither ran nor volunteered for the position. I was still too emotionally devastated. I think, however, that largely because of how I spoke up at our meetings, the issues I raised and questions I asked, my peers elected me President. I served in the position from 1970 to 1971. I was living with tremendous grief at that time over the loss of my mother, but I did the best I could in the position, and was actually quite successful in it. One of the things I most wanted to do in my life was make my mother proud of me. I was profoundly sad that she did not live to see me in that position at Bethany. She would have been very proud.

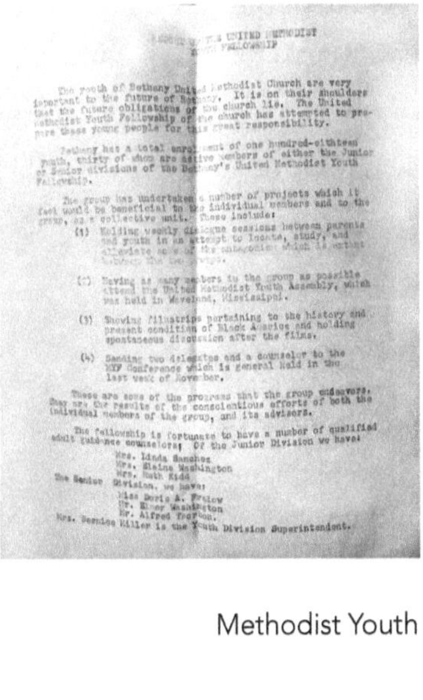

[illegible] THE UNITED METHODIST
[illegible] FELLOWSHIP

The youth of Bethany United Methodist Church are very important to the future of Bethany. It is on their shoulders that the future obligations of the church lie. The United Methodist Youth Fellowship of the church has attempted to prepare these young people for this great responsibility.

Bethany has a total enrollment of one hundred-eithteen youth, thirty of whom are active members of either the Junior or Senior divisions of the Bethany's United Methodist Youth Fellowship.

The group has undertaken a number of projects which it feel would be beneficial to the individual members and to the group, as a collective unit. These include:

(1) Holding weekly dialogue sessions between parents and youth in an attempt to locate, study, and alleviate some of the [illegible] which is extant between the two groups.

(2) Having as many members to the group as possible attend the United Methodist Youth Assembly, which was held in Waveland, Mississippi.

(3) Showing filmstrips pertaining to the history and present condition of Black America and holding spontaneous discussion after the films.

(4) Sending two delegates and a counselor to the MYF Conference which is general held in the last week of November.

These are some of the programs that the group endeavors. They are the results of the conscientious efforts of both the individual members of the group, and its advisors.

The fellowship is fortunate to have a number of qualified adult guidance counselors; Of the Junior Division we have:

Mrs. Linda Sanchez
Mrs. Elaine Washington
Mrs. Ruth Kidd

The Senior Division, we have:

Miss Doris A. Frelow
Mr. Elmer Washington
Mr. Alfred [illegible]

Mrs. Bernice Miller is the Youth Division Superintendent.

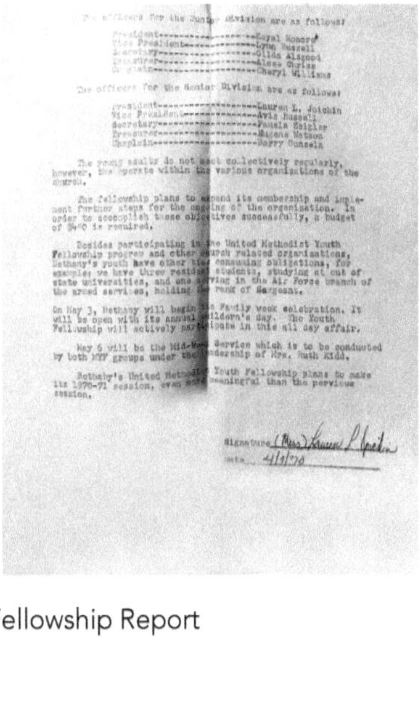

The officers for the Junior Division are as follows:

President----------Loyal Monore
Vice President----------Lynn Russell
Secretary----------Gilda Alsgood
Treasurer----------[illegible]
Chaplain----------Cheryl Williams

The officers for the Senior Division are as follows:

President----------Lauren L. Joichin
Vice President----------Avis Russell
Secretary----------Pamela Zeigler
Treasurer----------Eugene Watson
Chaplain----------Barry Gonsela

The young adults do not meet collectively regularly, however, they operate within the various organizations of the church.

The fellowship plans to expand its membership and implement further steps for the ongoing of the organization. In order to accomplish these objectives successfully, a budget of $[illegible] is required.

Besides participating in the United Methodist Youth Fellowship program and other church related organizations, Bethany's youth have other time consuming obligations, for example; we have three resident students, studying at out of state universities, and one serving in the Air Force branch of the armed services, holding the rank of Sergeant.

On May 3, Bethany will begin its Family week celebration. It will be open with its annual childern's day. The Youth Fellowship will actively participate in this all day affair.

May 6 will be the Mid-Week Service which is to be conducted by both MYF groups under the leadership of Mrs. Ruth Kidd.

Bethany's United Methodist Youth Fellowship plans to make its 1970-71 session, even more meaningful than the pervious session.

Signature (Miss) Lauren L. Joichin
Date 4/1/70

Methodist Youth Fellowship Report

HIGH SCHOOL—IN RETROSPECT

When I entered high school at thirteen, I had a profound fascination with The Mysteries and, as a result, a passion for science. By the time I graduated from high school at sixteen, while my obsession with The Mysteries was unquestionably **still** at my core, I had developed a second passion—opening minds and softening hearts; helping all people to see our shared humanity as human beings. Throughout those four years of high school (with the exception of the first semester of my senior year during which I was most immediately dealing with the shock and pain of having lost my mother the preceding summer), I often spoke to my friends about my social justice passion, racism specifically, since it was the social injustice with which I had the most life experience. Although I spoke much less of my love of science and fascination with The Mysteries, my love of them was not lost on my friends. As a result, I developed a dual reputation among my high school friends— "The Professor," Lauren the passionate social activist, and "The Nutty Professor", the somewhat brainy kid, Lauren the young scientist. The comments that my classmates wrote in my senior class book say it all:

> Dear Lauren,
> Good luck in your future. I will always remember you as the Nutty Professor.
> Joanie

> Dear Lauren,
> I have known you since Jr. High and it only took me a minute to find out that you are nutty. I'm glad we met. Stay nutty. It becomes you.
> A Friend to the End, Leslie. '70

Lauren,
Think of me one day when you are in front of your class known as "professor".
Friends Always, Anne

To Laurie, Professor Joichin,
Never lose your great personality or your individuality. Stay as sweet and nice as you are. Someday maybe I'll take a course in "Black Studies" under Professor Joichin. Best of luck in the future.
Love, Leona

Dear Professor,
Hi. You are one of the sweetest nuts I've come across in a long time. Don't ever change your precious little ways for anyone. Keep the black power drive. My dear philosopher, I'll miss you a lot. I'll always remember you as my inspiration for black justice. You really showed me all of the insights. You are a very good friend to have. I'm truly glad we met. You are one in a million. Never forget all of the fun we had in your class Professor. We've gone through a lot.... Love and friendship always, Good luck in the future.

Love always Aleta

Lauren Joichin!
You've really been a great friend! Always keep your beautiful ways and you will go beaucoup far and have zero problems. Knowing you has really made me have such a great love for black people and opened my eyes to see all of the horrible things done to ya'll. I only hope one

day we'll all be united in peace but until then all I can do is hope.

Love and power, "Kathy."

Dear Lauren
Well what can I say. Let's see. I know a lot of Black people for I grew up with some. But I must admit I know them better now thanks to you. If there is one thing I've learned in my Senior year, it's that I'll never be prejudice again. Thanks for everything, Laurie. Best of luck in the future.

Love Vanda

To Laurie,
Always stay as sweet and nice as you are. With your mind you can go far!
Love, Doris

Lauren,
It's been great knowing you and your smart brain. I'd like to know what I would have done without you. Keep the faith baby.

Love and friendship, Vida.

Looking back on my high school years in retrospect, I am exceedingly thankful that the racism that I experienced during those years did not affect me emotionally to the point of destroying or even diminishing my curiosity about both The Divine and the universe. The first twelve years of my life prior to high school in my family, in my community, in my church, and with all of my African American teachers who believed in and inspired me and all of their other young African American students had molded me far too powerfully for that to have happened. For that, I am eternally grateful.

I graduated from The Academy of the Holy Angels High School in May of 1970 and turned seventeen near the end of that summer.

My Senior Prom

Photo: Me, Fourth from Left with Five of the Ten African American Students in my Class of 125. Reverend Kennedy's son, Korkee was my date.

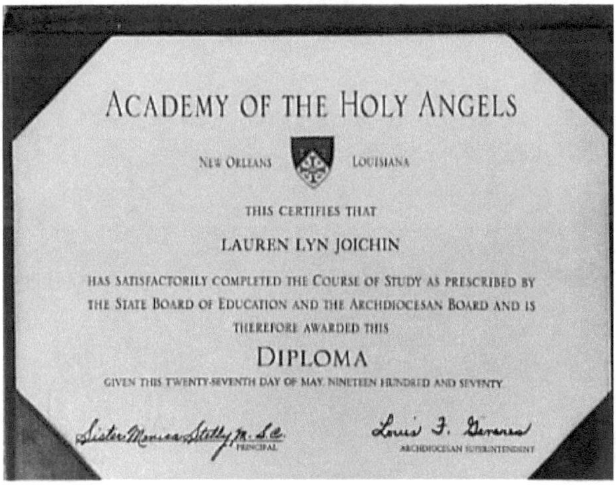

ACADEMY OF THE HOLY ANGELS

NEW ORLEANS LOUISIANA

THIS CERTIFIES THAT

LAUREN LYN JOICHIN

HAS SATISFACTORILY COMPLETED THE COURSE OF STUDY AS PRESCRIBED BY THE STATE BOARD OF EDUCATION AND THE ARCHDIOCESAN BOARD AND IS THEREFORE AWARDED THIS

DIPLOMA

GIVEN THIS TWENTY-SEVENTH DAY OF MAY, NINETEEN HUNDRED AND SEVENTY

PRINCIPAL

ARCHDIOCESAN SUPERINTENDENT

My High School Diploma

CHAPTER THREE

MY NEED TO GO DEEPER THAN SCIENCE

COLLEGE AND MY STUDY OF WESTERN PHILOSOPHY

Beginning in my sophomore year of college, I was on the outside, a young social activist in the LSUNO NAACP College Chapter. On the inside though, as I began to emerge from my two-year depression over losing my mother, my enthrallment with The Mysteries began to re-emerge.

At some point while I was in college, I learned about the Big Bang Theory, the hypothesis, now widely accepted as truth in much of the scientific community, that the universe began 13.4 billion years ago as an explosion of a miniscule primeval singularity, or point from which it is still expanding. That thought alone was intriguing enough, but what I found absolutely astounding was the related theory (held or perhaps speculated by some scientists) that the universe might ultimately expand to a maximum point after which it will then begin to contract. Even more astounding was the accompanying theory that the alternating expansion and contraction of the universe has already occurred countless times in the past, and will occur countless times again in the future.

But, what I was totally unable to let go of and to this day am still mystified about is what some physicists hypothesize happens during the split second in which the universe transitions from expansion to contraction—the millisecond during which it is perfectly still, perfectly motionless, as it must be at some point between the transition from expansion to contraction. Some physicists postulate that at that moment the laws of physics randomly reshuffle. The laws of physics randomly reshuffle?! What?! I was blown out of the water when I first heard that theory! What that means is that everything that our species has learned about how the universe works, everything that we have painstakingly discovered over the last few thousand years about how the universe is organized, everything that human beings have ever learned about things as fundamental as gravity will, in that moment, no longer be true. The universe itself will not cease to exist, but our universe certainly will. In other words, reality as we know it, will no longer exist. In the contracting universe (we are currently in the expansion mode), up may be down and down may be up. Gravity may not exist, and even time as we know it may not exist. If we could somehow experience that contracting universe, we'd probably feel we were deep in Alice's rabbit hole and the mad hatter was quite sane. I know that our rational human minds cannot even begin to fathom such a thing, but it was in learning the Big Bang Theory itself, i.e., that the entire known universe originated from a single point that I came to the realization that science was utterly unable to answer the ultimate question: "Where did that original point come from? What was its source?" I believed that even if we learned everything else about the universe, science would never be able to answer that, the most fundamental of all questions.[138]

I remained completely haunted by that, the ultimate mystery—What is the origin of the universe? If it is a Divine Creator, what is the origin of that Creator? Science, I thought, had utterly failed me in my quest for the answer. Still in need of an answer, however, I decided, at the beginning of my sophomore year, to major in Philosophy. Of all of the academic disciplines, Philosophy was the only one that allowed me to go both broadly enough, and deeply enough, to satisfy my need to focus on nothing but the deepest, most fundamental questions of reality.

Just as finding the LSUNO NAACP College Chapter was a lifeline to me as a social activist, my study of Philosophy that began at the same time, was a lifeline to me as a young seeker of Truth. It was, indeed, a second godsend. After spending two full years, my senior year of high school and freshman year of college, in deep mourning and a full-blown depression, in the Fall of 1971, both parts of me—the social activist **and** the seeker of answers to The Mysteries, found fulfillment that allowed me to actually feel a degree of happiness for the first time since I lost my mother.

"Introduction to Philosophy" was the very first Philosophy course I took as a Philosophy major. The course was essentially a survey of several major philosophical disciplines, and a wide range of topics. Among several others, one of the most interesting was the question within the field of Aesthetics— "What is beauty?" That was actually something I had wondered about for some time. Among the things I most love about life and being human is my ability to appreciate the beauty of the natural world. Mountain ranges, waterfalls, and forest streams are for me among the most beautiful sights on our magnificent Earth. I've spent a summer in the magnificent Blue Ridge Mountains of southeast Virginia, and

138 In a conversation several years ago with my physicist friend, Jack, he told me that evidence exists that it is possible for something to come from nothing! Apparently, physicists have discovered that in a total vacuum, a point can appear - out of nowhere, or more precisely, out of nothing. I cannot even begin to think about such a thing!

driven along the mesmerizing Skyline Drive of its Shenandoah National Park. I've driven through the enthralling Green Mountains of New Hampshire and the Berkshires of Upstate New York. I've flown over the majestic Rockies of Colorado more times than I can remember, and visited its southern rim. Recently, I've lived in the foothills of Southern California's beautiful, green San Gabriel Mountains, and my present home is surrounded by the captivating San Jacinto desert mountains. As I've looked at all of those absolutely captivating mountain ranges over many years, I remember wondering in total curiosity, "What makes these mountains, these giant dirt and tree-covered rocks so incredibly beautiful?" "What **is** it," I often wondered, "that makes me experience mountains as so incredibly beautiful? They are, after all, essentially just big mounds of dirt." I was pleasantly surprised to learn that that **very** question, among others, "What is beauty? What makes certain things and not others appear beautiful to us?" is the focus of an entire branch of Philosophy – aesthetics.

Philosophy majors were required to complete an introductory course in logic. I enjoyed the rigor of the intellectual exercise of applying the principles of logic to absolutely everything. That course, more than any other, taught me how to think critically and analytically. In The History of Philosophy, we studied the ancient Greeks, Thales, Plato (my favorite of the Greek philosophers), Aristotle, Anaximander, Anaximenes, and others. In my Phenomenology course, we read Hegel's *Phenomenology of Mind*, Kant's *Critique of Pure Reason*, and Descartes' *Meditations of First Philosophy*. In Epistemology, the philosophy of knowledge, we focused on questions such as "How do we know what we know?" In other words, how do we know that what we think we know is actually true? The ultimate epistemological question was, "What is knowledge?" I was captivated by those lectures and discussions. As a Philosophy major, I also studied Ethics, in which we discussed the questions, "What is ethical and unethical?" What is moral and immoral?

What does it mean to be amoral? Does moral relativism exist, or is there an absolute, universal, unchanging, unchangeable morality by which we must all live as human beings?" My other Philosophy courses included Philosophy of Law, Philosophical Psychology, and Special Topics in Philosophy.[139]

I very much enjoyed studying the works of Plato, Rene Descartes, Friedrich Hegel, Immanuel Kant, Jean-Paul Satre, Alfred Whitehead and others, but in none of my classes did we ever study the works of any African American or White women Philosophers, and I wondered whether there **were** any. To my knowledge, there were not. "It's the history," I thought. "It's the history. It's the historic discrimination against white women and Americans of color that's responsible for us not being in Philosophy." As I pursued my studies in Philosophy, I thought that if I decided to pursue an academic career in Philosophy, I would encourage as many of my students of color and European American women students as possible to consider a career in Philosophy. I wanted us to add our thoughts, our intellectual brilliance, our scholarly genius to humanity's body of Philosophical work.[140]

My Philosophy of Mind course was one of my three favorite Philosophy courses. I loved it. In it, we dealt with the mind/body question, i.e., whether as human beings, we are simply the sum total of the physical parts that comprise our bodies, or whether there is more to us, whether we are not only body and brain, but indeed body, brain, and mind. Is there, in other words, some non-physical component of ourselves that exists independently of our bodies?

139 My total fascination with questions of the origin of the universe made metaphysics (the branch of Philosophy concerned with explaining the fundamental nature of reality) particularly fascinating to me. I thought of it as the natural next step in the progression from biology to chemistry, from chemistry to physics, and crossing over from science to philosophy, from physics to metaphysics, taking one into the very depths of inquiry about the deepest mystery—the origin of the universe. Unfortunately, metaphysics was not offered by UNO's Philosophy Department during the time of my undergraduate studies.

140 I am happy that having as an adult researched the history of African and African American philosophers, I am now aware of brilliant African philosophers including Kwasi Wiredu, Sophie Oluwole, and Anton Amo, among others, and brilliant African-American philosophers including Angela Davis, Cornell West, W.E.B DuBois, Bell Hooks, and Frantz Fanon, among others. In my research of White women philosophers, I found the brilliant Simone de Beauvoir, Hannah Arendt, Philippa Foot, and others.

It was indeed the question of whether as human beings, we have souls. Renee Descartes, the French Philosopher and main figure in the Philosophy of Mind, thought unequivocally that we do. His iconic quote, "I think, therefore I am," summarizes his position that our minds can and do exist independently of our brains, i.e., that the "I" that thinks uses "my" brain to do so. About that, I also had no doubt. Despite my serious scientific orientation, the belief that as human beings we can and do exist independently of our bodies (i.e., that we indeed have souls) is one of my strongest personal convictions. I was, therefore, one of Descartes' few followers in my class, a rare Cartesian, as his followers are called, among my classmates of almost exclusively materialists, those who believe that nothing exists except matter and, by extension, that as human beings we have material brains that do not survive death.

A CRISIS OF FAITH

When I was an eighteen-year-old college sophomore, I experienced a serious crisis of faith. I had, since I was a very young child, wondered about some of the Christian doctrines with which I was being raised. Now, I had reached the point at which I no longer wondered about them—I simply didn't believe them anymore. While I still very intensely believed that a loving Divine Creator created our marvelously mysterious universe, I simply no longer believed many of the claims about The Creator that I had been taught in my childhood. Additionally, I was, at that time, very much aware that just as Catholics believed in the Catholic church as the one true church, in mortal sins, in purgatory, in the transmutation of the eucharist, in the infallibility of the Pope, and in the canonization of saints because they were **taught** to believe them, Protestant Christians believed in the Trinity, in Jesus' death as the purpose of his life, and in the necessity to accept Christ as one's personal Lord and Savior in order to avoid Hell because we were taught to believe **them**. It was at this point that my doubts and disbelief about three important matters of the Christian faith that I had been taught my entire life began to evolve from doubt and disbelief into a formulation of my own thoughts about them.

First was the idea that God was a trinity, three gods that were simultaneously only one. The concept felt faintly polytheistic to me, as if Christianity was a relic of the many polytheistic religions that preceded it. When I thought about the Christian belief in a father-son god, I thought about some of those religions and **their** belief in father-son gods. I had learned about some of them in school. Others I read about on my own—the Egyptians' belief in Ra and his son Osiris; Osiris and his son Horus; and Atum and his son Khonshu, among others. I thought about the Greeks' belief in father-son gods, some of which I learned about in school and others that I had independently researched. Among a host of others, Uranus and his son Cronus; Cronus and his son Zeus; Zeus and his son Apollo; Apollo and his son Asclepius; and Asclepius and his son Podalirius.[141] After grappling with the notion of The Creator of the universe being a father and a son, and thinking about the fact that that same God-construct was a central theme in some of Christianity's predecessor religions, I ultimately came to believe neither that The Creator was a trinity nor that The Creator had a son. I believed rather that there was one, indivisible grand Divine Creator of our magnificent universe.[142]

The Christian belief that Jesus' death was the purpose of his life was the second matter. I didn't believe that God would use, for **any** purpose, the worst instincts of human nature, our inclination toward brutality and cruelty, and one of the most wicked manifestations of that inclination ever devised, human crucifixion. The personal belief that I began to formulate about the purpose of Jesus' life was that he lived not to **die** for us, but rather to **teach**

141 Greek religion, like many other aspects of Greek culture, was significantly inspired by the ancient Egyptians.

142 As explained earlier, my questions about what I was being taught came from no outside source. My father was a staunch agnostic, but I never discussed religion with him, nor he with me. Not once. Rather, the concept of The Creator existing as a trinity was simply antithetical to the spiritual orientation I felt at my core, the orientation with which I very deeply feel I was born. Nothing else can explain why I was so young when I began my questioning.

us, to demonstrate to us through his own example what is possible for us and, not only what we can be, but indeed what as human beings, we truly **are**. I believe that he came to teach us that we are Divine, and that we are so both because we are made in the image and likeness of God, and because God is within us.[143] I'm not sure whether at that time I believed, as I now do, that God sends prophets to the Earth, but I am sure that if so, Jesus Christ was certainly one of them. Furthermore, I believe that both Jesus' life and his three-year ministry were among the most important events in human history. I very deeply believed then, as I do now, in the beautiful wisdom of the Beatitudes, and in Jesus' profound lessons of love and compassion toward all of humanity. I came to believe that the purpose of Jesus' life was not his death. I came to believe that the purpose of his life was his example.

Finally, I stopped believing in hell. It was an enigma to me as a child, and it still made no sense to me at all. "Why," I thought, "would God send Jesus to teach us to be loving **and forgiving** if God couldn't even forgive us for our sins if Jesus didn't die for them?" I knew that my mother's incredible love for me would never allow her to sentence me to eternal damnation, no matter what I had done, so I simply couldn't understand how God, who was infinitely loving and infinitely forgiving, could do so. "We human beings couldn't be more loving than God," I thought. I simply couldn't believe that God would allow us to live perhaps ninety years on Earth and then, depending upon how we lived those ninety years, would sentence us to spend all of eternity in utter misery and pain. It just intuitively felt to me on a very deep level that The Divine Being that created the majestic mountains, The Divinity that created the Earth's magnificent waterfalls, The Spirit that created the stunning forests, brooks, glens, and meadows, The Deity that created the billions of galaxies and trillions of stars in

143 I write about this extensively in *On Religion and Spirituality Humanity's Greatest Call: The Call to Spiritual Maturity*. In this work, I simply say that with his life, Jesus was attempting to teach us that we are literally made in the image and likeness of God and, for that reason, are capable of doing not only all of the things that he did while he was here on Earth, but indeed, even greater things than he was able to show us because his life was cut so short.

this universe, The Creator that is love, is infinitely beyond anger and retribution. I believed that those were human characteristics that we human beings were projecting onto The Creator. I thought that we were anthropomorphizing The Creator by believing that if we didn't follow The Creator's will, The Creator would become angry enough with us to sentence us to eternal damnation. The concept of a vengeful, wrathful God who sentences people to hell is one that I simply could no longer accept. I wondered about what happened to "bad" people after death, from child pornographers to the Adolph Hitlers of the world, and I had no answer to the question of their after-death fate, but I knew that I no longer believed in a Hell, or in a Creator that was capable of sending us to one.[144]

In addition to those three crises of **faith**, I was simultaneously becoming increasingly uncomfortable with two Christian **practices**, taking communion, and thinking of and referring to God as male.

In high school, I had been repelled by the Catholic belief that in taking communion, we were eating the actual body and drinking the actual blood of Christ. Now, taking communion at Bethany, even with our belief that the communion wafer and grape juice were only symbolic of Jesus' body and blood, became increasingly unpleasant to me. I was aware that the belief that The Creator sent a revered messenger to Earth was present in a number of religions, but I wasn't aware of any other religion in which it was the practice to eat the body and drink the blood of God's messenger, whether literally or symbolically.

I don't remember when, where or by whom the practice of referring to God as male was explained to me, but I do remember the explanation. It was probably in response to a question that I had raised about it. The explanation was that referring to God as

144 Years later, I heard an explanation of what happens to such people that resonates with me. I discuss the issue of what happens after death to people who commit acts of great evil in my book, *On Religion and Spirituality: Humanity's Greatest Call - The Call to Spiritual Maturity.*

"He" and "Him" didn't really mean anything because God is in reality neither male nor female, that God is beyond human sex categories. That explanation, however, didn't satisfy me in the least. I believed that the practice of referring to God as "He" and "Him" resulted in the belief by most Christians that God really is a male. After all, we referred to God as Jesus' father—his father, not his parent. Indeed, we were taught to believe that not only was God Jesus' father, but that he was our father as well. "Father," "God the Father," "Heavenly Father" and "Father-God" are, I believe, the four most common Christian references to God. The Christian use of only male pronouns to refer to God, combined with the Christian reference to God as a male parent only, simply made it impossible for me to believe that Christians do not believe that God is indeed a male entity.

I thought about how a discussion of this subject between myself and a sincere, devout Christian could go, and thought that it might likely proceed as follows. I've named the other speaker Randy.

Lauren: You know, Randy, for some time now, I've been uncomfortable with the practice of referring to God as He and Him and Father. I really think that for a lot of people, it results in an unconscious belief that God truly is male. But in my mind, and I believe in the minds of many other people, God is beyond all human categories—race, color, creed, nationality, and yes, also sex. And I think that creating the idea in people's minds that God is male can and indeed does have some pretty negative consequences in our thinking about the relative roles or the place of women and men in our species. I think it reinforces ideas about their supposed inequality.

Randy: Naw. God is beyond gender. God's neither male nor female. The words we use to describe God don't mean anything. You shouldn't be hung up on that. Those are just the words we use, but God is so much greater than the words. Stop focusing so much on the words, Lauren. You're giving them far too much importance.

Lauren: Wow. I never thought of it like that. OK, so since the words don't matter at all, it must be OK to refer to God as God the Mother, and to worship the Holy Trinity as God the Mother, God the Daughter, and God the Holy Spirit. So yeah, I really get it. The words that we use to refer to God are just words, so I can pray to **Mother** God when I feel like doing **that** and to **Father** God when I feel like doing **that**. I never ever thought of it that way. Thanks, Randy!

Randy: Well, uh…. Well, no, I didn't mean, uh that…. uh

Lauren: But you said that God is beyond sex and therefore neither male nor female, right?

Randy: Well yeah, but uh, well, I didn't mean that you could pray to **Mother** God.

Lauren: Oh, Ok. I'm sorry. Well what did you mean?"

Randy: Well, just that uh…. I mean uh….

In the end, my difficulty with the three articles of Christian faith and the two Christian practices discussed above, resulted in my inability to continue to believe the Christian doctrine I had been taught all my life. I continued, however, to have a very strong belief in what I was taught were Christian principles, those taught by Jesus, the principles of forgiveness, of non-violence, and most importantly, love.

THE END OF CHURCH IN MY LIFE: AMBIVALENCE AND SORROW

At about the same time as I was experiencing my crisis of faith, after serving as Bethany's minister for more than ten years, the hierarchy of the Methodist Church, to the utter dismay of Bethany's entire congregation, reassigned Reverend Kennedy to another church.[145] It was June 1972, my sophomore year of college. I attended church with Lorna for several weeks after Reverend Kennedy left, but have absolutely no memory of the minister who took his place. I do very clearly remember, however, that during those first few weeks when Reverend Kennedy was no longer at Bethany, my church experience felt very different, empty really. It no longer felt like the church that was such a wonderful part of my childhood, the church that meant so much to my mother. In response to the combination of those two factors, the crisis of faith that I was experiencing and Reverend Kennedy's simultaneous departure, I made, at the age of eighteen, what was for me, the very difficult decision to stop attending church. I said goodbye to Bethany.

Discontinuing my life at Bethany was a huge change in my life. It felt like an enormous loss of a connection to my mother and to a place that had been extremely significant in my life for as long as I could remember. My decision to stop attending Bethany was accompanied by feelings of both great ambivalence and deep sorrow.

145 The Church attempted to reassign Reverend Kennedy to another congregation several years prior. The Pastor Parish Relations Committee, however, under my mother's leadership as Committee Chair, was successful in convincing the church's regional leadership to allow Reverend Kennedy to continue to serve at Bethany for several more years.

GOING DEEPER THAN SCIENCE: MY PHILOSOPHICAL STUDY OF RELIGION - A PROFOUND AWAKENING

IT WAS DURING THE LAST YEAR OF MY UNDERGRADUATE PHILOSOPHY studies that I enrolled in my two favorite Philosophy courses—The Philosophy of Religion and Religions of the World. Philosophy of Religion was first. I loved that course. The Philosophy of Religion is the study of neither religious beliefs in general nor those of any particular religion. It is, rather, the study of the very nature of both religion itself and religious belief. It is the study of the very meaning of religion for human beings. We read and discussed the essays in *Philosophy of Religion*, by John Hick, *Basic Modern Philosophy of Religion*, by Frederick Ferre, *God, Man, and Religion: Readings in the Philosophy of Religion*, by Keith E. Yandell, and *From Religion to Philosophy: A Study in the Origins of Western Speculation*, by F. M. Cornford. The course was, for me, up to that point on my spiritual journey, **the** most exciting academic study of my life. While the course didn't focus on all of The Mysteries, to my utter delight, among the issues on which it did focus, was the question, "Does God exist?." I held a very strong personal belief in the existence of a Divine Creator, but being able to study the question of whether God exists was a kind of intellectual excitement I had never before experienced.

Among other issues that we considered in the course were the following:

- What is religion?
- What is it about human beings that accounts for countless societies, both throughout history and around the world, having started religions? Are our brains hard-wired for faith in The Divine? If so, what purpose would such hard wiring serve?
- Why have religions been so enduring throughout human history?

- The classical arguments for God's existence, including the classical deductive arguments; the rationalist arguments; the Cartesian approach; the cosmological argument; the ontological argument; and the empiricist argument.
- The classical case for skepticism of all of the arguments for God's existence.

What was to my mind among the most challenging questions that we studied in the course was what is known within Philosophy as "the problem of evil." It is the problem, essentially, of how evil can coexist with an all benevolent, omniscient, omnipotent, omnipresent God. I spent countless hours thinking about what were for me the two questions within the study of the problem of evil—the how and the why of its creation.

The "How" question: Since God created everything in the universe and nothing pre-dated His (using the pronoun that we used at the time) existence, He must have also created evil. But how can that be? If God is all, only and wholly goodness and love, there can be no evil in Him, so how is it even possible for Him to have created evil? I have never heard what was for me, a satisfactory answer to that question.

The "Why" question: Leaving aside the question of how it was even possible for God, a Being of pure and infinite goodness and love to have created evil, the question of why God would do so troubled me to no end. Why would God create evil and then allow it to both exist and thrive? Why does He allow hatred, murder, torture, rape, greed, selfishness, prejudice of many kinds, and all other forms of evil to exist among human beings? Many theists posit that evil comes not from God, but from an evil power at play in the universe. Within Christianity, that evil power would be the devil, known by his many names. The obviously ensuing question then is, "Why did God, The Creator of everything, create the devil in the first place?" The more specific questions for Christians and perhaps others are as follows:

- You believe that God is omniscient, i.e., all-knowing. If so, is it not true that He **had** to have known how evil, after He created it, was going to affect the world? If God is omniscient, wouldn't He have known, in advance, all of the specific forms of profound suffering that would result?
- You believe that God is omnipotent, i.e., all-powerful, so having created evil, God unquestionably has the power to end both it and the unspeakable suffering caused by it. Why doesn't He? Why does God allow evil and its excruciating consequences to **continue** to plague the world?
- You believe that God is omnipresent, i.e., existing everywhere at the same time. If that were so, how can evil exist anywhere? How can it co-exist in the same space with God?

The "why" question, however, the question of **why** The Creator created evil is, for me, one of the most difficult theological issues.

In speaking with Christians about the issue, I have only ever received two responses. The first is that God wanted to and indeed did create us with free will, not as non-thinking automatons, robots or puppets who blindly and unthinkingly follow His will. They say that God created us with free will because He wanted us to choose to follow Him. He did not want us to live essentially as marionettes at the end of strings that He pulls. Evil, they say, must therefore exist in order for us to be able to choose good over evil, to choose God over the devil, that it is a logical impossibility for us to choose good if there is no evil.

That response is not now, nor has it ever been, satisfactory to me. It is not so because it implies that The Divine Spirit was limited in the possibilities that were available to It in providing us with choice. My specific questions regarding that implied limitation are, "Then why did God set it up that way? Why couldn't God have created us with free will, without creating the evil that has resulted in human beings as a species living an abysmal existence, plagued by perpetual hatred, war, greed, selfishness, and corruption? After all, it's The Creator we're talking about here. Surely The Divine Spirit in Its infinite wisdom could have figured that out."

In my complete human intellectual finiteness, one possibility that occurs to me in that regard is that instead of giving us free will to choose between good and **evil**, The Creator **could** have given us free will to choose between good and **exceptional**. In other words, The Creator could have given us a choice between a world that is ordinary, and one that is essentially heaven on Earth. At least with the latter choice, if we did not choose to follow goodness, the consequence could perhaps be that as a species we would live only an **ordinary** existence as opposed to an **extraordinary** one. In our actual world, by contrast, with our choice between good and **evil**, and with our species having so often throughout our history **chosen** evil, our existence is one that has historically been beset by prejudice, war, genocide, human trafficking, large-scale rape, human slavery, the atrocious suffering of animals, and the horrendous trashing of the Earth.

Stated as clearly as possible, The Divine Creator could have organized the world very differently. If it was important for us to **choose** to follow The Creator, among what may have been a myriad of available possibilities, were those of:

A. Giving us a choice, as a species, to live either an ordinary life, **or** a divinely exceptional one; and,
B. Giving us a choice to live either an ordinary life, **or** a miserable one.

Why then, did The Creator choose the latter in which our world truly **is** miserable? Perhaps the answer is that we cannot evolve, we cannot develop the yearning for The Divine without suffering. It was, indeed, The Buddha's quest to find the answer to the question of why we suffer that ultimately led to his enlightenment. My question, in that case, would then be, "But why couldn't The Creator have created us to evolve in response to an **ordinary** existence? Why couldn't we have been created to yearn to seek The Divine in response to **mediocrity** as opposed to suffering?

The second response to the question of evil that I have received from Christians, i.e., the question of how and why God created evil that causes so much suffering is that God doesn't cause our suffering. We cause our own suffering. It is the choices that we make that cause us to suffer, the choice, specifically, to reject God and to choose evil. I find that response unsatisfactory because it begs the previously discussed question of why God even created evil in the first place.

A growing number of contemporary Christians are abandoning belief in a devil as a personality that is alive and active in the world, a fascinating development about which much can be written. One conceivable response to the question of evil from such an individual is that our species has historically lived and continues to live in abject misery not because we choose **evil**, but because we simply do not choose **God**, and whenever we do not choose God, i.e., wherever there is the **absence** of God, or godliness, or goodness, there is suffering. To that response, I have the same reply: "Why is the only available dichotomy God or suffering as opposed to God or mediocrity?"

Additionally, the suggestion that it is our act of choosing evil that results in our suffering, also fails miserably, in my opinion, to address the issue of innocent suffering—the contraction of disease, babies born with devastating disabilities, losing one's life in a natural disaster, and suddenly losing a loved one in a tragic accident, or to an act of random violence, among many other possibilities. I do not believe that there is a rational answer to the problem of evil, no answers that withstand logical scrutiny.[146]

As we grappled with those and other fundamental questions of faith in my Philosophy of Religion class, I wished that millions of people around the world could somehow engage their minds in a similar fashion. I wished that we could in some way develop a method of helping a critical mass of human beings to begin to look seriously, judiciously and analytically at both the substance of their religious beliefs, and why they hold them. I loved my Philosophy of Religion course.

Of all of the Philosophy courses I took as an undergraduate, however, my absolute favorite was, "Religions of the World." The course was essentially a survey of many of humanity's great religions. We studied the Western Abrahamic traditions of Judaism, Christianity and Islam, as well as the major Eastern religious traditions. Although I had been reared in the Christian tradition, of which Judaism is the foundational faith, I knew next to nothing about Judaism. I loved learning about the Jewish foundation of the religion in which I had been reared, and because the beliefs of Islam were also entirely new to me, I found the underpinnings of that faith intriguing as well. I was also fascinated by the information we learned in the course about the consequences of all three Western religions having succeeded their pagan predecessors. In the course, my instructor discussed a number of Christianity's predecessors in which a central figure was born of a virgin, in which the phenomenon of sacrifice was present, and in which the central figure of the religion had been severely persecuted. Learning about how around the world, earlier religions consistently influ-

146 The concept of pre-birth planning, i.e., the belief that prior to birth, we choose our parents and many of the circumstances of our lives, including all of its hardships, provides, for some theists, primarily members of some Eastern religions, another answer to the problem of evil. The belief is that in order to maximize opportunities for our soul to grow in wisdom, and thus achieve liberation, union with The Creator, we choose the life circumstances, including all of the painful ones that are most likely to cause us to grow. Many people find that notion highly offensive, however, because of its "blame the victim" connotation, i.e., its inference that whatever adversities one experiences in life are one's own fault for having chosen them.

enced their successors, and specifically how the three Abrahamic faiths, Judaism, Christianity, and Islam, had been influenced by religions that preceded them was, for me, absolutely fascinating. Additionally, I began comparing Christianity to Judaism, Islam and other faiths that believe in one indivisible God, other faiths that have no communion ritual, and religions in which the concept of sacrifice was not central, and in so doing, gained a true appreciation of them.

It was in that course, "Religions of the World", that I was introduced for the very first time to the great religions of the East. We studied the Eastern religions of Hinduism, Buddhism, Taoism, Shintoism, and the philosophy of Confucius (which is a philosophy, not a religion). Inexplicably, from the very beginning, the Eastern spiritual concepts to which I was being introduced very deeply resonated with me, particularly those that originated in India. Indeed, those concepts somehow actually felt familiar to me. It is categorically no exaggeration to say that it felt as if I had somehow known those concepts before. I am utterly unable to explain why that was the case. I only remember quite clearly that it just very much was so.

Learning some of the fundamental beliefs, concepts and principles of all of the faiths we studied, opened both my intellectual and my spiritual eyes in a way that I could never have imagined. It was the Hindu concept of enlightenment, however, that utterly captivated me — the belief that it is the purpose of human life to do three things. First, to slowly and steadily perfect ourselves, i.e., our character, becoming increasingly compassionate, increasingly patient, increasingly more peaceful, and increasingly wise, eventually becoming altruistic, enlightened beings. Second, as enlightened beings, to help others with whom we interact to understand and to reach **their** potential for enlightenment. Third and finally, to ultimately become one with The Creator, i.e., achieve God Realization. It is the Hindu conception of enlightenment. I distinctly remember feeling that in that concept, in that belief, the belief that we come from The Creator and that we are all on a long journey first to reflect, then to help others reflect, and then to ultimately return to The Creator, I had found my spiritual home. For that reason more than any other, my "Religions of the World" course was for me, no less than life-changing.

The Buddhist understanding of enlightenment, often referred to within Buddhism as "awakening" is very different. Buddhism is an agnostic religion in which the existence of a Divine Creator is neither confirmed nor denied. The concept of "God Realization", or reunion with God, is therefore not a part of the Buddhist concept of enlightenment. It is the notion, rather, of awakening. We awake from the dream-like state in which we live our daily lives, in which we are driven by our desires and fears and are utterly unaware of our potential to be enlightened, or "awake" beings. Buddhists think of enlightenment as spiritual liberation through the transcendence of desire and its resulting suffering. A liberated being is characterized as one who has achieved complete peace, infinite compassion and perfect wisdom. Buddhists believe that while Buddha achieved enlightenment, **every** human being is capable of achieving it. Among the most beautiful Buddhist concepts is that of the Bodhisattva, one who has dedicated their own liberation to helping all others become liberated.

I clearly remember that my "Religions of the World" course was also emotionally comforting to me. During the period in which I was experiencing a crisis in my faith, I felt spiritually lost. I had for some time questioned several aspects of the Christian theology in which I had been raised, and no longer attending church left me, for the first time in my life, feeling a spiritual void. Learning about some of the spiritual principles of the East that resonated so intensely with me, helped me fill that void, and was, therefore, indeed quite comforting.

After completing my "Religions of the World" course, I thought about how very little most of us who received religious training as children know about faiths other than the one in which we were reared. I know, for example, that among numerous other misunderstandings, many non-Hindus believe that Hindus worship millions of different gods, that many non-Buddhists believe that Buddhists worship Buddha as God, and that many non-Muslims believe that Muslims worship the Prophet Muhammad as God. I comprehend fully how such misunderstandings can exist. None of those beliefs, however, has any truth whatsoever. Once I became aware of how little I knew of religions other than the Christian faith in which I had been reared, I realized that most of the adults in my life likely also knew very little about other religions.

I was completely uncomfortable with the thought that my own beliefs about the questions that were so fundamentally important to me, my questions about The Mysteries, had been determined solely by what I had been taught as a child. I wanted my beliefs to not be the result of years of exposure to only one belief system. Rather, I wanted my beliefs to be the result of a very serious study of major theological questions, and the various answers to those questions found in humanity's great faiths.

After four years of college, in 1974, at the age of twenty, I earned a Bachelor of Arts degree in Philosophy from The University of New Orleans.[147] I absolutely adored my undergraduate study of Philosophy, and when I graduated, my desire/plan for my life was to have a career as a university Professor of Philosophy with a specialty in Eastern Religions and Comparative Philosophy. For that, I needed to earn a Ph.D., but I had to earn a master's degree first. I applied to and was accepted into the master's degree program in Philosophy at The University of Connecticut (UCONN). Lorna graduated from Coghill Elementary School the same

147 The University, while remaining in the Louisiana State University system, changed its name from "Louisiana State University in New Orleans", "LSUNO," to "The University of New Orleans", "UNO," just weeks before my graduation.

year and went to Washington, D.C. to live with my oldest brother, Lemar Jr., and his family, so that I could begin my graduate studies at UCONN.

Leaving Lorna was one of the hardest things that to that point, I had ever done. I had been her mother for five years, and she had bonded with me, and I with her. I knew, however, that I had to go to graduate school and work on making my dreams of having a career in academia a reality. If I hadn't gone to graduate school, I saw only two other alternatives after graduating from UNO. One was to return to UNO, enroll in and complete a one-year teacher certification program, and then teach high school in New Orleans for six years until Lorna graduated from high school, at which point I would have been twenty-seven years old. The other was to apply for a job with my mother's former employer, the New Orleans Urban League. If I had indeed stayed in New Orleans after college and done either of those, both our lives, mine and Lorna's, would have been extremely different. I knew, intuitively, that for both our futures, I had to leave New Orleans, and get Lorna out as well.[148]

I began my one-year Master's Degree program in Philosophy at The University of Connecticut in the Fall of 1974, two weeks after my twenty-first birthday. For primarily three reasons, I enjoyed my year at UCONN tremendously. First, after staying home for college and living in my childhood bedroom until I was almost twenty-one years old, I was finally living on my own. That alone was quite wonderful for me.

Second, after living in the city of New Orleans for my entire twenty-one years, the part of me that had always loved nature was

148 It was, I believe, no accident that the option was available for Lorna to live at that time with my brother and his family in Washington. I simply could not, nor would I in a million years, have left her at home in New Orleans with my father and older brother Lambert while I went off to graduate school in Connecticut. They would have taken very good care of her, and protected her, and my father would certainly have provided for all of her needs, but in leaving her with them I would have felt that I was abandoning her, which I could not have done. Having Lorna go to Washington to live with Lemar Jr. and his family when I went off to graduate school in Connecticut felt, in a sense, that I was taking her with me. I was certainly taking her with me out of New Orleans. It felt good that in Washington, she was going to be relatively close to me in Connecticut.

being gratified. I was, for the first time, living in a place that was filled with beautiful landscapes. The breathtaking New England Fall colors, the white winter snows, the rolling green hills, the forests with creeks and tiny waterfalls, the Atlantic beaches, the countryside with classic red barns and rusty wagons from what must have been the early 1900s or even earlier, the covered bridges—it was all like something straight out of a Norman Rockwell painting. During my year at UCONN, with the exception of end-of-semester exam time, I took long rides in my Volkswagen bug every Sunday afternoon, playing soft meditation music on my eight-track cassette player, often with sunlight streaming in from the open sunroof. At other times, overhead was a gray Fall or Spring sky filled with the mysteriousness and splendor of colossal, dark rain clouds. It was me alone on a beautiful, New England country road, often with very few other cars—the realization of many a daydream of little Lauren growing up in New Orleans collecting calendar pictures of beautiful landscapes.

Third, in my Master's Program I was studying only Philosophy, which pleased me to no end. I was studying Western philosophy, however, which is based upon rationality and reason. My courses included Moral Philosophy, Recent Social and Political Philosophy, and my two favorites, Metaphysics and the Philosophy of Mind. As much as I genuinely enjoyed my philosophical studies at UCONN, however, my Master's Degree studies clarified for me what I learned in my undergraduate Philosophy of Religion and Religions of the World courses—that I had to go deeper than Western philosophy could take me. I knew it was imperative for me to study the Wisdom Traditions of the East. I knew that Philosophy, as an intellectual discipline founded on reason, was entirely incapable of providing answers to the deepest mysteries that still plagued me.

I had a wonderful year in Connecticut as a graduate Philosophy student, and in May of 1975, at the age of twenty-one, earned a Master of Arts Degree in Philosophy from The University of Connecticut. Having earned both a Bachelor of Arts and a Master of Arts degree in Philosophy, I was now enthusiastic about starting the last chapter of my academic journey—a Ph.D. program in Eastern Philosophy and Comparative Religion.

HAVING AND LOSING GRAMZIE - MY HEART

Between my Masters and Doctoral programs, during my second year of working at Wesleyan, we lost Gramzie. I've said to many people on countless occasions, "That old lady was my heart." I cannot describe in any way that will even come close to being adequate Gramzie's love for us, her children and grandchildren, and her compassion for others. Gramzie, a woman of deep religious faith, was truly an angel on this Earth.

Toward all five of her grandchildren whom she had when I was very young, she showed the same loving kindness. When, for example, my cousin Drexel was in the process of doing something he shouldn't have been doing (and Drexel was **always** in the process of doing something he shouldn't have been doing), Gramzie, who spoke in the dialect that was typical of older New Orleaneans at that time, would call out to him in a voice in which even through her frustration and worry that he might hurt himself, her love could also be clearly heard. "Drexel Michael Gillard! Come down off of dat roof, lil boy. You could fall down! Na get down from there and come inside fo you hurt yoself. Yo Aint Selina's comin' to git ya'll soon." She had to speak loudly enough for Drexel to hear her from the roof, but it never felt like she was yelling at him. Gramzie never yelled at any of us - ever.

Gramzie's heart was so big that it had enough room for not only her tremendous love for her children and grandchildren, but also for her neighbors. I remember when she sent food over to Miss Nita, her Korean American neighbor in the Desire Project, when Miss Nita was running low on food for her children. It seemed as if Gramzie was a grandmother to all the children on her street, Desire Parkway. I can still hear her voice as she talked through the window to one of her neighbor's children. "Bobby don't play in the street, baby. A caw could hit chew. You know yo mama don't want you playin' in the street. Now come on and play right here on the grass where Miss Gramzie can see you." I remember that Gramzie used to babysit her European American neighbor's kids, Linda, Billie and Jimmy, and how kind she was to them. On more than one occasion when I was a child, after she'd once again seen a stray dog through the window, Gramzie put some food on a plate, handed it to me, and then said as she pointed to a spot just outside the door, "Here baby. Go right there and put this down for him."

I had allergies as a child, and was acutely allergic to almost everything I was tested for - oak, grass, pollen, and many of the other things that were abundantly present in the swampy New Orleans environment in which I lived. My allergies caused me to regularly suffer severe hay fever attacks with all of the typical symptoms, miserably itchy eyes and throat, sinuses that were totally blocked, and the feeling of having the worst head cold in the world. Whenever I was sick, my mother took me to Gramzie's house and Gramzie took care of me, as she did all of her grandchildren. She'd lay me on her bed saying, "Come here baby, let Gramzie doctor on you." She'd crush a baby Aspirin into a half cup of orange juice, hold the cup up to my mouth, and make me drink all of it. Afterwards, she dished up a small warm bowl of yellow grits from the pot of it that was on her stove **every** morning, and made me eat it. She'd then put Vicks VapoRub on my temples, my forehead and under my nose, slather it on my chest, then make me swallow a teaspoonful of Caster Oil. To this day, I still remember how horrible that Caster Oil tasted. Then, after she'd "doctored on me", Gramzie would "start to prayin" over me, as the old people referred to it. She'd hold me in her lap, and then placing her right hand on my forehead, she'd start asking Jesus to heal me. "Just heal this child, Lord. Please. Take her pain and her misery away from her, Lord. Make her feel better, Jesus. Lord, just take the sickness away from my child and help her feel better, please God." Throughout my entire life, and I'm sure for years before I was born, Gramzie had an altar in her bedroom that had a small number of religious statues, and at least thirty religious candles on it. In the front of the altar, right in the middle, was a small white, marble rectangular container of what she called "holy water." Although Gramzie grew up in the Baptist church, she periodically took a small vial of water to Corpus Christi Catholic Church, and asked the priest to bless it. The blessed water then became the holy water on Gramzie's altar. After many more pleas for my health, Gramzie would dip the four fingers of her right hand into the holy water, put them on the top of my head, and then end her prayer with the same words and in the same cadence. "I ask blessings for this child in your name, dear God, in the name of the Father and of the Son, and of the Holy Ghost. My Savior Christ. Amen." She held me until I fell asleep. When I woke up on her bed, I **always** felt better. I'm sure Gramzie's "doctoring" helped, but I wouldn't be surprised if there was also some magic in the passion of her prayers!

Several years later, when I was in college and driving my little red Volkswagen Bug, Gramzie would roll two dollars in a tight ball and put them in my hand saying, "Here baby. Put some gas in yo caw." I always protested. Because I took care of all of Gramzie's business, I knew that she lived on the $20.00 that was left of her $62.00 monthly Social Security check after she paid her $7.00 rent, bought her food stamps and paid for her medications. Every time she rolled up those two dollars, took my hand and put them in it, I said the same thing, "Gramzie, my Daddy gives me money for gas. You keep your money so you can buy what you need." Her response, said with determination, was also always the same, "Here I say. Take this money lil girl, and go 'head and put some gas in yo caw." I knew that my Uncle Ikee and Aunts Verlie and Johnnie also made sure that Gramzie had everything she needed, but it still didn't feel right for me to take money from her. Once, as I was on my way out of her apartment, Gramzie insisted that I take the two dollars. I refused, kissed her goodbye, and walked out. She then proceeded to throw the money out of the window on the ground so that I would **have** to pick the money up and take it. I just shook my head, smiled, and said, "Thank you, Gramzie", then left. From that time on, whenever Gramzie gave me the two dollars, I reluctantly took them, then went straight to Schwegmann's gas station near my house and with the two dollars, bought gas. As I remember, with those two dollars I actually got a third to a half tank of gas!

In July of 1976, after a terrifying flight over the Atlantic in a frightening rain, thunder and lightning storm following a month-long visit to Ghana, upon landing at JFK airport, I immediately called Gramzie to let her know that I had made it back home safely. Her response was, "You made it back home uh my baby?" I was relieved that after the pain of losing my mother, Gramzie did not have to also experience the pain of losing me.

My last visit with Gramzie was near the end of her life when she was in the hospital. Her bed was the last one in a long ward in Charity Hospital in which there appeared to have been perhaps ten beds on one wall and ten on the other. When I got to her bed, she introduced me to the woman who was in the bed next to hers, "Dis my granddaughter. Dis my dead daughter's daughter." Her words cut like a knife. After saying "hello" to her new friend, I asked Gramzie how she was doing, and sat, and held her hand. After I'd been there a minute or so, she noticed that the woman in the bed directly across from her was trying, unsuccessfully, to use her spittoon. Seeing that, Gramzie said to me, "Go help her spit, baby." Gramzie's compassionate heart was with her to the end, always caring about and trying to help others. After I'd helped the woman spit, I noticed a magazine with a religious theme on Gramzie's nightstand. I'm sure it wasn't hers because having completed only the third grade, Gramzie couldn't read. Someone must've brought it and left it there for her. Knowing how deeply religious Gramzie was, I thought that there may have been a passage in the magazine that she would enjoy hearing, so letting go of her hand, I picked it up and opened it. To my utter surprise and disbelief, the magazine opened to a page on which were printed the lyrics of Charles Meighs' hymn, "Others"! In that moment, I gasped, and my eyes filled with tears that flowed down my face. I tried to hide them from Gramzie, but my struggle to stop them was futile. I was **completely** moved by the fact that more than any other, **the** thought that comes to my mind if I were to describe Gramzie's life is that she lived it for others. Gramzie lived her life for others, for her children, for her grandchildren, and for her neighbors and friends. With my voice quivering uncontrollably, I read the words of the hymn to her.

Lord help me live from day to day
In such a self-forgetful way
That even when I kneel to pray
My prayer shall be for others.

Others, Lord, yes others.
Let this my motto be.
Help me to live for others
That I may live like thee.

I was taken by how very fitting it was for **those** to be the words that appeared for me to share with Gramzie. After I read the words of the hymn to her, I sat with her for a while and held her hand again while struggling with the awareness that I was going to have to leave her. I had stopped at the hospital on my way to the airport. I was traveling with several colleagues from other colleges and because I had stayed so long with Gramzie, I was aware of the small window I had to get to the airport and on my flight. Leaving Gramzie was one of the hardest things I'd ever done in my life. As I sat there with her, I actually thought about **not** leaving her. I stayed with her until the very last minute I could, and then said to her, "Gramzie, I have to go now, but I'm coming back soon to see you. You're going to be alright, Gramzie." She looked at me, smiled and said, "Gramzie's just tired, baby." My final words to my grandmother were, "I love you so much, Gramzie." She smiled again and said, "Gramzie loves you too. Bye my baby." I walked the long length of the ward, and before walking through the door, looked back at Gramzie and threw her a kiss. She smiled at me once again.

I arrived at the airport within minutes of my flight's departure, and when I stepped into the plane, my colleagues broke out in spontaneous applause. When they asked me what happened, all I could say, tearfully, was, "It's my grandmother. She's in the hospital."

Several days later, when I was back home in Connecticut, my father called and told me that Gramzie had died. My heart ached. At the same time, I felt tremendous gratitude that I was able to see her one last time. I did not fly back home to attend Gramzie's funeral. I wanted to remember her as she was in life, my grandmother who deeply loved me.

I have experienced tremendous good fortune throughout my life, doors that have opened for me just when I needed them to, and seeming coincidences that occurred at the most opportune time. Having to be in New Orleans for work when Gramzie was in the hospital was one such experience. As I look back at the many times I've had such experiences over the course of my life, I no longer believe that any of them **were** coincidences.

Barbara has heard my stories about Gramzie for the past twenty-two years. At first, every time she heard Bill Wither's song, "Grandma's Hands," Bill Withers - Grandma's Hands (Official

Audio) - YouTube she'd say to me, "That song reminds me of your Gramzie." Now, whenever we hear it, she says simply, "There's Gramzie's song." I smile and say, "Yeah." Not all of the lyrics weren't applicable to Gramzie, but the **spirit** of the song certainly is.

Having Gramzie was, for me, like having a second loving mother. I was at her house every day both before and after school during my elementary school years at Moton, so she truly did **feel** like my second mom. During the twenty-three years that I knew her, I never once saw Gramzie become angry, never heard her raise her voice, and never, not once, did I ever hear her use a curse word. She told me several times that my father's mother, my Grandma Emma, was a very sweet woman. Unfortunately, Grandma Emma died nearly a decade before I was born. I look forward to meeting her someday. In **this** life, however, Gramzie was the only grandmother I ever had, and ever knew.

Gramzie lived on this Earth from 1906 until 1976. She left it two months before her 70th birthday. In some respects, she lived a very small life. To my knowledge, she never rode on a train, never traveled on an airplane, and indeed never left the city. I can count on one hand the number of times I remember Gramzie even leaving her apartment. By those measures, Gramzie's life may have been quite limited, quite small. To her four children, my Uncle Isaac, my mother, and my Aunts Verlie and Johnnie, and to all thirteen of her grandchildren, Lemar Jr., Lambert, Gerard, Drexel, Lauren, Elliott, Kevin, Lorna, Neville, Shelly, Keith, Tonya, and Joe Jr. , however, Gramzie was a giant. She was a giant in all of our lives. She was certainly a **gigantic** loving presence in mine.

Nearly a half-century after Gramzie left us, at 69 years and ten months old, I am now the age that Gramzie was when she died. I can only hope that I have touched at least one person's life in as profound a way that Gramzie touched so many.

I have often thought that in having had Selina Gray Joichin as my mother, and Victoria Edwards Gray as my grandmother, experiencing in my early life, such **deep** and **profound** love, I won the birth lottery. I cannot imagine the person I would be today had I not begun life feeling such powerful love, without having known such great love from my mother and my grandmother. Gramzie's love for me, her compassion for and resulting kindness toward others, and her amazing gentleness of spirit had a **tremendous** influence on me as a child, ultimately, molding me into the person I became as an adult. My love for her will never diminish. That old lady, to whom this spiritual memoir is dedicated, truly was and always shall be my heart.

My Gramzie

CHAPTER FOUR

MY NEED TO GO DEEPER THAN WESTERN PHILOSOPHY

GRADUATE SCHOOL AND MY STUDY OF EASTERN PHILOSOPHY

I entered the Ph.D. program in the Department of Religious Studies at The University of Pennsylvania in the Fall of 1977. I loved my Ph.D. studies! As a student of Eastern Philosophy and Comparative Religion, my intellectual and spiritual lives had finally been integrated. I was now studying some of the world's oldest and what I considered to be its most profound religious and philosophical principles. I was studying the religions of ancient India.[149] I wanted to earn my doctorate from Penn and, with a career as a Professor of Eastern Philosophy and Comparative Religion,

149 I have since learned a good deal about some of the religions of ancient Africa and in so doing, have developed an appreciation of some of them as well. As an African American, I am comforted by that. It is Hinduism, however, the religion of ancient India, that powerfully, compellingly tugs my spiritual heart strings.

spend my life teaching humanity's most ancient wisdom. My hope was that I would be of help to others who, like me, were haunted by The Mysteries.

Among my doctoral courses were an Introduction to Indian Philosophy and Elementary Sanskrit, the language in which the Bhagavad Gita, the sacred text of Hinduism, was written. In my classes, I was delving deeply into the Eastern wisdom traditions that in my undergraduate Religions of the World course we simply touched upon. It was my intellectual dream that was preparing me for my career dream. I was following my dream, and I was enthralled. In essence, we were studying what the ancient Indian rishis and other wise ones of the East had written about the most profound mysteries of the universe thousands of years before the advent of any Western religions.[150] My mind was absolutely captivated. I thought, "These are the predecessors of The Wise Men of the East who visited Christ at his birth." I thought that they must have followed the Star of Bethlehem and made that pilgrimage because, in their wisdom, they knew that Jesus was born as a fully Enlightened Being who would try to teach others that they too have the capacity, indeed the calling, to find their own divinity and become enlightened. I believed that that was the purpose of Christ's life. I wondered why the profound spiritual wisdom of the East was not present in the West. Going even deeper into my studies of Eastern spiritual wisdom, as I did during my Ph.D. studies, made me even more determined to share, as a professor here in the West, that knowledge, that profound spiritual wisdom of the East. Later in my personal spiritual studies, in learning about the ancient, esoteric mystical or contemplative traditions of the Jewish, Christian, and Muslim faiths, I learned that that wisdom was indeed in the West, and that it **had** been for centuries, just known by very few. Simultaneously, I was introduced to Perennial Philosophy, or Perennial Wisdom, the view that the beliefs of many of humanity's religious traditions stem from a common metaphysical

150 Unfortunately, but not surprisingly, we studied no female Indian sages.

truth long veiled in the West, that God is within, that for each and every one of us, the Kingdom of God is therefore literally at hand, that it is possible for us to live as true reflections of God, and that doing so is the purpose of human life. I believed those concepts as deeply as one can believe anything.[151]

Unfortunately, at the same time that I was enjoying my studies at Penn, I was also learning from fourth-year students in the Religious Studies Department, some of whom were ABD ("all but dissertation," i.e.,those who had completed their course work and comprehensive exams, and had only their dissertation to complete in order to earn their Ph.D.) that at that time, there were very few academic jobs available anywhere in the country in the arcane disciplines of Eastern Philosophy and Comparative Religion. While at Penn, I also got to know graduates of the program, Teaching Assistants (TAs) who had completed the program, had their Ph.D. in hand, and were willing to go anywhere in the country to teach, none of whom had a single job prospect. I was seeing in real life what the American Philosophical Association (APA) had informed me of in a form letter that had been enclosed with my M.A. and Ph.D. admission applications. In the letter (that the APA requested graduate programs in Philosophy include with all admission applications), the APA informed the applicant that the job prospects for Ph.D. graduates in Philosophy were extremely limited, and not likely to improve for at least the next decade.[152] As a result, upon completing my first year in the doctoral program and actually seeing all of the exceedingly well-qualified ABD students and actual graduates of Penn's Ph.D. Religious Studies Program (which was ranked second in the nation at the time) who had no job prospects, it was with considerable reservation that I decided to take a year off to seriously consider whether I would continue in the program. The very real prospect of living in a West Philadelphia

151 I discuss Perennial Wisdom in much greater detail in *On Religion and Spirituality: Humanity's Greatest Calling: The Call to Spiritual Maturity.*

152 Despite that warning, I enrolled in both my M.A. and Ph.D. programs with the conviction that if there was only **one** teaching job available in my field, in the country, I would get it!

group house with four or five other ABD students or Teaching Assistants and working as a TA for an undetermined number of years in my 30's after having earned my degree was not in the least bit appealing to me. I wanted to earn my degree, secure a teaching position at a small, liberal arts university, teach, conduct research, write articles and books, attend and present at academic conferences about matters of religion and spirituality, live in a house in the woods, and regularly travel to India. That was the life I very much wanted.

During my year off, I did a tremendous amount of soul-searching about whether to return to my Ph.D. program. At the end of that year, after doing all of my intense thinking, and meditating about the matter, I made the very difficult decision to not return. I had earned my BA in Philosophy, I had earned my MA in Philosophy, and I was now abandoning my Ph.D. program in Philosophy. I was painfully aware that in so doing, I was deserting the only plan I had for my life that I had devotedly pursued for years. I knew that I was walking away from my life dream of being a Professor of Eastern Philosophy and Comparative Religion, my dream of spending my life opening my students' minds, teaching them to think critically and analytically about matters of religion and spirituality, and exposing them to what some of humanity's most ancient Wisdom Traditions thought about reality's most profound mysteries. It was an **extremely** difficult thing for me to do. I was twenty-five years old.[153]

153 Quite fortuitously, thirty years after beginning my Ph.D. studies in 1977 in preparation for an academic career, I began working for the California State University (CSU) system in October, 2007. I retired from two of the CSU campuses as Director of Training and Professional Development, a position in which I conducted the same kinds of workshops for members of the faculty and staff that I had facilitated as an Organizational Development trainer and consultant. Although in not quite the manner and with not quite the focus I had planned, I had, through a very circuitous route, ultimately ended up teaching in a university setting as I had aspired to do thirty years prior upon beginning my Ph.D. studies in 1977. It was a long, meandering journey back to academe, but one that I wouldn't trade for a treasure.

CHAPTER FIVE

MY POST-GRADUATE SPIRITUAL JOURNEY

While I had left my doctoral program in which I was studying what some of humanity's most ancient religious traditions have taught throughout the ages about The Mysteries, I was still plagued by them. I had once read that it is possible for a seeker to learn and spiritually grow a great deal on her own, but there eventually comes a time at which, in order to continue her spiritual growth, she will need a community of people who are pilgrims on the same or a similar path. I had also read that "when the student is ready, the teacher will come." After leaving my Ph.D. program, throughout the rest of my twenties and for the first half of my thirties, I sought both. I was in search of the wisdom of The Three Wise Men of the East. I **wanted** the wisdom of the East. I moved to New York City and there visited various spiritual communities that followed the teachings of Eastern mystics. I attended meetings of the followers of Sri Chinmoy, visited and had lunch at the Hare Krishna Center a number of times, attended several classes at the Transcendental Meditation Center, Transcendental Meditation - Wikipedia and practiced Transcendental Meditation for a time. Over the years, I studied Rosicrucian texts. I visited Sri Chivilasananda's ashram in upstate New York and practiced her tradition's Siddha Yoga for a while. I read Paramahansa Yogananda's *Autobiography of a Yogi*, Autobiography of a Yogi - Wikipedia intermittently attended his Self-Realization Fellowship (SRF) Self-Realization Fellowship - Wikipedia services, and was a member of a local SRF meditation group for a time. I investigated the principles of the Science of Mind The Science of Mind - Wikipedia theology (not to be confused with Scientology). I was totally taken by the movie "Meetings with Remarkable Men," Meetings with Remarkable Men - YouTube that dramatized George Gurdjieff's search for Ultimate Truth, and as a result, read his writings with much interest. I was a young mystic in search of a mystical community and its teacher.

Despite my many attempts to find a spiritual community that both resonated with me spiritually, and made me feel personally comfortable, I was unfortunately never able to do so. I was uncomfortable in all of them. Everyone in the various communities was always very warm and I believe genuinely so, but the greeting I received upon my initial visit to them always left me cold. After watching European American first-time visitors be received with, "Welcome. Is this your first time here? Wonderful. Happy to see you," I was greeted with what I refer to as the "Oh, hi Black person!" greeting, and I received it in every community I visited. The exact words differed from one experience to another, but generally, at some point during my visit, someone would say something one or more of the following to me: "Welcome! " "What brings you here?" , or "Are you here for the Transcendental Meditation session?" or "How did you hear about us?" In the midst of that interaction, it was absolutely clear to me that my greeters had no ill intention whatsoever toward me. Nonetheless, their response left me feeling absolutely racially objectified because, based upon my observation, none of the European American first-time guests were asked how they found the community or what brought them to it. It was likely assumed that their interest in the topic of the event brought them to it. Those questions were often combined with the stares that I inevitably received throughout the evening from various people at the event. At one particular meditation I attended at a Vipassana Buddhist retreat center, no one sat next to me. We were sitting on pillows on the floor, and all four pillows around me, the two on either side of me, the one in front, and the one behind me, were empty. All of the other guests were sitting next to each other. It felt as if I was on my own private pillow island. Needless to say, I left every such experience with the strong and very familiar feeling I had felt since I was a thirteen-year-old high school freshman, that the people who were behaving that way toward me were not experiencing me as an ordinary human being. They weren't experiencing me as just a person. It felt that they were experiencing me, instead, as a Black person.[154] It was quite apparent to me that they did not, and were not able to see me. They were unable to see the person I truly am—simply a pilgrim on a path in search of Divine Wisdom. Despite the fact that I doubted there was any conscious animus toward me on the part of most people, I was nonetheless disillusioned and deeply disappointed because of the ways in which the unconscious bias

154 I **am** a black person, of course, but I agree with Pat Parker's poem, *For the white person who wants to know how to be my friend*, https://lithub.com/three-poems-by-pat-parker, "The first thing you do is to forget that I'm Black. Second, you must never forget that I'm Black." I cannot say with certainty, but I suspect that perhaps the following is the meaning behind Pat Parker's statement: When you meet me, the first thing I want you to do is to connect with me on a human level, to see and to respond to me as a human being. I want you to see and acknowledge our shared humanity. I want you to see and respond to my full personhood. Then, **after** that, the **second** thing I want you to do **is** to see my blackness, to always remember that my blackness results in my having had a very different life experience than you. I need you to acknowledge that difference, and to be respectful of it. In other words, I need you to never joke about it or take it lightly, no matter how well we may come to know each other, no matter how close we may become. I'm not sure whether Pat Parker would agree with my interpretation of her statement, but that is certainly **my** dual wish for my first encounters with White Americans.

of the members of the spiritual communities I visited was directed toward me. I expected people on a spiritual path to be more conscious, more self-aware, more highly evolved.[155] Unfortunately, I never found a spiritual community in which I was comfortable, one in which people sincerely welcomed me as just another pilgrim on the spiritual path.

155 I realized some years later that that expectation stemmed from what was, at that time, my youth and naïveté. I have since learned over many years that being on a spiritual path alone does not necessarily result in heightened emotional intelligence in general and self-awareness in particular. Progress in those areas, especially awareness of one's unconscious biases, at the beginning of one's spiritual path, requires its own concerted effort. As one progresses farther along the spiritual path, however, with the benefit of persistent meditation, the veil of experiencing our fellow human beings as different, does begin to drop, and one gradually attains the ability to see all people lovingly as their sisters and brothers. Living in that way lends a kind of personal freedom that can never be fully described. It can only be experienced.

CHAPTER SIX

THE END OF MY SEARCH BUT CONTINUATION OF MY JOURNEY

MY QUEST FOR A SPIRITUAL HOME

Having not found a spiritual community, I simply pursued my spiritual path on my own, as a lone seeker, primarily meditating and reading books that fed my spiritual needs. I was on a mystical spiritual path, the process of which is meditation, and the goal of which is enlightenment – gradual self-perfection, leading to great compassion for and assistance to others, and ultimately to oneness with The Divine Creator. It is for that reason that I thought of myself then and continue to think of myself now as a mystic – one in search of enlightenment. Some years later, however, I attended a few Quaker About Quakers - Friends General Conference (fgcquaker.org) meetings, several Baha'i The Bahá'í Faith - Home (bahai.org) firesides, and a number of Unitarian Our Unitarian Universalist Faith | UUA.org services. None of those traditions can be described as mystical, but I was attracted to them for their social justice orientation. Eventually, however, my deeply seated, life-long feeling returned, my feeling that while working on fairness and equality issues is my **social** path, mysticism is my **spiritual** path.

I returned to the mystical path over twenty-five years ago. I study the teachings of several disciplines of Perennial Wisdom, accepting those aspects of their tradition that resonate with me, and not accepting those that do not. The traditions that I study advance a number of shared principles. Generally speaking, however, the following four are the most fundamental:

- Because they share a set of inherent principles, no conflict exists between religion and science.
- Ultimate wisdom and compassion through unity with The Creator, i.e., enlightenment, is possible, and is, indeed, the journey that we as human beings, are all on.
- Serious, persistent meditation ultimately leads to enlightenment.
- The purpose of human life **is** enlightenment.

Throughout my quest for a spiritual home, what I was really in search of was a community focused on obtaining the highest wisdom, one dedicated to a pathway to enlightenment, to helping its members achieve union with The Divine. I was not, however, looking for the one community that held the "true wisdom." Throughout my search, I was open to a variety of spiritual communities because, as a believer in Perennial Wisdom, I believed then, as I do now, that there are many paths to Ultimate Truth and to The Divine. I simply wanted a spiritual community that felt right for me. I fantasized for years that that community might actually be a formal, residential religious community, perhaps an ashram in the foothills of the Himalayas. The thought of living a contemplative monastic life in a monastery or ashram, being in meditation and practicing silence for many hours each day as a means of actually experiencing God, has captivated me since my thirty-second visit to Sister Mary Rose Elizabeth's room in the AHA convent as a sixteen-year-old senior at Holy Angels High School. I now believe that while it may be tremendously helpful to one's spiritual growth to be in an environment in which everyone is focused on their spiritual maturity, it is possible, with keen focus, to achieve enlightenment in any setting. Still, one day, I do hope to make a pilgrimage to India and spend significant time at an ashram in meditation. It is one of the things that I feel very strongly pulled to do before my life ends.

AMAZING SPIRITUAL EXPERIENCES

The last thing I would like to share with you on this, my spiritual journey, is the following: As a child, I had faith in a Divine Creator based upon a deep intuitive feeling in Its existence. As an adult, based upon a number of spiritual experiences I have had, it feels as if that faith has become knowledge. They are experiences I cannot explain. Indeed, they are experiences that defy reason and logic. Among them are the following:

- Very infrequently, perhaps once or twice in a year, as I'm doing some task around the house, I will sing one of the hymns we sang at Bethany when I was a child. On one such occasion, I was singing my favorite hymn while looking out of a window that faced beautiful, dense, lush woods—my favorite natural setting. When I reached the hymn's crescendo and sang at the top of my lungs the phrase that is its refrain, I had an experience for an unknown time period, but what was possibly only a few seconds, that completely defies verbal description.

The experience was both a physical and an emotional feeling. I can best describe the physical feeling as that of my body having no weight and that neither it nor the place in which it existed had any boundaries. There was no distinction between my body and the space in which it was present. It was as close as perhaps the experience of floating on air would be, except that I didn't feel any air. I also didn't feel my body. I didn't feel anything physical. Emotionally, the feeling was one of peace—total peace. The two words, "total peace" describe it entirely. Dear reader, in every account I have ever read of a feeling to which the words "ecstasy" and "bliss" have been applied, the person who had experienced and wrote about it, reported that there are no words to describe it. I may now add my name to that list of people. I have by necessity used words to try to describe the feeling, and from those words you may get some sense of it, but the feeling itself defies any and all verbal descriptions. As one who appreciates logical, rational explanations of everything, I am well aware that for the millions of people for whom that is also true, such a description is deeply dissatisfying. I know beyond any doubt, however, that try though I may, and no matter how hard I try, I will fail miserably at any attempt to describe the experience, for it exists in a realm that is not of this world, a realm that is beyond the limitations of the speech. What I'm sure may be most shocking to you, however, is that I experienced it as a realm that while utterly ethereal, is also indescribably more substantive, more "real" than the one in which we live our normal, everyday lives. As I write these words, I fully acknowledge the complete irrationality of what I report.

- For many years, I had an experience that occurred only in the car. I noticed that while driving, in a moment during which I was thinking particularly hard about my mother, a song would come on the radio that seemed to be a direct response to the specific thought I was having about her in that very moment. The experience became so very consistent that in disbelief that it was happening, and also to convince myself that it was actually happening I began to record the experiences—my thought and the lyrics of the song that played while I was having it. I wound up with a very long list of those experiences. I would have loved to have shared the specifics of those experiences with you, as they truly were amazing. Unfortunately, however, I lost the list many years ago. The experiences stopped when satellite radio became available, and I began playing ambient, new age, meditation music in the car almost exclusively. I do, however, remember two experiences on the list. During one, I was thinking about how much my mother's example, the person that she was, has always been my inspiration, and how that inspiration has so significantly shaped my character, and impacted my life. Just as I was in the middle of that thought, Bette Midler's song, "You are the Wind Beneath My Wings," began playing. Not all of the lyrics of the song correspond to what I was thinking, but the chorus, the refrain, matched my thought exactly. The other such experience I remember was the occasion on which I was thinking that regardless of how much time had passed since my mother's death, the amount and depth of love that I feel for her could never diminish. I was thinking that no matter how much time had passed since I was last with her, I still loved her as if I had just been with her yesterday. At some point during that thought, the Intruders' song, "I'll Always Love My Mama," came on the radio. No matter how many times I had the experience, it always astounded me. After it happened four or five times, I began to just smile, and actually laugh when it happened. My thought then, and even now, is, "What can possibly account for this? How can it be? It **must** be coincidence. To believe otherwise is pure madness." Yet, the experience was so frequent that I began to think, "But this happens so much that it can't be coincidence, can it? It's just too frequent, too consistent. It's amazing!" I wish I had my list of those experiences. I kept it in my car, and somehow over the many times I entered, exited, cleaned out, and washed it, I lost the list. I am so sorry that I am unable to share with you each item that was on it. It was truly astonishing.

- Sometime in the mid-90's a dearly trusted friend told me about an absolutely incredible reading she had just had with an astrologer. Amazed by her account of the reading, I subsequently followed up and scheduled a reading with him for myself.[156]

  Prior to the reading, I had never met the astrologer, Rob, in person. We had only a very brief telephone conversation during which he asked me for my birth date, time, and place, and for three areas in which I'd like him to focus during the reading I was to have with him. I remember two of the three - my career (specifically whether I was going to impact the world in the way that I so badly wanted to), and the possibility I may find a life partner in the future. I subsequently emailed the information to him. It was a telephone reading because

156 Although I have always had a very strong intellectual inclination toward science and the scientific method, I also believe that science cannot explain many things that exist in our reality. Astrology, practiced responsibly, I believe, is among them. Indeed, many astrologers, most likely the best among them, believe that astrology actually **is** a science.

the room of Rob's home in which he provided readings was being remodeled at that time. During a short introduction, Rob explained that he was solely an astrologer, not clairvoyant, and neither a psychic nor a medium. He said that while he believes there are those who possess those gifts, he was not among them. He said that in reading people's astrological charts, he merely "crunches numbers." Rob then went on to inform me that he uses the ancient system of astrology, not the more contemporary one, and gave me a brief explanation of the difference between them. I honestly understood very little of what he explained. He then began the formal reading of my complete astrology chart.

At one point during the reading, Rob asked me, "Now are you gay?" I said, "Yes, I am. But why do you ask?" He replied, "Because you have a chart that's pretty typical of gay people." I was very, very surprised![157]

Further on in the reading, Rob said, "Now, you asked about romance. Well, I do see something coming up, and it's going to be sometime around your 49th birthday." He told me that the person wasn't here, that she was quite far away, and that this was the one that I'd been waiting for. I met Barbara some years later, in 2002, months before my 49th birthday. At the time of my reading with Rob, I lived in Virginia, and Barbara lived in California. We have been together now for twenty-one years.

The most astonishing part of the reading, however, occurred at the point at which Rob asked me, "Now you said that you were born at 4:50 P.M.?" I answered, "Yes. That's right." In response, he replied something

157 While I have used quotation marks in recounting this and the other dialogues reported in this section, the dialogues as written are not actually verbatim accounts. They are, however, very close to verbatim.

very close to, "Well, based upon when your mother died, you should've been born closer to 4:5**8** P.M. And your mother left right on time." In utter astonishment, I replied, "What?! My mother died nearly sixteen years after I was born? How could the date and time of her death possibly have anything to do with the time of my birth?" After being speechless for a few seconds, I asked Rob to hold on for a minute while I got my birth certificate, which was in my desk filing cabinet. I then pulled my birth certificate out of the file and saw the time of my birth. I was born at 4:58 P.M! The 4 and the 5 on the document were not very clear, but the 8 was clearly visible! **Based upon the date and time of my mother's death that occurred nearly sixteen years after my birth, Rob was able to determine the exact time of my birth**! To say that I was totally and utterly flabbergasted would be a huge understatement! In that moment, I could've been knocked out of my desk chair with a wet noodle. After another few seconds of silence, I asked, "Rob, how do you know these things? How, in heaven's name, can you **possibly** know this stuff? How do you figure it out?" Rob's reply was, "All I can tell you, Lauren, is that these things are determined in a realm that is beyond time and space as we know them to be."

To the many readers who will quite understandably be very skeptical of this claim, it is with pleasure that I am able to inform you that I have, somewhere in my garage, the original tape recording of the conversation, which I assume can be scientifically dated for its age. I would gladly place the contents of the tape online for the world to hear were I able to acquire Rob's permission to do so. Since, however, we lost touch years ago and I have not been able to acquire any current contact information for him, doing so without his permission is legally impermissible as it would violate his privacy. I am happy to make the recording available, however, to any certified forensics expert who would like to both listen to it and determine its age.

I had one more reading with Rob several years later, in the early 2000s before we lost contact. Unfortunately, and to my utter surprise and disappointment, I got very little from that reading. It was both vague and very general. It was also over the phone, and both Rob's voice and his manner of speaking had changed quite noticeably. He had clearly aged. Rob and I never met, but the first of his two readings with me is an experience I shall never forget. I have no explanation of the events just described, and fully acknowledge their complete non-rationality.

- Several years later, I had experiences with three individuals who, like Rob, were very highly referred to me by a trusted friend, but who, unlike Rob, were psychics/mediums.

  The first was with Reverend Brown, a man whom, like Rob, I had never met. Rev. Brown began the reading with a prayer, asking for blessings for me, and for the reading that was about to take place. At the start of the reading, my mother came through and told me how proud she was of me. If there is one thing my mother would know I would want to hear from her, it is that she is proud of me. It is the first thing that Reverend Brown reported that my mother said. I smiled with the biggest, brightest smile I could ever have. Gramzie showed up next. Reverend Brown didn't report that Gramzie said anything, but commented that her love for me was very strong and that her energy for me felt like an octopus, as if she had eight arms around me, hugging me tightly, squeezing me with every one of them. I had to leave the room at that point because I was unable to control my tears. When I went back into the room, after talking about my mother and grandmother for a while, I asked about my father. Reverend Brown's response, revealing a degree of surprise, was, "Your father is in spirit?" to which I responded, "Yes." He then said, "I don't feel him. I don't feel him at all." My father had been gone for many years by then, so I couldn't understand why that was the case. I then shared with Reverend Brown that I was disappointed because I really wanted to know how my father was doing since before he died, he confided in my aunt at one point, telling her that he had a tremendous amount of guilt about not being a better husband to my mother. Reverend Brown responded, "When people cross over and they're not at peace, if the pain of their guilt or remorse or whatever negative feeling they crossed over with is too great for them to bear, angels put them to sleep and then work on them while they're sleeping. Then, when they've achieved a certain amount of peace, they're awakened to begin their life there. Oh yes, yes. Your mother is telling me that your father is asleep right now. She said that they're working on him." I didn't know what I thought about that at the time, or if I even believed it. Before the reading ended, Reverend Brown told me about the home in the woods of Manassas, Virginia that I was in the process of building, describing it correctly with a level of detail that was no less than utterly remarkable. At the time of the reading, the foundation of the house had been completed, but construction of the house itself had not yet even begun. In that moment, therefore, I wondered exactly what it was that Reverend Brown was actually "seeing." I was both bewildered and amazed at the accuracy of his description of my home that, at the time, existed only on paper.

My second experience with a reading by a psychic medium wasn't actually my experience. It was Barbara's that I merely witnessed, but it left me in utter astonishment. Barbara is a foundling adoptee, and the reading concerned the circumstances of her birth. She was found, at ninety minutes old, in a phone booth that was in the basement of the Newark, New Jersey City Hall, placed with a foster family for her first eighteen months, and then with her adopted parents. After many years of wondering about her birth family, who they were, whether her birth mother was still alive, why her mother didn't keep her and why she left her under the circumstances that she did, Barbara decided to try to find the answers. We told a dear friend that Barbara was about to begin her search for her birth mother and family and, in response, our friend recommended that Barbara begin with a consultation with a psychic whom she very highly recommended. Barbara took the person's contact information, called her, and scheduled the consultation. It had to be a phone consultation because Cathy, the psychic, lived in the Midwest, and we were in Pasadena, California. Barbara used the phone's speaker for the session. I was in the room, and with Cathy's permission, listened to the entire conversation, throughout which Barbara took extensive notes. It turned out to be the very first step in Barbara's long journey to find her biological family. Cathy began the reading with a prayer to The Creator, giving thanks for the opportunity to help Barbara and asking for guidance in her attempt to do so. Among the many things that Cathy told Barbara were the following:

◊ Someone helped Barbara's mother with her birth and then took Barbara to the phone booth. "It feels like it was a relative, an older relative that helped her."
◊ "Ok, so you asked about a family name. I see 'Hall.' Now it could be Hallman or Hallmond, but I definitely see 'Hall'."
◊ Her birth mother died in an automobile accident in 1964. Cathy described the accident as if she were actually able to see it. Her words were to the effect of "Oh, how tragic. How tragic. Very tragic accident."
◊ "You can find your birth family if you search for them. You can definitely find them."

On July 26, 2006, Barbara requested and received her non-identifying information from the state of New Jersey. Non-identifying information is what adoption or government agencies provide to adoptees who request information on their adoption. While it provides details on the circumstances of the inquirer's adoption, it does not provide any information on the identity of their birth parents. They remain non-identified. Barbara's non-identifying information stated that her birth name was Leonia Hall. Remembering her conversation with Cathy, Barbara was utterly amazed. The document stated that, "The nurses in the hospital wanted to name you Leonia Hall. They chose that name because the mayor of Newark at the time was Leo Carlin and you were found in City Hall." Barbara was perplexed by that explanation of her birth name, however, because as a retired social worker, she was well aware that it is highly unusual for hospital nurses to name abandoned babies. In the hospital, the babies are usually assigned the name Baby Doe, after which whatever foster family the child goes to chooses a name of record for them until hopefully, they are adopted.

After fifteen years of searching, in June of 2020, as the result of both a lot of very persistent research and the identification, through Ancestry.com, of two second cousins, Barbara identified the extended biological family to which she thought she belonged. Emotionally, she was thrilled, but cautious. Through further research, she acquired the names of four sisters in the family, one of whom, she thought, had to be her mother. Fortunately, at this juncture, Barbara obtained the help of three very kind women who provide a free service to adoptees and others who are searching for their birth family. The women with whom Barbara worked identified which of the four sisters was indeed her biological mother. It was the one who Barbara was unable to trace after the 1940 census because she changed her last name...to **"Hall."** Remembering her conversation with Cathy, Barbara was again astonished.

Having acquired her birth mother's name, Barbara was then able to conduct research on her. Through that research, she discovered two newspaper articles that described a head-on collision in which her mother had died on a slick road on a rainy day in 1964. Remembering once again, her conversation with Cathy, Barbara was stunned.

After searching for fifteen years, through the help of DNA evidence submitted to Ancestry.com and 23 and Me, and the assistance of the three kind women who helped Barbara, she found her birth family! For Barbara, it was the accomplishment of a lifetime! I could write an entire book about her journey and the feeling of satisfaction, elation, completion and accomplishment that she experienced after searching for her birth family for a full decade and a half. Her family's subsequent very warm and loving welcome gave her a second experience of pure elation. Her elation was quickly followed by feelings, once again, of surprise, incredulity, and wonderment because in an early conversation with her aunt, Barbara learned that her biological mother's "favorite" sibling, the one to whom she felt closest by far, was her sister...Leona. Upon learning that, Barbara was shocked, and immediately wondered if her name, "Leonia", in her mother's mind, meant "Little Leona."[158]

Barbara is still in possession of the notes that she took during her conversation with Cathy that contain the information here reported. Barbara dated the notes, of course, but their age can be independently verified through the chemical process of ink dating.

- Third and finally was my experience, during the years of Barbara's search, with psychic/medium Margaret. Margaret was from Scotland, and a total stranger to me when we met. Over approximately five years, I had several readings with her.

  Margaret began every reading with a prayer, asking the Divine Spirit to bless the reading as the partition be-

158 Barbara and I have speculated that if her birth mother, and not the hospital nurses, named her, her mother had to have done so by leaving a note with Barbara with her name on it. To this day, however, both Barbara and I marvel at the improbability of there being two different, plausible explanations of her birth name. The two relevant questions in this regard are, "How likely is it that a foundling infant whose birth mother named her, **"Leonia Hall"** would be left in a City **Hall** of a city, the mayor of which, at the time, was **Leo** Carlin?"; and conversely, "How likely is it that **"Hall"** would be the last name of the biological mother, and **"Leona"** the first name of the biological aunt of a foundling infant who was named Leonia Hall by hospital nurses?" We have often thought about how utterly remarkable it is that both explanations of Barbara's birth name are possible.

tween the two worlds fades. During my first reading, as happened during my reading with Reverend Brown, my mother immediately came through. Margaret, upon experiencing her spirit for the first time, said, "Now, there's an energy building up here that feels like a mother's energy. Yes, it's a mother's energy. Oh what a lovely spirit!" In that moment, I thought, "Wow, even in death, Mama's personhood shines through." Margaret then went on to tell me several things that left me with absolutely no doubt that it was indeed my mother with whom she was in contact. She told me several times that my mother was saying to her that she is proud of me. Of course I smiled and also teared up quite a bit. Margaret, I'm sure as a result of her experience providing readings, had a big box of tissues next to the chair in which I was sitting. I was happy they were there.

Later during the reading, Margaret said, "Now your mother's saying that your home is beautiful." Upon hearing that, I was speechless. My mother **loved** interior decorating and was always engaged in some cosmetic improvement or another to the house. Among the magazines to which she subscribed for as long as I can remember were, "Beautiful Homes and Gardens" and "House Beautiful." My home at that time was a mid-century modern, built in 1952, that was similar, in a number of ways, to 5019 New York Circle, my childhood home in Pontchartrain Park that was completed in 1955. Upon hearing Margaret report my mother's appreciation of my home, the only thing that I was able to verbalize was, "Wow."

Margaret then said that my mother was telling her that her going from this world to that one was very sudden. Margaret said, "Now, your mother's saying that she was there (on Earth) one minute, and here, the next, and she's doing her hands like this (Margaret moved her right hand, then her left), showing how sudden it was." Margaret then said, "It feels heart related. Did your mother die of a heart attack?" I told her that it wasn't a heart attack, but that she did pass away as the result of a cardiac arrest following a simple surgery.

Through Margaret, my mother also told me that she did not like the way a loved one was treating me. I knew, instantly, what my mother was referring to – the way in which that loved one treated me as a result of my sexual orientation. I was surprised, however, that it was present enough with her, on the elevated plane on which her spirit now existed, to make mention of it. It actually saddened me that that painful situation was in her consciousness.

The most astounding part of my reading by far, however, was the point during the reading at which Margaret said, "Now, your mother just said, 'All the prayers that you said for me when I first got here really helped,' and she thanks you for them." After hearing that, the old adage, "You could have knocked me over with a wet noodle" was totally applicable to me. Immediately upon my mother's death, and for perhaps a full two months thereafter, I prayed **incessantly** for her. Specifically, I prayed for her peace—constantly. I knew that my mother, finding herself on the other side, would be terribly worried about Lorna and me, and that thought, the thought of her being in a state of extreme worry about and fear for us was very painful to me. I prayed, and prayed, and prayed, all throughout the day, and until I went to sleep, asking The Creator to please let my mother know that Lorna and I were going to be just fine, to please, just let her be happy and at peace. That was my constant prayer for several weeks immediately after my mother died. Over the course of the forty-five years that passed between the time of my mother's death and that reading, I told no one, not a single person, of my prayers. When Margaret told me that my mother told me that my many prayers for her were very helpful, and that she thanked me for them, I was flabbergasted. Again, I cried.

Gramzie also visited during that reading. Margaret didn't report that she said anything to me, but said that her energy, her spirit, was coming through as a gigantic, bright, glowing, golden globe of warm, nurturing grandmotherly love. On a purely intuitive level, that made sense to me. It just felt true. It felt like a description of Gramzie. I remembered my reading with Reverend Brown years earlier, and was amazed that Margaret's reading of Gramzie was so similar to his. She didn't speak in either session, but in both, her tremendous love came through brilliantly.

My father was also present this time. The following exchange took place between Margaret and me regarding him:

Margaret: "Now, was your father a well-built man?"

Lauren: "No, he wasn't." (My father had always been quite thin.)

Margaret: "Well, I mean was he lean? He wasn't stocky at all?"

Lauren: "Oh no. Not at all. He was a thin man."

Margaret: "Because I'm seeing a man who is fit, he's trim, standing slightly behind your mother, and he has one hand on her shoulder as if he's supporting her. Yes, and now he's saying that he's proud of you too."

I was in that moment, once again really glad that the box of tissues was within arm's reach. Remembering my reading with Reverend Brown some years earlier in which I learned that my father was "asleep" while angels were working on him, I was happy he was now conscious and experiencing his life on that plane. Additionally, I was moved not only by what my father said, but also because he was with my mother in what sounded like a loving, supportive manner, a manner in which he was never able to be with her in life. I hoped they were now happy together, and I felt happy whenever, after that reading, I thought about my father with his hand on my mother's shoulder.

In yet another reading with Margaret, she said, "Now, there's what feels like a female energy building up and it feels like it could be a sister-in-law. And the feeling that's coming through is gratitude. It's gratitude. She's so thankful to you for what you did for her, and she's saying, 'And as busy as you are, you still took the time to do that for me.' She's so grateful." Although Margaret had no idea exactly who was speaking and why she communicated to me what she did, I knew it was my brother Lambert's wife, Debbie, who had died the preceding year, and whom, after she suffered a massive stroke, I sat with for a week in her hospital room, subsequently coordinated her transition from the hospital to a rehabilitation facility and got her settled in and comfortable there. Once again, I was dumbfounded!

At one point, Barbara and I had a joint reading with Margaret. During that reading, she asked us, "Now, who is it that has the problem with their feet?" Barbara and I looked at each other in bewilderment, after which one of us (I don't remember who) said, "Neither of us." Margaret responded with a simple, "Oh," but it very much felt like a **knowing** "Oh," one that rather than being a simple, "Oh, I see", felt much more like an "Oh, ok well, then it's coming." Two weeks later, Barbara woke up and was unable to walk. She had suddenly, and without warning, developed a case of planter fasciitis in her feet that made walking excruciating. Fortunately, the condition was temporary and she made a full recovery within weeks.

Barbara's father by adoption also visited during that session. Margaret told Barbara that a fatherly energy was showing up for her, and that he was mentioning the dance shoes of two little girls. After thinking for a minute, during which she was unable to connect to the reference in any way, Barbara realized that her father was referring to the ballet shoes of her younger twin sisters (also by adoption), Valerie and Sonia. Margaret then said to Barbara, "Your father's saying that you were always his favorite. 'You were always my favorite' he said." Needless to say, Barbara was touched.

During that same reading, Margaret asked us, "Now, are you mortgage free?" Barbara and I looked at each other and laughed in great amusement. Barbara said, "Um, no," to which I added, "I **wish** we were mortgage free!" We both laughed. Margaret replied, "Well you're going to be. You're going to be mortgage free." Barbara and I just looked at each other, both smiling, and in utter amazement. In a later discussion at home, we acknowledged that with twelve more years of mortgage payments still in our future, we had absolutely no clue how that was going to happen. Two years later, after a conversation with a few friends who live in the Palm Springs area of California (we lived in Pasadena at the time) and after several months of much thought and careful research, we decided to move to Palm Springs for retirement. Because the real estate market in Los Angeles County, in which Pasadena is located, is significantly stronger than the market of Riverside County, in which Palm Springs is located, even with twelve more years of mortgage payments owed on our Pasadena home, we were able to sell it, and pay cash for our home in the Palm Springs area. Incredibly, it wasn't until a full year after we had lived in our new home that we remembered what Margaret told us. It was actually Barbara who remembered. Out of the blue one day, she asked me, "Hey, do you remember what Margaret told us about us being mortgage free?" I responded, "Oh my goodness! I do remember that! She told us that we were going to be mortgage free, and I remember we both laughed, thinking, 'Not within the next twelve years!'" We just looked at each other in disbelief both that Margaret had correctly told us that it was going to happen, and that we hadn't remembered until then that she had!

The final incredible thing that I remember about that particular reading is that Margaret asked, "Now, who is the writer in the family?" I responded that I was. She then went on to describe in surprising detail what I was writing about. She said that the angels who are my spiritual guides are strongly encouraging me to write. She said that they were saying to her, Margaret, "Tell her to write. Tell her again. Tell her to write." She said, "They're saying that your computer has a name." For three decades now, I have called my various notebook computers, "Brainiac." To say that I was shocked is a mammoth understatement.

- Dear reader, as powerful as all of my spiritual experiences described thus far were when they occurred, none of them comes even close to the one that follows:

Sometime in the late nineties when I was living in the home in the woods that Reverend Brown saw so clearly in my reading with him, while driving to Newport News, Virginia for work, I felt what in the faith tradition in which I was raised, was referred to as heaven. **I literally felt heaven**. It happened on one of the several bridges that must be crossed when traveling south to Newport News. I was thinking of my mother and feeling intense guilt about her death. The night before the surgery that ended my mother's life, I had powerful feelings of fear. I felt that something just wasn't right; that my mother shouldn't have the surgery. I was tremendously afraid that something very bad would happen if she did. That night, I thought I should wait until my father fell asleep, and then take the car keys off of his dresser, drive up to the hospital, and throw a tantrum until they let my mother go home with me. (The act of throwing a tantrum was totally antithetical to the young person that I was at that time, but I was so distraught about my mother's surgery the night before it occurred, that I actually considered doing it.) I ultimately talked myself out of throwing a tantrum at the hospital, telling myself I was just afraid because Mama had never had surgery before, and that the operation was going to help her a great deal, making her life much easier and more comfortable. When the next morning, minutes after the short surgery was over, my mother suffered a cardiac arrest in the recovery room and died three days later, I felt guilty. I'm now aware that young people (I was not quite sixteen at the time) often blame themselves for the various kinds of difficulties their parents may experience, and, at the time, I did blame myself. On my drive down to Newport News, I thought, "If I'd only gone up to that hospital and thrown that tantrum, demanding that Mama come home with me! If I had only followed my 'first mind'! Why didn't I? My feeling was so strong! Why didn't I do it? If I had done it, Mama would've been alive all these years. She'd still be here if only I'd done it!" While that feeling lessened significantly once I became active in the UNO NAACP College Chapter and indeed eventually went away, the "what if" thought of what would have happened had I actually driven up to the hospital and thrown a tantrum to take my mother home the night before her surgery occurred to me several times over many years.

On the day in question on which I was driving to Newport News, that is the thought that, out of nowhere, indeed occurred to me. For some reason, however, on this particular occasion, the thought didn't just occur to me—it walloped me. For a reason I cannot explain, when the thought entered my mind that time, it did so with a kind of power, strength and force I hadn't felt in decades. As I was driving with the "what if" thought in my mind, I began to cry nearly uncontrollably. I wanted to get off the highway, but before I was able to change lanes to do so, I suddenly heard my mother speaking to me. It wasn't normal auditory hearing that I experienced. I didn't actually hear my mother's voice with my ears. What I experienced was her speaking to me mentally. I heard her, not with my ears, but in my mind. Her communication to me was what is referred to as telepathic—and it was as clear as day. "Laurie, I don't want you to feel bad about what happened. It was not your fault. It was God's will. I never want you to feel this guilty about it again. I'm going to show you what my life is like now because I don't want you to **ever** feel these feelings again." In the next instant, what I experienced (not unlike what I felt in the experience of singing the hymn described earlier) can never be described in words. For an amount of time I cannot quantify, but that since I was driving, could not have lasted more than a few seconds, I had a feeling that was unlike any other I had ever experienced. It was beyond happiness. If joy is beyond happiness, it was joy. If ecstasy is beyond joy, it was ecstasy, and if bliss is beyond ecstasy, it was bliss. In what must have been only a few seconds, I felt a depth of bliss that not only had I never before experienced, but that I also did not know existed and could not possibly have ever imagined in my present life—ever. I could use all of those descriptors, happiness, joy, ecstasy, bliss, and still I write those words knowing that they absolutely fail at relaying the actual experience. I know that the experience can be known **only** by having it.[159]

In short, I felt heaven. After the experience, my mother said again, "Now Laurie, I want you to let the guilt go. I love you, and I don't want you to **ever** feel that again." In the more than twenty years that have passed since, I never have. The indelible effect of that experience is that it not only freed me from the guilt that I felt about my mother's death, it also left me with a secure knowl-

159 I suspect that what I felt might have been a glimpse of what highly advanced yogis report as the experience of samadhi. In my experience singing the hymn, I felt indescribable peace. In this experience, I felt indescribable bliss. I believe that the experience described by advanced yogis as enlightenment, or samadhi, and the experience of ordinary people who have meditated for many years, as well as the experiences of ordinary people who have spontaneously had a "mystical experience" encompasses both. Indescribable peace and indescribable bliss. In such experiences, however, people also report a third feeling, that of being in the presence of infinite love - The Divine.

edge that beyond this life, literally only a heartbeat away for every human being, is an existence that in this life we can believe in, but that without years of significant spiritual work, spiritual practice, we cannot know. It is to this day, the pinnacle of **all** of my spiritual experiences.

If before my experiences with loved ones who have died, I had any doubt at all about whether we continue to exist after Earthly death, about whether those who loved us in life continue to love us in death, indeed, if I had had any doubt at all about whether a spiritual universe exists, I have absolutely no doubt after them. Since, however, I never did have any doubts about any of those things, my experiences, rather than dispelling doubts, confirmed my long and deeply held beliefs in every one of those things.

A FINAL EXPERIENCE AND MY SPIRITUAL LIFE TODAY

My final spiritual experience I will share with you is the one that I have when I am meditating. I have had a meditation practice for many years now, and it is the focal point of my spiritual life. When I begin my meditation, initially, I notice my many, many thoughts that are constantly present. I notice how very busy my mind is. I observe what Buddhists refer to as "monkey mind"—my thoughts jumping, figuratively speaking, non-stop, from one branch, i.e.one thought, to another.

I have spoken over many years to people who have said to me, "I just can't meditate. I've tried it, but my mind is much too busy. I just can't sit there still like that because my thoughts just keep coming and going, and I can't control them. I try to be quiet inside, but I have too much going on in my life to be internally quiet. Between my family and work that are always on my mind, I just can't do it." I understand... TOTALLY. I started there, in that very place as well. Everyone does. Indeed at times, I am there still, even after many years of meditating. It is simply the nature of the human mind. It takes time, a **lot** of time, to slow our thoughts and calm our mind. It takes time to be still.

The practice of being still, of achieving stillness, is found in a number of humanity's spiritual traditions. Hinduism, Buddhism and other Eastern religious traditions, as well as the Jewish, Christian, and Muslim contemplative or mystical traditions, hold that we can experience being in the presence of and even in unity with The Creator once we achieve the goal of stillness of mind, i.e., peace of mind. The concept is specifically mentioned in the Hebrew Bible or the Old Testament. Psalm 46:10 says, "Be still and know that I am God." The process of doing so first requires achieving total stillness of body, which gradually leads to stillness of mind, which in turn, over time, leads to the ultimate experience of enlightenment – being in the presence of, and even in unity with The Creator – being still and knowing God. During the years of mediation practice, our character transforms and, in due course, we feel a deep need to help others transform. The ultimate goal of meditation practice, however, is "knowing God." It is referred to as a practice because that is exactly what it is – a practice. It is practicing being patient and compassionate in both thought and deed, in every moment, in every interaction, often referred to as "mindfulness." It is practicing sitting in perfect stillness (even with what is at first and often remains for a prolonged time, a very busy mind) until our mind begins to still, until, with continued practice, we begin to feel more and more peace, until we ultimately begin to feel the peace that passeth all understanding.

For most of us, our minds are totally out of control, out of our control. Most of us aren't able to have a quiet still mind for more than a few seconds. It is for that reason that years of practice are required to still our constantly very busy minds jump from one branch, one thought to another. Along the way, however, long before we reach the ultimate goal, we acquire tremendous benefits from our practice – more peace, more poise, more self-awareness and thus self-control, and more wisdom. We become more peaceful, and convey that peacefulness in the world.

I have heard it said that, "Prayer is talking to God, and meditation is listening to God." Our world would be a very different place if a critical mass of humanity, in addition to talking to God, would regularly meditate, would practice listening to God.

I always begin my meditation with music, meditation music, of course—soft, ambient tones. At times, it is Gregorian chant. The music very much helps to center, quiet and still my mind. As much as I absolutely enjoy the music, however, it is a crutch that I hope, at some point, I will no longer need. After the music goes off, I'm much more mentally, i.e., internally quiet. As my meditation continues in silence, my mind becomes more and more quiet, more and more still. I become increasingly more present in the moment. That presence allows me to hear whatever is happening in present time—a bird chirping outdoors; the wind in the trees on a windy day; a gurgle of my stomach or the settling noises of the house. I am able to feel whatever is happening in present time—the coolness of the floor on the bottom of my feet; my arms resting in my lap; an itch behind my ear; the temperature of the air in the room; any tension in the various parts of my body and my torso expanding and contracting as I breathe in and out. As I continue to sit in perfect stillness, experiencing, but not scratching an itch (that shortly goes away), becoming conscious of and then consciously releasing the tension in various parts of my body—my forehead, face, shoulders, arms, hands, fingers, and legs, as I continue to sit in silence and in total stillness, I begin to have an experience that, as with all of my other experiences I refer to as "spiritual," defies verbal description. I can say, however, that the feeling begins in the middle of my lower forehead, in the space between my eyes. It feels as if it originates and then emanates from that spot. The feeling that then comes is simply peace. It is peaceful, and utterly calm—a mental and emotional oasis. I think of meditation as a kind of shower for the mind. Showering, i.e., the cleansing of our bodies, is inarguably important for our physical health and wellbeing. Meditating, i.e., the cleansing of our minds is equally important for our spiritual health and wellbeing. Furthermore, it is a necessity not only for our spiritual health and wellbeing, but also for our spiritual growth and evolution. Practicing **physical** stillness helps us to achieve **mental** stillness, and mental stillness is our very first step in developing the ability to actually feel The Divine. It is, I believe, the true meaning of Psalm 46:10 of the Christian Bible, "Be still and <u>know</u> that I am God."

My friends, it has taken me years of meditation practice to be able to sit in meditation free of monkey mind, to be able to sit in mental peace. Having read the accounts of those who are very spiritually advanced, however, I know that although I have been meditating for years, the peace I experience in many of my meditations is just the beginning of my meditation journey. I know that as I advance in my practice, I will eventually experience what Hindus refer to as samadhi—union with The Creator.[160]

Today, my spiritual life consists of my personal meditation practice, attending group talks, meditations, and spiritual services with seekers who are on a similar path, and going on personal meditation (and sometimes silent) retreats. The most important part of my spiritual life, however, is my personal meditation practice – the time that I spend alone, in stillness. I practice (and still often fail) mindfulness in every moment. I practice slowing down. Slowing down gives us the opportunity to live an examined life, one in which we actually think about our thoughts and their accompanying emotions. In so doing, we gain the opportunity to consciously decide what thoughts and feelings we want to have, and to then practice having them. We think about our actions,

160 I am a firm believer in reincarnation and thus believe that if I do not reach samadhi in this life, I will, without question, do so in a future life. I believe that that is, after all, the purpose of our human lives here on Earth—perfection of our character that then leads to reunion with our Divine Creator. I write much more extensively about this subject in my book of which this spiritual memoir is the first chapter, *On Religion and Spirituality Humanity's Greatest Call: The Call to Spiritual Maturity*.

decide how we want to behave, and then practice behaving in that way, in a way that is compassionate to all living beings and to the Earth. It is the practice of perfecting our character. Spiritual evolution **requires** practice. Spiritual evolution **is** a practice. We practice being a conscious, patient, wise, compassionate reflection of The Creator. Along the way, we begin to notice subtle changes in ourselves, in our character – that we are not so quick to judge, to respond, and to be impatient or short with others, that we are becoming more charitable, more understanding, and indeed, more compassionate.

FINDING FULFILLMENT, FINDING PEACE

IN THIS, THE AUTUMN OF MY LIFE, I AM EXCEPTIONALLY HAPPY TO have found a way to combine my two passions – my passion for helping my fellow human beings to comprehend the beautiful oneness of humanity, and my passion for spiritual evolution. I, with my dear friends Theresa and Jack, am developing a workshop that we hope will be a spiritual path to racial healing. In the session, we will use the ancient spiritual practices of meditation and visualization to help participants uncover whatever unconscious bias they may have toward people who are racially different from themselves. Our **belief** is that unconscious bias is a powerful source of personal racism. Our **hope** is that the spiritual work that we do during the workshop will help participants to identify, release, and transform any unconscious racial bias that they may have. While the focus of the session is on racism, we will certainly also give voice to other "isms", other prejudices.

I know from my own experience that when we can spiritually go deep enough, when in meditation **we can be still**, we can significantly slow down our constantly racing minds. In so doing, we can experience a level of internal peace that I believe can make it possible for us to both become aware of and to release self-limiting beliefs about our inability to live our lives free of the emotional prison of prejudice. It is at that point of stillness, that point of peace, that we have the potential to deeply feel our oneness with all things, and the shared humanity, the oneness, of all human beings. Jack, Theresa and I, in our workshops, are going to do our very best to help our attendees accomplish that profound goal.

In facilitating these workshops it feels to me that my life has now come full circle. I am using my spirituality, my spiritual practice, in service of my commitment to helping my fellow human beings to be aware of, to deeply understand, and to profoundly appreciate that all human beings, irrespective or race and other superficial differences, are equally human, and indeed, members of one very large human family. In this, the autumn of my life, my two passions have now united. With that, I am fulfilled.

I am and always have been a mystic, a seeker of The Divine. My search for a **path** toward The Divine, however, ended many years ago when I found one that is in full alignment with my spiritual beliefs and needs, the path of meditation. Today, however, I am still on a spiritual journey. It is a mystical journey back to The Divine Creator from which I, and from which we **all** originated. It is a journey in which I engage in my spiritual practice of meditation in order to attain God Realization, union with The Divine, what is often referred to as enlightenment. My deeply rooted belief is that in **attaining** enlightenment, not only will I find all of the answers to The Mysteries that captivated me as a child, I will also possess a level of understanding of all of reality that I cannot, at my present level of spiritual development, even begin to imagine. It is for that reason that I am also no longer in search of answers to The Mysteries, for the path of enlightenment always and inevitably leads one to them. I have learned over the past five decades, however, to not be anxious while on the path of enlightenment, of God Realization, but instead to relax as I travel the path; to live with as much self-awareness, peace, grace, compassion and love as is possible for me at my present level of personal and spiritual development; to live with myself and all others in a constant state of dignity, acceptance and kindness, knowing that my understanding of The Divine, and all of creation, indeed **union** with The Divine, will come.

I began my journey from Jim Crow to Mysticism seeing some of our lowest human instincts. I ended it understanding our highest human potential. With that, I am at peace.

EPILOGUE

In order for us to **survive**, in order for us to have a future, our human species must mature beyond all of the isms, i.e., all of our prejudices, and all of our phobias, racism, colorism, sexism, anti-semitism, ageism, classism, heterosexism, Islamophobia, homophobia, and transphobia, among them. We must become aware that all human beings, regardless of how different we look and behave, are members of the same species - homo sapiens. We must learn that the differences among us are entirely superficial, and that **underneath** our differences, **deeper** than our differences, is the homo sapiens brain and heart that are the same in us all. If we are to survive, we **must** mature beyond our tendency to be prejudiced against and cruel to one another based upon the racial or any other groups into which, as an accident of birth, we happened to have been born. One need only consider the havoc that racism, homophobia and other prejudices have wreaked in the United States over the course of its entire history, and particularly over the past six years, in order to see the potentially devastating impact that hatred based upon our differences can have on our human societies. In order for us to escape the ravages of both the emotional and physical violence in which racial, religious, and other hatreds often result, we must learn to live in respect for, in peace and harmony and indeed in **love** with all of our fellow human beings. We must learn that in our humanness is our sameness, regardless of all of our exterior differences. We must become deeply aware that as human beings, all seven-plus billion of us on planet Earth are one.

In order for us to **thrive**, we must spiritually mature. We must become spiritually curious, and through that curiosity, we must become spiritually literate. We must become aware of our capacity to be compassionate and self-aware in every moment, and then, most importantly, we must **attempt** to be so. If, as a species, we were spiritually mature, all prejudice would end and none of the geo-political conflicts that result in the horrific, utterly uncivilized atrocity of war would exist. As a species, we would be **significantly** advanced in every imaginable way. I hold little hope that we can continue for very much longer on our current path of spiritual ignorance and intolerance. I hold great hope for humanity, however, if we pivot, if we change course, and begin traveling down the path of wisdom-in-general, and spiritual wisdom, in particular. My hope is that spiritual maturity is indeed in our future. Only time will tell whether it will be. The choice is ours.

ABOUT THE AUTHOR

www.LaurenNile.com

Lauren Joichin Nile is an author, keynote speaker and retired attorney. Lauren spent thirty years as an organizational development trainer. The goal of her work with organizations was to help create environments in which understanding and kindness are valued and, as a result, every person is equally welcomed, uniformly appreciated, and treated with equal kindness, irrespective of all demographic differences.

The goal of Lauren's speaking and training in the greater society is to help the human species grow in both wisdom and compassion. Her fervent desire is to help all people to deeply understand the oneness of humanity, to see The Divine in themselves and themselves in each other.

NOTES

NOTES

NOTES

www.ingramcontent.com/pod-product-compliance
Lightning Source LLC
Chambersburg PA
CBHW030355130626
46549CB00004B/1503